Irish Queer Cinema

Allison Macleod

Edinburgh University Press is one of the leading university presses in the UK. We publish academic books and journals in our selected subject areas across the humanities and social sciences, combining cutting-edge scholarship with high editorial and production values to produce academic works of lasting importance. For more information visit our website: edinburghuniversitypress.com

© Allison Macleod, 2018, 2019

Edinburgh University Press Ltd
The Tun – Holyrood Road
12 (2f) Jackson's Entry
Edinburgh EH8 8PJ

First published in hardback by Edinburgh University Press 2018

Typeset in Monotype Ehrhardt by
Servis Filmsetting Ltd, Stockport, Cheshire,
Printed and bound by CPI Group (UK) Ltd, Croydon, CR0 4YY

A CIP record for this book is available from the British Library

ISBN 978 1 4744 1148 6 (hardback)
ISBN 978 1 4744 5508 4 (paperback)
ISBN 978 1 4744 1149 3 (webready PDF)
ISBN 978 1 4744 1150 9 (epub)

The right of Allison Macleod to be identified as author of this work has been asserted in accordance with the Copyright, Designs and Patents Act 1988 and the Copyright and Related Rights Regulations 2003 (SI No. 2498).

An early version of Chapter 4, entitled 'Queer bodies and contested space within the Irish pub in *A Man of No Importance* and *Garage*', appeared in the *Canadian Journal of Film Studies* 24.1 (2015): 45–65.

An early version of Chapter 5, entitled 'Compartmentalized cosmopolitans: constructions of urban space in queer Irish cinema', appeared in *Irish Masculinity and Popular Culture: Tiger's Tales* (2014): 42–57, published by Palgrave.

An early version of Chapter 7, entitled 'Queer mobility, Irish masculinity and the reconfigured road movie in *I Went Down*', appeared in *Cinephile* 10.2 (2014): 21–5.

Irish Queer Cinema

Contents

List of Figures vii
Acknowledgements viii

1 Queerly National and Nationally Queer: Paradoxes of an Irish Queer Cinema 1
   Queer 5
   Irish 9
   Space 13

2 Mapping Ireland's Queer Films 18
   First Wave Queer Cinema 20
   Celtic Tiger Queer Cinema 22
   Post-Celtic Tiger Queer Cinema 25

3 Re-imagined Kinship and Failed Communities 28
   Queering the Family 30
   Pigs 33
   The Last Bus Home 39
   Conclusion 47

4 The Contested Space of the Irish Pub 48
   The Male Homosocial Space of the Irish Pub 50
   A Man of No Importance 54
   Garage 60
   Conclusion 65

5 Compartmentalised Cosmopolitans and Rigid Fluidity 67
   Cowboys and Angels 69
   Goldfish Memory 76
   Situating Irish Lesbianism within Urban Space 80
   Conclusion 88

6	The Queerly Productive Constraints of Rural Space	91
	Reefer and the Model	94
	Clash of the Ash	98
	The Stag	104
	Conclusion	106
7	Queer Mobilities and Disassociated Masculinities	109
	I Went Down	111
	The Disappearance of Finbar and *Breakfast on Pluto*	117
	Conclusion	126
8	Contested Belongings within Diasporic Space	128
	Reconstituting 'Home' within Diaspora	130
	2by4	131
	Borstal Boy	138
	Conclusion	144
9	The Irish Queer Short Film	146
	The Contestation of Public Space	148
	Disrupting Domestic Spaces	152
	The Spatiality of Lesbian Desire	155
	Conclusion	159
10	Concluding Remarks	160

Select Filmography	162
Bibliography	163
Index	174

Figures

3.1	George, Ronnie, Jimmy and Tom sit down to a family dinner in *Pigs*	34
3.2	Petie and Billy embrace in the forest, unaware they are being watched, in *The Last Bus Home*	43
4.1	Alfred peeks out from behind the partition in the pub in *A Man of No Importance*	56
4.2	After being pushed away by Carmel, Josie stands confused and alone as Breffni watches in the background in *Garage*	64
5.1	Shane is refused entry to the nightclub while Vincent is inside dancing in *Cowboys and Angels*	71
5.2	Clara and Isolde's kiss in *Goldfish Memory* is watched by Tom	79
6.1	Phil's confession to Rosie about feeling trapped is reflected by his fenced-in surroundings in *Clash of the Ash*	99
7.1	A circular journey in *I Went Down*	114
7.2	Finbar maintains eye contact with Danny as he gropes Katie in *The Disappearance of Finbar*	118
7.3	Billy Hatchett shifts from hard-bodied republican masculinity to glam rock performer in *Breakfast on Pluto*	123
8.1	Johnnie and Christian lie in bed together in *2by4*	134
8.2	The borstal boys' tangled intertwined bodies as they celebrate their rugby win in *Borstal Boy*	140
9.1	Man shows moment of intimacy to his partner through the safety of the café window in *Elephant Shoe*	151
9.2	Forced back into the 'closet', boy performs a defiant dance in *Fantabulous*	154

Acknowledgements

This book would never have been achieved without the massive support given to me by family, friends and colleagues. As this project has taken me on my own personal journey, I am indebted to those who make up my support system and who have helped me in so many different ways. While it is impossible to thank everyone involved, I would like to give particular mention to Gaby Smith, Phil Fillis, Stuart Bell, Becky Bartlett, Richard Horner, Graeme Gillespie, Graeme Spurr, the University of Glasgow Film and Television Department, Conn Holohan, Tony Tracy, the Irish Film Archives, Sue Clayton, Cathal Black and Colette Cullen. Thanks to Gillian Leslie and everyone at Edinburgh University Press for supporting this project. I also want to thank Dimitris Eleftheriotis and Katie Gough, who started this journey with me and who helped shape many of the conversations that led me here.

A special thank you to my mother, Becky Reuber, who has shown me unfailing love and support throughout what I am sure seemed to her at times a never-ending project, and to my sisters, Julia Macleod and Fiona Macleod. Finally I want to thank my partner, Ian Thomson, who has been with me every step of this long road and who has never wavered in his enthusiasm, patience and love.

CHAPTER 1

Queerly National and Nationally Queer: Paradoxes of an Irish Queer Cinema

On 22 May 2015, Irish citizens voted in favour of legalising same-sex marriage. This referendum was the first time that a federal government had left the legal question of same-sex marriage to be decided by popular vote. Through the overwhelming yes vote, Irish citizens presented a more liberal and inclusive Ireland to the world that broke away from its historical image as a conservative nation. As well, the international campaign for Irish people living around the world to return to Ireland to vote in the referendum (documented on Twitter through the hashtag #hometovote) was evidence of how Ireland's imagined national community extends beyond the nation-state's geographical borders to become a global community.

In an article in *The Irish Times*, journalist Fintan O'Toole framed the referendum as more than a victory for 'Liberal Ireland over Conservative Ireland'; instead, 'it's the end of that whole, sterile, useless, unproductive division. There is no longer a Liberal Ireland and a Conservative Ireland. The cleavage between rural and urban, tradition and modernity that has shaped so many of the debates of the last four decades has been repaired. This is a truly national moment' (O'Toole 2015). O'Toole's comment reveals the extent to which Irish identity has historically been defined through oppositions (Irish/British; Nationalist/Unionist; Catholic/Protestant) as well as underlines the potential for a new form of national imagining to emerge through the break-down of such divisions.

Irish Queer Cinema is located within this context of an Ireland in a state of national re-imagining. This book provides an analysis of representations of queer sexualities in contemporary Irish films to examine the complex role played by Irish cinema in the socio-cultural production, marginalisation, normalisation and interrogation of queerness. In recent years images of LGBTQ (lesbian, gay, bisexual, trans, queer) identities have become increasingly visible in Irish cinema. This growing queer cultural visibility has been linked to global factors, such as Ireland's integration into a European community, global campaigns for gay political rights and social inclusion, and the normalising sexual politics of neoliberalism. It has also been linked to political, socio-economic and cultural developments taking place within Ireland, including the decriminalisation of homosexuality in 1993, shifting demographics and cultural practices in response to Ireland's economic boom and subsequent recession, and the Irish Film Board's (IFB) revised mandate in 1993 of encouraging Irish filmmakers to cater to international audiences and mainstream appeal. This book investigates Irish queer cinema as a constantly shifting constellation of tensions surrounding the local and the global, shaped and reshaped by changes taking place in the Irish film industry, Irish society and the global economy.

While the term 'national' implies a unifying impulse, 'queer' operates as a disruptive tool that undermines identity categories, and those systems of power and language that produce and sustain them. By bringing these terms together, this book considers how the relationship between Irishness and queerness manifests in diverse ways through cinematic representations of non-normative sexual identities. *Irish Queer Cinema* draws together feature-length and short films released between 1984 and 2016 as depictive of an Irish queer cinema. It argues that Irish queer cinema is unlike the queer cinemas of other nations, where queer films tend to be manifestations of an oppositional and marginal culture. Instead, this book considers how Irish queer cinema emerges as a product of the complex, interdependent and inherently conflicted relationship between nationalist discourses and sexual politics in Ireland. Many of the films examined in this book were funded, at least in part, by the IFB, Ireland's national film funding body, and are consequently tied to its nationalist agenda. The IFB has not only been instrumental in the development of an indigenous film industry in Ireland, but its organisational policies have had a direct impact on the shape of Irish queer cinema, as discussed in Chapter 2. An understanding of Irish queer cinema therefore needs to take into account the institutional context from which many of these films emerge, and how cinematic representations of queerness participate in the national imaginings promoted by public funding bodies such as the IFB.

Historical antagonisms between dominant strains of nationalism in Ireland and homosexuality have produced 'Irish' and 'queer' as mutually repellent terms. Writing in 1997, Lance Pettitt argues that these tensions have resulted in cinematic representations which 'conceptualize "gay" as a highly problematic form of identity: socially, politically and morally marginalized within Irish culture and society' (1997: 254). In films such as *Pigs* (Black 1984), *Reefer and the Model* (Comerford 1987) and *The Last Bus Home* (Gogan 1997), non-normative sexuality is framed as a form of deviance that is subject to homophobic violence and discrimination. Yet more recent representations of queerness in Irish cinema are frequently tied to discourses of cosmopolitanism and neoliberalism. For instance, both *Goldfish Memory* (Gill 2002) and *Cowboys & Angels* (Gleeson 2003) present the Irish queer subject as a sexually liberated positive contributor to Irish society.

As globalisation and Ireland's 'Celtic Tiger' economic boom from the mid-1990s to the mid-2000s have broadened national boundaries and redefined traditional signifiers of Irishness, representations of Irish queer identities have become more visible on-screen. Such visibility, however, does not necessarily equate progressive sexual politics, and this more visible image of the Irish queer subject often fulfils a largely symbolic role while perpetuating negative and homophobic sexual stereotypes. As Ed Madden (2011) suggests, Irish cultural texts about homosexuality are rarely about homosexuality; instead, as Michael G. Cronin has argued with regards to Irish gay fiction in the 1990s, 'homosexuality inevitably functions as an icon of Irish modernity, symbolizing the social liberalization of the Celtic Tiger but defusing the radical potential of gay politics' (2004: 254–5).

Through its different case studies *Irish Queer Cinema* explores how Irish queer films participate in the ideological construction of the Irish 'nation' even as they may use queerness to challenge social norms and dominant modes of representation. The reason for this book is twofold. First, it responds to a need to provide a sustained analysis of Irish queer filmmaking culture. This book extends on previous work on gender and sexual representation in Irish cinema, and on earlier debates surrounding Irish cinematic representations of queerness initiated by Lance Pettitt (1997; 1999), Jenny Murphy (2003) and Fintan Walsh (2008; 2012). Further works by Ruth Barton (2004), Debbie Ging (2008; 2013), Martin McLoone (2000) and Conn Holohan (2010a) provide invaluable insights into the role that Ireland's film industry has played in both perpetuating and challenging dominant gender and sexual ideologies. *Irish Queer Cinema* builds on these works to offer the first extensive critical study of Irish queer cinema.

Second, *Irish Queer Cinema* offers a new approach to the study of Irish cinema via theories of space. Analysing spatial relationships between films enables new interpretations of individual texts. Within the wealth of critical work on Irish cinema, many discussions tend to focus on the same films and to analyse these films in relation to their historical contexts. This book broadens these debates by examining films in terms of space, focusing on how films represent specific socio-cultural spaces and how these spaces operate through social and sexual norms. Social exclusion is frequently expressed as exclusion from space; as a result, 'struggles for citizenship claims are increasingly expressed in the assertion of . . . the right to occupy space' (Bell and Binnie 2000: 80). Cultural representations produce particular spatial meanings, and are a means through which sexual ideologies and social relations are legitimated and normalised. For Brian Graham, cultural landscapes are implicated within the construction of power within a society, whereby 'social power requires space, its exercise shapes space, and this in turn shapes social power' (1997: 4). Through an approach of close textual analysis that interrogates films in terms of a sexual politics of space, *Irish Queer Cinema* explores cinematic space as a complex system of signification that is at once produced by and implicated within dominant social imaginaries.

Irish Queer Cinema is centrally focused on feature-length fiction films. As Ireland began to develop a film industry in the 1970s and 1980s, fiction emerged as an arena where indigenous filmmakers could challenge the wealth of fictional representations of Ireland and the Irish produced by foreign filmmakers; Irish filmmakers 'began to explore the contradictions of a changing society in a form of culture (the fiction film) in which there was little in the way of a national tradition or precedence' (McLoone 2000: 131). Growing institutional support and financing opportunities for commercial filmmaking further made fiction an increasingly appealing form to work within (see Rockett 1987: 128). The production of feature-length fiction films can therefore be understood as intimately linked to the inherently political project of re-imagining Irishness for both local and global audiences. In addition, a central focus in this book is on the relationship between cinematic representations of queerness and Irish nationalist discourses. Feature-length filmmaking, which, out of financial necessity, relies more heavily on national funding bodies such as the IFB, offers a compelling case study for exploring this relationship. Although the focus of this book is primarily on feature films, Chapter 9 begins to open up this focus by considering the unique queer potential of the Irish short film.

This study of Irish queer cinema does not include films from Northern Ireland. The lack of queer films from Northern Ireland in comparison to the Republic of Ireland prevents the identification of possible representational trends. Further, in establishing an Irish queer cinema this book is focused on socio-economic and cultural developments that are specific to the Republic of Ireland. As Holohan (2010a) acknowledges, the political and cultural conflicts within Northern Ireland are a direct consequence of the historical relationship between Britain and Ireland, and are therefore an implicit presence within any study of Irish national culture. Addressing the full complexity of these conflicts is beyond the immediate scope of this book. This book's deployment of the term 'Irish' therefore refers to the Republic of Ireland, unless otherwise stated.

Although this is a book on Irish queer cinema, the majority of queer representations examined here involve male characters. At the same time that queer identities have become increasingly visible in Irish cinema, queer masculinities dominate this new cultural visibility. Madden argues that the proliferation of texts focused on issues of masculinity 'are very much part of a cultural moment obsessed with the nature of masculinity and its possibilities for crisis, interrogation and transformation' (2011: 79). For Debbie Ging (2013), the cultural visibility of Irish masculinities can be attributed to the deconstructive and polysemic impulses of postmodern culture, public debates about men's roles in a changing society and the rise of masculinity studies out of feminist and queer scholarship.

The absence of Irish queer women on-screen can be further linked to the general invisibility of lesbianism within Irish public and cultural discourses. In her introduction to *Sex, Nation and Dissent in Irish Writing*, Éibhear Walshe notes that in contrast to the relationship that male homosexuality has had with Irish nationalist discourses, the issue of national identity for Irish lesbians has been 'more complicated because of the lack of a public identity, even a criminalised one' (1997: 6). Unlike male homosexuality, lesbianism was never criminalised in Ireland and therefore 'Irish lesbians were both outside the law and at the same time rendered invisible by lack of official recognition or even condemnation' (1997: 6). Such political invisibility has led to minimal cultural visibility, particularly in film. While queer women are found in five of the feature-film case studies in this book, only *Goldfish Memory* and *A Date for Mad Mary* (Thornton 2016) offer these female characters any strong narrative agency. In *Snakes and Ladders* (McAdam 1996) and *Crush Proof* (Tickell 1998) queer female characters only make brief appearances and are peripheral to the films' central narratives, and in *Cowboys & Angels* non-normative female sexuality is invoked only to be immediately disavowed through a celebration of heterosexuality. The lack of queer female representation within Irish cinema is an issue explored in more detail in Chapter 5. The following sections establish the three key paradigms framing this book's discussion of Irish queer cinema, namely 'queer', 'Irish' and 'space'.

Queer

Irish Queer Cinema's deployment of the term 'queer' can be read in two ways. First, *Irish Queer Cinema* uses 'queer' to establish its focus of study on films which feature non-normative sexual identities that include homosexual, bisexual and transgender identities. 'Queer' is frequently used as an umbrella term for diverse sexual identities, desires and behaviours that do not fit into institutional and socially sanctioned categories. Through such a broad conceptualisation of 'queer', *Irish Queer Cinema* draws together a group of films as representative of an 'Irish queer cinema' even as these films represent very diverse articulations of sexuality.

Second, this book extends 'queer' beyond sexuality to more broadly critique normative social structures and hierarchies of privilege. Queer theory emerges out of the deconstructive strategies of postmodernism and poststructuralism, and encompasses a wide range of theoretical approaches and methodologies. Broadly, queer theory operates as a discursive tool for challenging social norms and identity categories by exposing and undermining those dominant systems of power and language that have constructed and sustained them. It not only critiques heteronormative systems that inscribe a heterosexual identity as a dominant norm, but simultaneously exposes the constructed nature of identity; a queer critique 'problematises normative consolidations of sex, gender and sexuality [and] is critical of all those versions of identity, community and politics that are believed to evolve "naturally" from such consolidations' (Jagose 1996: 99). Defining itself against the norm rather than the heterosexual, 'Queer is by definition whatever is at odds with the normal, the legitimate, the dominant' (Halperin 1995: 62). Queer emerges then as a powerfully disruptive position of alterity that encompasses new forms of social relations: non-normative lifestyles, oppositional and subcultural practices, and alternative models of alliance and community.

The rise of queer scholarship within Film Studies demonstrates the value of queer theory for rethinking issues around identity and representation in film as well as exposing the ideological and cultural role that film plays in the construction of meaning. By applying queer theory to the study of Irish cinema, this book contributes to these ongoing debates whilst investigating how 'queer' operates in unique ways in relation to Irish culture. Even as this analysis of films reveals ways in which they begin to unpack ideas of normality and disrupt dominant structures and meanings, many of these films also delimit identity within stereotyped representations, depoliticise and desexualise sexuality through allegory, privilege heterosexist norms and appropriate mainstream conventions. Subsequently, the most interesting and significant tensions emerge in the ways in which Irish queer cinema is at once 'queer' and 'not-queer': neither completely mainstream nor marginal, neither fully radically subversive nor assimilationist.

As Walsh (2008; 2012) has noted, the difficulty in arguing for an Irish queer cinema stems from the lack of films which overtly explore the conceptual fluidity and slipperiness of sexuality. Rather than using sexuality as a strong affective, erotic and disruptive force, Irish films tend to use sexuality as allegory for the nation: as 'an instrument of national reflection, rather than as a complex web of identifications, desires and affects' (2012: 216). In an earlier essay, he suggests that Irish films perpetuate negative representations of homosexuality, with homosexuality typically linked to 'trauma, perversion, paedophilia, and social and political tension' (2008: 16). Focusing specifically on the on-screen male homosexual subject, Walsh argues that he tends to be largely evacuated of his sexuality to become a symbol of national dystopia and utopia: marking 'the outermost limits of social degradation (usually associated with a past that we are trying to forget) and future possibility (the ideal Ireland we imagine, and attempt to purchase into being)' (2008: 17). Further, as Murphy has argued, representations of queerness in Irish cinema tend to be subordinated within a heteronormative narrative, with films 'suppressing the homosexual "threat" through the marginalisation of homosexual storylines' (2003: 70).

Pettitt (1997; 1999), Murphy (2003) and Walsh (2008) propose alternative frameworks for interpreting representations of queer sexuality in Irish cinema and, in doing so, suggest that the queerness of Irish queer cinema can be understood in unique terms. Pettitt claims that even as Irish films frequently use homosexuality to signify 'a range of aberrant, negative types' (1997: 254), these stereotyped images can be reinterpreted as subversive forms of resistance against a heteronormative society. For example, while *Pigs* and *Reefer and the Model* associate homosexuality with criminality and deviance, both films can be read in terms of their critique of the Irish State and the socio-political struggles that have produced these queer characters as criminals and deviants. In a later essay, Pettitt argues against simply documenting instances of gay characters in Irish film and instead stresses the need to more rigorously interrogate sexual categories. Referencing the influence of the US-based New Queer Cinema (NQC) movement, progressive political reform and the growing critical attention on sexual minorities in Ireland, he claims that 'the point now should be to problematise the category "gay" itself' (Pettitt 1999: 61).

As Irish cinema in the 1990s and 2000s has become increasingly guided by commercial imperatives, Murphy suggests the need to consider how Irish films can challenge heterosexual and homosocial norms even as they replicate mainstream narrative conventions. Expressing doubt about the possibility of inventing a new language of cinema that could represent gay viewpoints, Murphy instead argues that the representation and interrogation of gender and sexual issues are best suited to mainstream narrative cinema, since it offers the greatest opportunity for accessing the mass audience and subsequently shifting cultural attitudes. She therefore proposes that the potential of a more subversive Irish queer cinema can emerge through the subversion of mainstream cinematic conventions. Specifically, Murphy identifies humour, and the use of homosexuality as a comic device, as a strategy for eliciting a new self-awareness and self-reflexivity amongst Irish audiences. Using *I Went Down* (Breathnach 1997) and *About Adam* (Stembridge 2000) as examples, she argues that the use of humour in these films reveals a possible new direction for Irish queer cinema: 'through the use of wit, Irish society can see itself in all its bigotry and assimilate alternative images without ever feeling berated or threatened by the "other" on screen' (2003: 76).

Murphy posits this strategy as one that will undermine homosocial norms to eventually lead to more progressive social attitudes and representations of homosexuality in the public sphere. While the transgressive potential of this strategy remains questionable, Murphy nevertheless introduces a new approach to analysing the queerness of Irish cinema in terms of its articulation via mainstream conventions. The influence of her approach is found in Chapters 5 and 7, where queer representation is analysed as a product of the mainstream, with a particular emphasis on how such images can be reread in more political and subversive terms.

Walsh extends on earlier arguments made by Pettitt and Murphy to consider the possibility of 'a queer representational aesthetic in Irish film' (2012: 216) that subverts and challenges aesthetic and cultural conventions. Shifting beyond overt homosexual representation, he locates the queerness of *Adam & Paul* (Abrahamson 2004) and *Garage* (Abrahamson 2007) in terms of how they feature 'a range of non-normative identities and relationalities which, although not expressly homosexual, are queerly unfixed and unsettling' (Walsh 2012: 218). Rather than using the sexual subject as a symbol of national trauma or economic success, these films situate their protagonists 'within a complex, unresolved domain of desire and otherness' to enable particular queer resonances (218). Walsh's conceptualisation of queerness in terms of alterity is developed further in this book through a spatial approach, whereby queerness is analysed not only in terms of representation but in terms of inclusion (or exclusion) from space.

Subsequently, while 'queer' is initially used in this book to refer to films that feature non-normative sexualities, it is simultaneously used to reveal identity as a process of becoming rather than a static state of being:

'always an identity under construction, a site of permanent becoming' (Jagose 1996: 131). In positing identity as inherently unstable, discursively constructed and historically contingent, *Irish Queer Cinema* exposes how normative regimes maintain the perceived hegemony of social identities and formations, such as the national citizen and the nation, through the reiteration of gender and sexual norms. This book does not attempt to identify 'positive' or 'negative' queer images in Irish cinema; rather, it explores how cinematic queerness functions to challenge social norms and dominant modes of representation.

Irish

The homosexual subject, and particularly the male homosexual subject, has occupied a key role within Irish discourses in both historical and contemporary contexts, operating simultaneously as evidence of colonial perversion, a marker of national treason and a symbol of modernisation. By applying queer theory to the study of Irish national cinema, this book investigates how sexual norms are deployed within dominant culture to participate in the ideological construction of the Irish 'nation'.

Ireland's political history with Britain and the strong social influence and political power of the Roman Catholic Church in Irish affairs have shaped Ireland's dominant national narrative and privileged political and sectarian identities over other forms of identification. Anxieties surrounding the nation and national stability in Ireland have historically justified and sanctioned State and Church intervention in the private realms of the individual and the family, and the public policing and regulation of gender and sexuality. Nationalist and religious discourses encouraged the tenacity of conservative values and moral ideals that were framed as integral to Ireland's national character and cultural legacy. They also promoted rigid gender and sexual norms that in turn prescribed certain kinds of social roles of Irish men and women.

Michel Foucault's assertion that 'homosexuality threatens people as a "way of life" rather than as a way of having sex' reveals that the threat that non-normative sexuality poses to the dominant social order is not rooted solely in non-procreative sex (1996: 310). In particular, queer bodies which refuse to comply with the State-sanctioned heterosexual imperative of citizenship are framed as 'a profound threat to the very survival of the nation' (Alexander 1994: 6). These queer bodies thus are positioned as anti-national deviants that need to be regulated and controlled by the State. For both British colonial powers and Irish nationalists, homosexuality has historically operated as a threat to national stability. Kieran Rose cites Jeffrey Weeks' explanation of the homosexual purges of the 1880s and the 1885 legislation, which criminalised sexual practices between men, as part of the general British concern with 'imperialism and national decline' (Rose 1994: 6). Homophobia was also perpetuated by the Irish nationalist press by pursuing 'homosexual scandals' in order to undermine officials in the colonial administration in Dublin. For Rose, 'It is significant that Irish nationalist ideology developed during such a homophobic period in European history' (1994: 7).

Anxieties surrounding masculinity, sexuality and the nation-building project are further evident in the cases of Roger Casement and Oscar Wilde. Casement, a British diplomat, was arrested for attempting to supply the Irish nationalist forces with arms for the Easter Rising in 1916. Kathryn Conrad (2004) argues that while the British case of treason against Casement was justified, he was further attacked by the press for his suspected homosexuality after the discovery of his diaries (known as the 'Black Diaries') which contained details of homosexual encounters. These dual accusations solidified a link between national treason and homosexuality. Yet Conrad notes that the Irish response to these accusations also implied the foreignness of homosexuality, whereby characterisations of Casement as an 'Irish patriot' were accompanied by rejections of his alleged homosexuality and dismissals of the Black Diaries as forgeries.

Drawing from B. L. Reid's biography of Casement, Conrad suggests that the anxiety Casement provoked can be attributed to the fluidity and incoherence of his identity. Embodying conflicting identity categories and allegiances, he was unable to be easily accommodated within nationalist discourses and threatened the reproduction of a coherent national self-image. Similar claims have been made with regards to Irish playwright Oscar Wilde, whose multiple identifications position him at once inside and outside the nation. The cultural anxiety surrounding Wilde is examined in more detail in Chapter 4's analysis of *A Man of No Importance* (Krishnamma 1994).

For Conrad, inherent assumptions regarding the foreignness of homosexuality and its threat to the family and, by extension, the nation reveal 'a profound anxiety not only about sexual identity but also about the stability of the nation and state and the security of their borders' (2004: 25). As Ireland sought to establish a strong post-colonial identity in the twentieth century, homosexuality was positioned as a potential threat to the nation-building project, 'seen to threaten not only the reproduction of bodies but the system of alliances between men, providing affective bonds and allegiances that might undermine both the family cell and the public sphere' (Conrad 2004: 7). Thus homosexuality operated within the nationalist project as 'a ready discursive tool that can be conflated with any enemy of the state, in the process becoming the enemy within' (Stychin 1998: 194).

Over the past five decades, the cultural visibility and political support of LGBTQ people in Ireland have grown substantially. In Rose's (1994) seminal historical mapping of gay and lesbian politics in Ireland, he argues that a series of political, economic and socio-cultural events starting in the 1960s were instrumental in establishing and increasing the visibility of gay and lesbian movements in Ireland. As Ireland became increasingly industrialised, a new economic policy was introduced that relaxed protectionism and implemented incentive strategies for encouraging foreign investment in Ireland. Ireland applied for European Union (EU) membership, gaining admittance in 1973. In 1962 the nation's State television station, Radio Telefís Éireann (RTÉ), was established, and in 1964 and 1967, bills were passed that liberalised film and literature censorship laws, respectively. Furthermore, in 1965 a report on education in Ireland was published that sought to remove the school from the sacristy. These changes suggested Ireland's shift towards becoming a more globalised and socially liberal society, creating the conditions for gay and lesbian movements to take shape.

Following the Stonewall Riots in New York in 1969, the Irish Gay Rights Movement (IGRM) was founded in Dublin in 1974 with the social and political aims of creating a space in which gay people could socialise while working to neutralise Ireland's anti-gay laws. Several members of the IGRM soon split off to form the Cork Gay Collective in 1980, with a Dublin-based counterpart established shortly after. Described by Rose to be 'at the cutting edge of gay political action in the 1980s', the Collective adopted a manifesto that encouraged gay Irish people 'to have a positive view of their sexuality, to live fully and to challenge society's control by coming out in the family, work, church and social life' (Rose 1994: 16). The Collective also aligned its cause with other social movements, particularly the women's movement in Ireland, by claiming that 'gay liberation involves the freeing of all oppressed groups ... recognising that our shared oppression derives from the abuse of sexuality as a tool of oppression which necessitated strict gender stereotyping and the denial of sexual fulfilment' (1994: 16). The Collective's stated aim of aligning itself with other social movements was not limited to Ireland; the group positioned itself as 'internationalist' and aligned itself with gay and lesbian causes worldwide (1994: 16).

Yet despite this early drive for the legal and social recognition of sexual minorities in Ireland in the 1970s, Rose notes that by the mid-1980s there was a noticeable decline in political activism, not only within the gay rights movement but also within other political activist groups such as the women's movement. He attributes this decline to the economic recession Ireland faced in the 1980s. This period has been widely characterised as a deeply conflicted period in Irish history, torn between the project of modernisation and industrialisation that signalled social and economic progress, and the continuing hold of those deeply ingrained conservative nationalist ideals of the Catholic Church and republican politics (Baudrillard 1996; McCarthy 2000; McLoone 2000; Barton 2004). The failed divorce referendum in 1986, a series of highly publicised scandals of violence, rape and sexual abuse within the family (namely the Granard tragedy in 1984, the Kerry babies case in 1984, the 'X' case in 1992 and the Kilkenny Incest Case also in 1992),[1] high unemployment rates and increasing emigration rates all suggested that Ireland was in a state of economic, social and political regression; as Baudrillard claims, 'the equation of urbanisation and industrial development with enlightenment values of progress, secularisation and cosmopolitanism proved no longer viable in the austere cultural climate of the 1980s' (1996: 84). Baudrillard's statement resonates with Irish feminist and lesbian activist Ailbhe Smyth's 1988 assertion that the confidence and energy previously driving the women's movement was 'well nigh quenched by the fundamentalist repression and the economic recession' in the mid-1980s (Smyth quoted in Rose 1994: 21).

From the late 1980s onwards, the influence of global politics and economic forces on Irish identity politics has become increasingly apparent. Between 1988 and 2006, Ireland underwent rapid socio-economic and cultural transformation. Ireland's economic boom, popularly referred to as the Celtic Tiger, is largely attributed to an influx in foreign investment and Ireland's central position within the European market, and has been

---

[1] The Granard tragedy refers to the death of Ann Lovett, a fifteen-year-old schoolgirl who died giving birth beside a grotto in Granard, County Longford. Her infant son also died. The Kerry babies case later that year involved the discovery of an infant stabbed to death and abandoned on a beach in County Kerry. A young woman named Joanne Hayes was arrested and confessed to the crime, only for authorities to discover that she had given birth to a different baby that she and her family had then buried in her garden. In the media storm that followed the case, police were criticised for intimidation tactics and unlawfully coercing a confession from Hayes. The 'X' case in 1992 involved a pregnant fourteen-year-old girl who had been raped by a family friend and was banned by the Irish State from travelling to Britain to get an abortion since abortion is outlawed under the Constitution of Ireland. Only once the victim was proven to be suicidal did the Supreme Court grant her permission to travel to Britain. Finally, the Kilkenny Incest Case refers to the case of a young woman who was systematically abused and raped by her father for over sixteen years and had a son by him.

linked to decreasing rates of unemployment and government debt, increasing patterns of urban living and rising standards of living (McLoone 2000; Coulter 2003; Barton 2004). While Irish history has been characterised by a narrative of emigration, with net emigration rates peaking in the 1950s, by the mid-2000s this became reversed as Ireland became an increasingly desirable immigration destination. In line with these changes, Celtic Tiger Ireland became a new commodity market, with consumer spending rates rising dramatically in the late 1990s. Ireland also began to find a place within the global export market, as local artists, cultures and traditions found popularity on the world stage.

Celtic Tiger Ireland is further characterised by a series of significant political events. Both McLoone (2000) and Barton (2004) note that a series of political reforms in the 1990s, including the legalisation of divorce in 1997 and the signing of the Belfast Agreement in 1998, indicated that Ireland was moving away from a past shaped by a tumultuous political history with Britain, the nationalist ideals of Irish republicanism and the repressive doctrine of the Catholic Church. In 1993, homosexuality was decriminalised in Ireland following a twenty-year campaign for reform that was linked to a broader struggle for liberalisation against censorship laws and repressive legal control around sexuality. Further, the Employment Equality Act (1998) and the Equal Status Act (2000), which prohibit discrimination in the workplace and in the provision of goods and services, and the Marriage Equality Act (2015) have resulted in greater freedoms for sexual minorities.

In addition to cinema, a growing queer cultural visibility has emerged in Ireland through queer theatre and performance, the rise of Irish drag queen Panti Bliss as a cultural icon (she performed on the Abbey Stage in 2014 and was the subject of the 2015 documentary film *The Queen of Ireland* – Horgan 2015), and annual events such as the Dublin-based GAZE International LGBT Film Festival and the Dublin Gay Theatre Festival. There is also growing critical attention to this new cultural visibility, evidenced by such recent publications as *Deviant Acts: Essays on Queer Performance* (Cregan 2009), *Queer Notions: New Plays and Performances from Ireland* (Walsh 2010), *Theory on the Edge: Irish Studies and the Politics of Sexual Difference* (Giffney and Shildrick 2013), and *Queer Performance and Contemporary Ireland: Dissent and Disorientation* (Walsh 2015).

Space

Irish Queer Cinema approaches the study of Irish queer cinema through the sexual politics of space, exploring how social and spatial relations are structured by gender and sexual norms and how these are represented in terms of cinematic space. It takes as an assumption the constructed nature of space, building on canonical theories put forward by Lefebvre, Foucault and Soja to conceptualise space in postmodern terms as heterogeneous, contested and dynamic rather than homogenous and static. Social identities and relations must be interrogated in relation to spatial practice; as Soja argues, 'we are becoming increasing aware that we are, and always have been, intrinsically spatial beings, active participants in the social construction of our embracing spatialities' (1996: 1). The social is thus materialised through its spatialisation: 'the social relations of production have a social existence to the extent that they have a spatial existence; they project themselves into a space, becoming inscribed there, and in the process producing that space itself' (Lefebvre 1991: 129). Dominant systems of power and knowledge rely on the coherent and ordered mapping of space, and those bodies within it, to construct a dominant social order, and that social order is maintained through material actions.

Issues of space are central to nation-building and the formation of the national subject. An imagined national space is constructed by social imaginaries that operate through both ideological and material practices. The national 'imagined political community' (Anderson 1983: 6) is imagined not only as homogenous and cohesive but as bounded within a specific socio-physical space. As globalisation has transformed traditional understandings of the nation, such transformation can be understood in terms of the transformation of space. Ireland's growing economic and cultural ties to Europe and the increasingly global mobility of people, information and capital have produced new spatialities and subjectivities associated with urbanisation, deterritorialisation and transnational mobility. *Irish Queer Cinema* explores how these changes are mapped out in cinematic space, examining how films shape an imagined national space even as they problematise the construct of nation by 'exposing its masquerade of unity' (Hayward 2000: 101). Within these films, space becomes 'an ideologically charged cultural creation whereby meanings of place and society are made, legitimised, contested, and obscured' (Hopkins 1994: 47).

Just as issues of space shape the nation, they are implicated within the production of gendered and sexualised identities; for Browne, Lim and Brown, 'sexuality – its regulation, norms, institutions, pleasures and desires – cannot be understood without understanding the spaces through which it is constituted, practiced and lived' (2007: 4). The discursive positioning of homosexuality within the Irish nation-building project in the nineteenth and twentieth centuries and the recent campaign surrounding same-sex marriage in Ireland reveal how sexuality has historically been and continues to be implicated within spatial models of citizenship. The characterisation of homosexuality as outside the nation, as a foreign threat or colonial pollutant, brings sexuality out of the private sphere into the public sphere only to position it as neither private nor public, subject to State monitoring and regulation. More recently the 2015 same-sex marriage campaign in Ireland revealed how private rights to marriage and family continue to be negotiated within the public sphere.

Work on the spatial politics of sexual citizenship argues for how sexual identities are organised, divided and confined across public and private spaces, and seeks to problematise the public/private divide. Private and public spaces are not natural and stable entities; rather, they are discursive constructions that are actively maintained through social practices. Sexuality is often assumed to be, or suggested that it should be, confined to the private sphere, with this assumption promoting an understanding of sexuality as apolitical. Yet the private sphere reproduces sexual ideologies that are inherently political and it should therefore be considered in dialogue with the wider public realm; as Elizabeth M. Schneider describes, 'The decision about what we protect as "private" is a political decision that always has important "public" ramifications' (1991: 978). Lauren Berlant and Michael Warner (2002) argue that intimacy is itself publicly mediated, and that the hegemony of heterosexual culture is achieved through ideologies and institutions of intimacy, such as marriage and reproduction; for example, as explored in Chapter 3, the Irish Constitution explicitly frames the heterosexual family unit as a necessary building-block of the nation and makes a direct correlation between the woman's position in the home and the well-being of the State.

The relegation of sexuality to the private sphere obscures the sexualisation of public space. While ostensibly a democratic space, public space operates through uneven power relations and hierarchies of privilege that reinforce the naturalisation of heterosexual norms. Jean-Ulrick Désert (1997) argues that the unequal claims to public space for heterosexuals and homosexuals means that heterosexual desire can be publically expressed while homosexual lives must be lived in secrecy. Yet he further theorises how queer bodies have the disruptive potential to reveal such space as both constructed and contested. A dominant strategy deployed within LGBTQ activism has been to transgress space to destabilise its heterosexual identity and undermine processes of homophobic oppression. Forms of activism such as public displays of same-sex 'kiss ins', large-scale protests and marches, and pride parades use the queer body to make visible the normalisation and spatialisation of sexual ideologies.

By exposing and challenging the heteronormativity of public space, spatial tactics of queer politics become what Tim Cresswell calls 'crisis points in the normal functioning of everyday expectations' (1996: 22). Gill Valentine considers how such disruptive performances of dissident sexualities are 'about empowerment and being "in control" ', re-territorialising space normalised as heterosexual and publicising 'private' identities to reveal the public/private divide as a heteronormative construction (1996: 154). In Ireland, public space continues to be a central site for sexual contestation. In 1974, Gay Pride Day was established when a small group of activists protested outside the Department of Justice and the British Embassy, and in 1983 Dublin's first recognisable pride parade took place. Earlier that same year, Ireland's largest gay and lesbian march was organised in response to the murder of a gay man, Declan Flynn,[2] and the leniency given to his murderers, which was viewed as official tolerance of anti-gay violence. Protestors marched from the city centre to Fairview Park in the north of the city, and through the areas where Flynn's attackers lived: as Rose explains, 'It was to be a defiant public statement that gay people would not be frightened off the streets and out of public spaces' (1994: 20). In one of the few early accounts of Irish lesbian feminist political and social activities, Joni Crone (1988) describes how lesbian activists in the 1970s countered their invisibility and challenged the media's refusal to print any form of gay or lesbian advertising by printing stickers with the number of a gay and lesbian telephone support line and placing them on bathroom doors in pubs and hotels across the country.

Public space can therefore operate as a crisis space characterised by the complex negotiation of multiple sexualities and spatialities. In addition to the disruptive potential of queer bodies within heteronormative organisations of space, queer bodies may embody non-normative relations to time and space. Judith Halberstam uses Foucault's assertion that 'homosexuality threatens people as a "way of life" rather than as a way of having sex' to propose a 'queer way of life' that encompasses 'subcultural practices, alternate methods of alliance, forms of transgender embodiment, and those forms of representation dedicated to capturing these wilfully eccentric modes of being' (2005: 1). For Halberstam, such subcultural practices enable queer subjects to explore new life modes and social relations outside of the normative, linear life course of birth, marriage, reproduction and death.

---

[2] Flynn was attacked by a group of young men who chased him through Fairview Park and beat him to death. The young men were given five-year suspended sentences and held a 'victory march' in Fairview Park where they proclaimed 'we are the champions' and celebrated homophobic violence.

Her argument for queer spatialities and temporalities dovetails with Sarah Ahmed's (2006a; 2006b) concept of 'queer orientations', which she uses to suggest the possibility of specifically queer modes of living. Ahmed develops 'orientations' as a spatial and temporal model for understanding how the body is directed to follow certain life paths that in turn reinforces dominant social norms. Arguing for sexual orientation as a process of residing in space, she conceptualises it in terms of 'how we inhabit spaces as well as "who" or "what" we inhabit spaces with' (2006a: 1). She suggests that living a queer life involves some degree of disorientation, since the queer body is unable to fully inhabit a world shaped by heterosexual structures. Through the act of 'turning away' from those objects given by heterosexual culture, 'the queer subject within straight culture hence deviates and is made socially present as a deviant' (2006a: 21). Compulsory heterosexuality can thus be likened to a straightening device, whereby bodies become straight by 'lining up' with heteronormative lines and become queer when they fail to do so and consequently appear 'out of line' (2006a: 22).

Halberstam and Ahmed's arguments for how queer ways of being open up alternative relations to time and space heavily inform the following case study chapters. Throughout this book, close textual analysis is combined with queer and spatial theory to analyse films in terms of a sexual politics of space. A key focus is on the relationship between bodies and space, exploring how gender and sexual norms are embedded within spatial practices and structures, how these in turn produce, shape and regulate social identities and life modes, and how these are represented in terms of cinematic space. *Irish Queer Cinema* argues that space plays a central role in the construction, articulation and transformation of social identities and sexual politics, and that cinematic space reflects, reinforces and re-imagines broader ideological and political processes taking place within the material spaces of the nation.

This book is structured by spatial models of queer sociality that are used to organise and analyse its different case studies. It consists of ten chapters that analyse specific films in relation to different socio-cultural spaces: the family, the pub, the city, the rural, the journey, diaspora and the short film. Within these spaces, tensions between public/private, visibility/invisibility, inclusion/exclusion and normality/deviance emerge as productive sites for exploring how Irish queer cinema re-imagines the parameters of national identity, sexual citizenship and Irish culture.

CHAPTER 2

Mapping Ireland's Queer Films

This chapter provides a historical context for the following case study chapters. It frames individual films in relation to significant developments and debates shaping Irish society and the Irish film industry, mapping out Irish queer cinema against three different periods of indigenous filmmaking in Ireland: the First Wave, Celtic Tiger and post-Celtic Tiger. In doing so, it establishes the parameters for this study of Irish queer cinema whilst outlining the rationalisation for and value of considering these films as Irish.

Discussions of national cinema generally define it in terms of its ability to express a distinct national culture and are based on the premise that the national origin of a film is a unique marker. The concept of national cinema has been undermined by critics who argue that it assumes a homogenous and stable national community that in turn obscures cultural diversity and transnational forms of belonging. Yet this book argues for the potential of a national cinema to reveal the inconsistencies and incoherencies that underlie the discursive construction of the nation. Aligning itself with approaches to national cinema taken by Tom O'Regan (1996) and Susan Hayward (2000), it explores how Irish queer films affect and are an effect of 'the way in which society as a national whole is problematized and the kind of nation that has been projected through such problematization' (O'Regan quoted in Hayward 2000: 93). Rather than using the national to imply a coherent and cohesive whole, it becomes a tool for examining how films situate Irish queer stories, identities, spaces and themes in relation to local, transnational and global processes.

In 1992 perhaps one of the most internationally recognised Irish queer films, *The Crying Game* (Jordan 1992), was released to critical acclaim. Centred on a love triangle between IRA member Fergus (Stephen Rea), black British transgender hairdresser Dil (Jaye Davidson) and Antiguan black British soldier Jody (Forest Whitaker), the film plays out anxieties surrounding nationalism, the Irish/British relationship and race through the subversion of norms surrounding masculinity and sexuality. *The Crying Game* garnered high levels of visibility on the international festival circuit and was nominated for six Academy Awards, winning one for Best Screenplay. It also helped to invigorate the Irish film industry, with its international success helping to relaunch the IFB in 1993. Twenty-five years later the film remains a significant cultural text in discussions of both Irish cinema and queer representation, not only in terms of its content but also in terms of the polarising debates it continues to provoke. Arguments surrounding the film's 'queerness' as well as competing claims regarding its 'nationality' are indicative of broader issues and debates shaping this study of Irish queer cinema.

Critics have praised *The Crying Game* for its attempts to deconstruct an Irish nationalism predicated on violent republican politics, Catholic virtues and compulsory heterosexuality. Jordan uses queerness as a signifier for a fluid and postmodern identity that transcends rigid national identity politics, and characters' sexual transgressions become rejections of those political, religious and social norms embedded within nationalism. However, some critics have argued that the film actually reinstates rigid representational strategies by using Dil as a narrative device and refusing her any strong agency or voice, by subordinating racial politics and privileging the white subject, and by presenting a regressive and misogynistic female stereotype through the character of Jude (Simpson 1994; Edge 1995; McIvor 2009). Jordan's heterosexual identity has also been cited as problematic, with Mark Simpson (1994) claiming that the film presents a male heterosexual view of homosexuality. Yet for Lance Pettitt the significance of *The Crying Game* lies in how it has produced these debates. Rather than being seen as a 'culmination' film, 'the film's contrariness expresses a moment of ideological contest between the dominant political/cultural blocs and subordinate groupings which have a specific location within an Irish context' (Pettitt 1997: 273).

Competing claims about the nationality of *The Crying Game* also reflect ongoing issues surrounding the Irishness of Irish queer cinema. While written and directed by an Irish man, Neil Jordan, and centrally focused on violence and IRA politics during the Troubles, *The Crying Game* was funded and produced by British companies Palace Pictures and Channel Four Films. Even as the film uses the historical setting of the Troubles in Ireland, it fails to offer any strong interrogation into the reasons behind the political violence. Instead the film is framed in more global terms as an individual's journey of self-discovery and its international success has helped to mark Irish cinema as 'a global art form' (McIvor 2009: 171).

At the same time, Pettitt claims that characterising the film as Irish is crucial for understanding its significance. By fusing sexual anxieties with national antagonisms, the film questions how homosexuality has figured within dominant formations of political power within both British and Irish contexts. In addition, Jordan has stated that the idea for the film emerged out of his own ambivalent relationship to Ireland. Having immigrated to the UK due to a lack of opportunities and funding for filmmaking in Ireland, Jordan continues to identify as Irish and has stated that he feels like an outsider in England. For Jordan, 'the attempt to imagine another state of living, another way of being, is I believe very Irish' (Jordan quoted in Barton 2004: 10).

Similar issues surrounding 'queerness' and 'nationality' emerge in relation to many of the Irish queer films examined here. As discussed in Chapter 1, the Irish queer subject on-screen frequently operates as national allegory. Even as queerness functions as a disruptive signifier of fluidity and excess in Irish cinema to challenge rigid identity categories and normative structures, such disruptive potential is often diffused through the queer subject's containment within sexual stereotypes, mainstream conventions and narrative function.

However, in line with Pettitt's approach to *The Crying Game*, this book is interested in how these films provoke interesting and troubling questions surrounding gender, sexuality and nationalism within contemporary Ireland. Analysing them in terms of their sexual and spatial politics enables new understandings of how these films are implicated within and yet intervene in current cultural and political debates surrounding Irish and queer cinemas. Like *The Crying Game*, several of the films examined here can also be characterised by competing nationalities because of, for instance, the transnational funding structures of *I Went Down* and *The Disappearance of Finbar* (Clayton 1996) and the primary settings of *2by4* and *Borstal Boy* (set in New York and England, respectively). Framing Irish queer cinema as a distinctly national mode of cultural expression enables a more productive understanding of how these films participate in the ideological and cultural construction of the nation even as they may not necessarily be exclusively bounded by this paradigm. The following sections map this book's case studies against three distinct periods of Irish filmmaking.

First Wave Queer Cinema

Ireland began to develop a distinctive film industry in the 1970s and 1980s. According to Martin McLoone (1994), the turning point for film production in Ireland was the 1973 Arts Act, which recognized film as an art form and made it eligible for State funding. Ireland's First Wave film movement, labelled by Ging as Irish cinema's 'golden age' (2013: 2), was led by a group of independent filmmakers who employed film as a political tool. The works of Cathal Black, Joe Comerford, Fergus Tighe, Bob Quinn, Thaddeus O'Sullivan and Pat Murphy (the only woman filmmaker regularly included in this group) sought to interrogate established understandings of Irishness with regards to nationalism, religion, class, gender and sexuality. Critical in tone and deploying a cinematic language influenced by experimental and avant-garde filmmaking, First Wave films sought to 'deconstruct received notions of Irish images and themes' (Barton 2004: 85) and focused on Ireland's fractured, conflicted and excluded individuals, narratives and spaces.

The First Wave film movement was the product of the conflicted state of Irish society. From the late 1960s to the late 1970s, processes of modernisation in Ireland led to rapid economic growth and indicated its shift towards becoming a more urban, secular and liberal society. However, by the 1980s the climate of optimism and liberalism surrounding this project of modernisation had dispelled. Economic stagnation, high unemployment rates and increasing numbers of young Irish people emigrating abroad suggested that Ireland was in a state of economic and social regression. The failed divorce referendum in 1986 and a series of highly publicised scandals of violence, rape and sexual abuse further revealed the continuing hold of deeply ingrained conservative religious and nationalist ideologies.

Irish queer films emerging during this time reflect a conflicted moment in Irish history, caught between competing pressures of traditionalism and modernity. *Pigs* (Black 1984) and *Reefer and the Model* (Comerford 1988) each focus on a group of disparate individuals who band together through their shared experiences of social marginalisation. Both films are landmark Irish queer films for making homosexuality visible rather than simply inferring its existence. *Pigs* portrays what has been described as Ireland's first gay bar on-screen, and *Reefer and the Model* presents the first on-screen kiss between two men in an Irish film. Even as the films make homosexuality explicitly visible, they situate such representation in relation to other kinds of socio-political struggle. Subsequently, struggles surrounding sexuality in these films are imbricated in issues of class, gender, nationalism and religion to suggest a broader state of crisis taking place in 1980s Ireland.

While *Pigs* and *Reefer and the Model* engage explicitly with themes of homosexuality, the queer themes embedded within *Clash of the Ash* (Tighe 1987) emerge implicitly through a queer reading of the film that focuses on its interrogation of normative Irish masculinity. The film's protagonist, Phil Kelly, experiences a crisis of masculinity as he struggles against conforming to social pressures and the expectations of his family and rural town community. The film reveals the lack of opportunities that exist for young people, particularly in rural Ireland, in the 1980s and suggests emigration as a necessary act of escape. *Pigs*, *Reefer and the Model* and *Clash of the Ash* also share aesthetic strategies associated with the First Wave: a realistic and naturalistic filming style, on-location filming with non-professional actors, and cinematic conventions associated with radical or independent cinema, such as spatial ambiguity and narrative disjuncture.

The development of the First Wave was aided in part by the establishment of the IFB in 1980. Operating under the mandate of supporting works that met 'the need for the expression of national culture through the medium of filmmaking' (Irish Film Board Act 1980), the IFB aimed to boost the local economy by funding the development and production of Irish film and television. From 1980 to 1987, the IFB helped to finance ten feature films, funded various television documentaries and film shorts, provided grant-supported script development and made what Kevin Rockett declares as 'the most significant contribution to the development of Irish cinema' (1994: 128).

At the same time, it became subject to scrutiny after its decision to allocate a substantial portion of its annual budget to fund Neil Jordan's *Angel* (1982), a film executively produced by then-IFB chairman John Boorman. First Wave filmmakers therefore felt some animosity towards the intentions of the IFB. Suspicion surrounding those who were running the IFB along with the IFB's poor financial return on its investment led to its closure in 1987. The re-establishment of the IFB in 1993, the same year that homosexuality was decriminalised in Ireland, marks the start of Ireland's 'Second Wave', or 'Celtic Tiger', film movement.

Celtic Tiger Queer Cinema

The majority of the films examined in this book belong to Ireland's 'Second Wave' film movement and were produced during the Celtic Tiger economic boom. Ireland's rapid economic growth was accompanied by cultural responses imbued with a new outward-looking optimism whereby 'Ireland's contemporary culture is seen as an eloquent expression of new-found confidence where the liberalisation of internal markets is matched by the celebration of individual rights and liberties' (Kirby *et al.* 2002: 7). For Ruth Barton (2004), the Celtic Tiger encompassed a cultural shift away from the expression of a collective national identity, linked to the nation-building project, and towards an emphasis on plurality and multiplicity informed by a postmodern identity politics. Films emerging during this period also reflect the demands of the global market, moving towards a more commercialised form of filmmaking aimed at international audiences.

The commercial imperative underpinning this Second Wave film movement has been directly attributed to the IFB's revised mandate in 1993 that encouraged filmmakers to be 'market-responsive auteurs': filmmakers who cater to market demand by making films with mainstream appeal to ensure greater financial return. This mandate sought to meld local specificity with international appeal, and operated through the rationalisation that producing films with significant economic outcomes would finance an increased number of future films, thereby enhancing cultural impact.

Rod Stoneman, who served as the CEO of the IFB from 1993 to 2003, described its revised mandate as combining cultural and economic aims by setting out 'to construct a practice of filmmaking that came from, and spoke to, its own national imaginary with authenticity and integrity, whilst also navigating the implications of international finance from a market dominated by doxa from elsewhere' (2005: 251). For Stoneman, this model of producing a larger number of smaller budget films, with the minority succeeding sufficiently financially to cover the majority (which would fail commercially), is 'the only basis of any non-industrial version of cinema to play to its strengths, maintain its authenticity and integrity, and in the longer term to reinvent itself' (2005: 249).

Stoneman further acknowledges the IFB's role in modernising national and international perceptions of Irish film by providing alternatives to the well-established Irish tropes based on historical, rural and art-house sensibilities: 'shift[ing] those residual perceptions and transmit[ting] a sharper sense that many of the new films were more urban, comic, violent, sexual' (2005: 254). Under this new film policy, Irish filmmakers looked outwards for alternative cinematic models and modes of representation.

In its second stage, the IFB became instrumental to the development of Ireland's queer cinema. For Walsh (2008), the most overt explorations of sexuality in Irish cinema emerged in the wake of the IFB's re-establishment. Second Wave queer films include: *A Man of No Importance* (Krishnamma 1994), *The Disappearance of Finbar* (Clayton 1996), *Snakes and Ladders* (McAdam 1996), *I Went Down* (Breathnach 1997), *Crush Proof* (Tickell 1997), *2by4* (Smallhorne 1998), *Borstal Boy* (Sheridan 2000), *About Adam* (Stembridge 2000), *Goldfish Memory* (Gill 2002), *Cowboys & Angels* (Gleeson 2003), *Breakfast on Pluto* (Jordan 2005) and *Garage* (Abrahamson 2007). In contrast to the radical aesthetics and inward-looking critique found in the First Wave queer films, queer films emerging in this second wave tend to adopt mainstream film conventions borrowed from Hollywood and British cinemas and explore broader universal themes relating to identity, sexuality and desire that open them up to global audiences. For example, the romantic comedy is revisited in *About Adam* and *Goldfish Memory*, the buddy film informs *Cowboys & Angels*, and *I Went Down* adapts the conventions of the American road movie.

In addition to showcasing queer sexualities, Celtic Tiger queer films represent the growing range of Irish identities on-screen, particularly marginalised or deviant identities excluded from dominant nationalist discourses. *The Last Bus Home*, *Snakes & Ladders* and *The Disappearance of Finbar* focus on young adults struggling to find modes of cultural expression and personal independence outside the shadow of their parents' generation, while *Crush Proof* and *I Went Down* feature criminal male characters and are associated with a similar cycle of 'lad' films emerging in Britain (Ging 2013). Even as these films contribute to the growing visibility of youth cultures and marginalised identities on-screen, they frequently present them in apolitical and ahistorical terms, with social exclusion framed as a subcultural lifestyle rather than a social problem.

I Went Down and *The Disappearance of Finbar* further represent the Irish film industry's growing reliance on EU funding schemes. Both films received funding from the European MEDIA program, and discussions of these films frequently cite their European influences. At the same time that Irish cinema was being informed by a European sensibility, McLoone (2000) argues for a renewed interest in Irish cinema in the 1990s in exploring the American-Irish relationship. *2by4*, written and directed by Jimmy Smallhorne (who also stars in the film), draws from Smallhorne's own experiences as an Irish immigrant living in New York. The film explores the contemporary implications of the Irish diaspora in the United States.

This second wave of filmmaking is also defined by a postmodern sensibility found in films that return to the past as a site of socio-political contestation (Walsh 2008; Barton 2004). *A Man of No Importance*, *Borstal Boy* and *Breakfast on Pluto* use Irish history to interrogate the effects of religious and nationalist ideologies on individual lives. These films project a type of retrospective liberalism around their characters' queer sexualities and reinforce the more universal themes of love and belonging rather than articulate an explicitly political agenda. *Breakfast in Pluto* in particular deploys a fragmented postmodern style through the instability of its protagonist, Patrick 'Kitten' Brady. The film's action is mediated through Kitten's subjectivity, with this subjectivity rendered inherently unstable through fantasy sequences, unreliable narration and temporal ellipses.

Finally, *Garage* is informed by an art-house sensibility that contrasts it stylistically with many of the earlier Celtic Tiger queer films and creates what Coinín Moore terms 'a new approach to Irish cinema' (2009: 112) with its lack of dialogue, long takes and slow pace. Produced during the Celtic Tiger, *Garage* provides a critique of that moment in Irish history through a character study of gas station attendant Josie. Josie's experience of liminality reflects 'the problems and uncertainties of a society in rapid transition' (McLoone 2009) and offers a critique of those more celebratory Celtic Tiger narratives. *Garage* can be viewed as one of the precursors of a more critical form of Irish filmmaking that emerged in response to the Celtic Tiger in the wake of Ireland's economic downturn.

Post-Celtic Tiger Queer Cinema

Ireland's post-Celtic Tiger cinema is shaped by the issues and debates that emerged during the Celtic Tiger. The Celtic Tiger economic phenomenon became a 'powerful cultural signifier for progress and newness' that changed Irish society on many levels (Buchanan 2009: 300). For Battel (2003: 101), 'Celtic Tigerhood was an important stage in the construction of postcolonial Irish identity, arguably the first one that was not constructed on "otherness", on being anti- nor not-British.' As the previous discussion of Celtic Tiger queer cinema revealed, films emerging within this context are difficult to classify due to their shift away from more traditional Irish cinema and incorporation of European and American cinematic sensibilities. Thus, the films can be seen as reflecting Alessandra Boller's claim that 'Ireland has become more open-minded but the fast transition, especially since the 1990s, also seems to have robbed many people of a stable basis when it comes to issues of (national) identity' (2017: 16).

Ireland's experience of such rapid economic growth and then decline has resulted in films that comment on Irish society's 'unease with transition' and its impact on people's individual and collective identity. Thus, a dominant theme in Ireland's post-Celtic Tiger cinema is around deepening social divisions and experiences of liminality and alienation, reflected in films such as *Parked* (Byrne 2010), *What Richard Did* (Abrahamson 2012), *Calvary* (McDonagh 2014), *I Used to Live Here* (Berry 2014) and *Frank* (Abrahamson 2014). Incorporating an inward-looking gaze that can be aligned with the First Wave, these more recent films focus on the marginalisation and isolation of Ireland's 'inner' outsiders in order to challenge the Celtic Tiger discourse of prosperity and liberalisation.

In queer films emerging out of this post-Celtic Tiger era there is an emphasis on the ongoing reconstruction of the (Irish) self within contemporary Ireland. These films include *A Date for Mad Mary* (Thornton 2016), *The Stag* (Butler 2013) and *Handsome Devil* (Butler 2016). In *A Date for Mad Mary*, Mary is released from prison where she was imprisoned for violent assault to discover that her best friend Charlene has distanced herself from her. Determined to get a date for Charlene's upcoming wedding, Mary signs up for a dating agency and goes on a series of unsuccessful dates with different men. She simultaneously develops a close friendship with Charlene's wedding videographer, Jess, with this friendship evolving into a romantic relationship. Unlike the Celtic Tiger romantic comedy *Goldfish Memory*, where a utopian modern-day Ireland serves as the backdrop for different sexual couplings, *A Date for Mad Mary* employs a more social realist style that highlights Mary's search for companionship and belonging amidst feelings of isolation. The film also subverts the masculinist 'lad' film that emerged in the UK in the 1990s and early 2000s. Whereas this genre generally focuses on male criminality and disenfranchisement as a subcultural lifestyle, *A Date for Mad Mary* puts a woman at the centre of its narrative and provides a more intricate exploration into the personal and social factors behind Mary's experience of social exclusion.

Díóg O'Connell (2016) locates a trend in recent Irish cinema of revisiting traditional Irish themes of rural life and Catholicism in order to deal with the legacy of Ireland's past. Both *The Stag* and *Handsome Devil* revisit these tropes to offer a more nuanced and complex representation of the Irish rural and Catholic character. *The Stag* is about a group of men going on a stag camping trip in rural Ireland. The film avoids representing an idyllic Irish pastoralism that has been historically tied to the Irish nationalist imaginary as well as the more bleak images of rurality found in First Wave queer films such as *Reefer and the Model* and *Clash of the Ash*. Instead, the film uses the rural setting as a catalyst for forcing its characters to confront issues facing men in contemporary Ireland that gained greater public attention following the Celtic Tiger, such as depression, financial hardship, emotional damage and social marginalisation.

Finally, *Handsome Devil* is set in a Catholic boarding school where rugby is treated as a religion. New student Ned becomes subject to the rugby team's homophobic taunting. When another new student, Conor, who is also a talented rugby player, is assigned as Ned's roommate, Ned anticipates they will not get along. However, after Ned witnesses Conor going to a gay bar one night, he realises that the two have more in common. Alongside the boys' growing friendship, their English teacher Dan Sherry emerges as a mentor figure. Dan is also gay, but has not come out to his colleagues.

Through these three queer male characters, the film represents different experiences of queer struggle. Ned fights to maintain a sense of individualism despite the bullying of his classmates. Conor struggles with how to reconcile his sexuality with his love of rugby as he tries to keep his sexuality a secret from his fellow teammates. Finally, while Dan urges the boys in his class to use their own voices, he is uneasy with how to be open about his own sexuality. Across these struggles, the film also breaks down the Catholic stereotype to show how Catholic identities can emerge in relation to, rather than in opposition to, queerness. While the rugby coach is openly homophobic, demanding Dan's resignation upon suspicion of his sexuality and refusing to allow Conor to play rugby after discovering he is gay, the school headmaster, Walter Curly, displays a more liberal attitude by comparison. Walter defends Dan to the rugby coach and at the end of the film Dan introduces his boyfriend to Walter. The film at once shows the continued presence of homophobia in contemporary Irish society and breaks down the Catholic stereotype to show the multiplicity of identities that exist.

Post-Celtic Tiger queer cinema is both shaped by and a response to the previous two Irish film movements. This periodisation of Irish queer cinema identifies common themes, aesthetics and representational trends linking films in each of the First Wave, Celtic Tiger and post-Celtic Tiger periods of indigenous filmmaking. It further shows how these film movements are shaped by broader socio-political, economic and cultural developments. The following case study chapters shift from this historical mapping to focus on how grouping films in terms of their spatial politics enables new productive comparisons across film movements.

CHAPTER 3

Re-imagined Kinship and Failed Communities

The Irish family is a consistent trope in Irish cinema, from the unhappy, poverty stricken Catholic upbringing Frank McCourt experiences in *Angela's Ashes* (Parker 1999) to the resilient and suffering matriarchal figure of Mrs Brown in *My Left Foot* (Sheridan 1989), to the troubled father-son and brother relationships that structure the narratives of *In the Name of the Father* (Sheridan 1993), *How Harry Became a Tree* (Paskaljevic 2001) and *The Wind that Shakes the Barley* (Loach 2006). Frequently operating as microcosms for Irish society, these on-screen families are subject to those greater forces affecting Ireland as a whole: economic poverty, mass emigration, political violence and religious oppression.

Such family narratives reflect the central position that the Irish family has historically occupied within Irish nationalist discourses and in the doctrine and teachings of the Catholic Church. Article 41 of the 1937 Constitution of Ireland directly positions a stable family unit as synonymous with stable social institutions and a stable nation-state with its decrees that 'the State recognises the Family as the natural primary and fundamental unit group of Society' and 'the State, therefore, guarantees to protect the Family in its constitution and authority, as the necessary basis of social order and as indispensable to the welfare of the Nation and the State' (*Bunreacht na hÉireann* 1999). From the 1970s onwards, successive legislative battles surrounding the legalisation of contraception, abortion, divorce and homosexuality in Ireland revealed the active roles played by the Irish State and the Catholic Church in regulating sexual practices and sexuality through the institution of the family. The Granard tragedy, the Kerry babies, the 'X' case and the Kilkenny Incest case further exposed the family as a space of crisis (see note 1 on page 12).

As these highly publicised legislative battles and sexual scandals brought issues surrounding Irish family life and the regulation of sexuality to the forefront of the public consciousness, Irish filmmakers responded by using family narratives to signify a profound national crisis. Ruth Barton argues that First Wave films frequently used a counter-narrative of the Irish family (as nation) to critique contemporary Irish society and its imagined national community: 'The discursive trope of denying the notional happy family and of refictionalising it as an oppressive, verging on dysfunctional, institution ... refutes the ideal of the Irish as "one happy family" and legitimises social alternatives to the biological family' (2004: 96). This approach enabled filmmakers to explore the 'surrogate' family: 'usually a coming together of a group of marginalised contemporaries' (2004: 97).

This chapter examines how *Pigs* (Black 1984) and *The Last Bus Home* (Gogan 1997) offer such a counter-narrative of the Irish family as nation by at once emulating and queering traditional kinship structures. Both films feature individuals who feel marginalised by and excluded from dominant Irish society and who congregate together to form subaltern communities to which they feel they can belong. Each of these communities also includes a queer male subject, Jimmy (Jimmy Brennan) in *Pigs* and Petie (John Cronin) in *The Last Bus Home*. Both men are aligned with the other members of their alternative families in terms of a shared sense of social marginalisation.

Pigs is centred on a group of squatters who take up illegal residence in an abandoned townhouse in inner-city Dublin. The group consists of Jimmy, a queer and largely silent figure who is legally married but does not live with his wife and is shown cruising for sex with men in a local bar; George (George Shane), an unemployed and chronically ill businessman; Tom (Maurice O'Donoghue), a paranoid schizophrenic; Ronnie (Liam Halligan), a drug dealer; Orwell (Kwesi Kay), a Jamaican immigrant and pimp with dreams of becoming a pop star; and Mary (Joan Harpur), Orwell's prostitute girlfriend. Near the end of the film, Jimmy is the target of homophobic violence when four boys break into the house and attack him after witnessing him picking up a man in a bar. After violence permeates the house, its community begins to break down and the inhabitants leave one by one. Only Jimmy is left until two Gardaí arrive to arrest him for social welfare fraud. The film ends with Jimmy being taken away in a police car.

In *The Last Bus Home* a group of young adults come together to form a band called the Dead Patriots within Dublin's underground punk rock scene. The band consists of Jessop (Brían F. O'Byrne), the lead singer; Reena (Annie Ryan), the band's self-elected manager and Jessop's girlfriend; Joe (Barry Comerford), the bass player; and Petie, the drummer who is also struggling with his sexuality. They set up a steady weekend gig in a city bingo hall and begin to attract a small but dedicated fan base in Dublin. When an interested scout from a London record label, Steve

Burkett (Brendan Coyle), comes to see them play, all four band members are initially optimistic and excited about their chances at more major success. However, disagreements among them about whether or not to move to London to pursue an opportunity with Steve's label, as well as Jessop's growing paranoia that he is losing control over the band and Reena, cause fractures within the group. Jessop witnesses Petie embracing Billy, another local musician, and shortly after Jessop confronts Petie onstage and accuses him of keeping secrets. Afraid Jessop is about to 'out' him, Petie runs out of the venue and into the street, and is run over and killed by a passing bus. The band breaks up and the film shifts forward several years later to show Reena and Jessop reuniting in Dublin shortly after the decriminalisation of homosexuality in Ireland.

Critics have already likened the communities in these films to an alternative form of family. Barton claims that in *Pigs* 'the disparate group of squatters forms its own family' (2004: 98) while Martin McLoone describes the band members in *The Last Bus Home* as building 'their alternative family' (2000: 173). Both critics' statements are supported by how these communities are marked by traditional kinship structures, with certain characters assuming more conventional patriarchal and matriarchal roles, and how they make similar claims to protection and self-preservation that characterise the traditional family unit. Yet what Barton and McLoone do not examine in depth is how the formation of these communities depends on the characters' occupation of spaces that are physically peripheral (the abandoned Georgian townhouse in *Pigs*) and culturally peripheral (Dublin's underground punk rock scene in *The Last Bus Home*). The survival of these communities appears contingent on them remaining physically and culturally insular; once they come into contact with dominant Irish society violence ensues, the bonds between characters break down and characters become physically dispersed. Specifically with regards to the queer male subject, both films end with him isolated and contained, either through state imprisonment (*Pigs*) or through his death (*The Last Bus Home*).

Queering the Family

Jeffrey Weeks (2010) argues that family and kinship systems are crucial to the social organisation of sexuality. While family and kinship may appear as fundamental and static social constructs, and are central to individuals' understandings of their own sexual identities and needs, they are not natural entities; rather, they are shaped by wider social relations and economic forces, and are a mechanism through which government and religious institutions exercise political and social control. In her work on the Irish family and the regulation of sexuality, Kathryn A. Conrad (2004) draws from Foucault's (1978) notion of the 'family cell', which he describes as a social, economic and political structure of alliance that anchors sexuality and sustains particular sexual relations. For Conrad, Foucault's family cell 'shapes both normative heterosexuality and that which falls outside of it' (2004: 4). She suggests that this has broader cultural implications when considering the family unit as a microcosm for the dominant national order: 'the centrality of the family cell to social, economic, and political organisation defines and limits not only acceptable sexuality but also the contours of the private sphere, the public sphere, and the nation itself' (2004: 4). Social relations within the private realm of the family serve as the foundation for the public sphere, and this reveals the illusory separation between the two spheres and the role of the family cell as 'a regulatory ideology, one that defines roles and choices' (Conrad 2004: 14). Conrad argues that the Irish family further operates as a mechanism for self-regulation and self-preservation, working to contain transgressions within the family in order to present itself as a unified whole.

The Irish State and the Catholic Church have historically sought to regulate gender hierarchies and sexual relations within the family in order to shape national borders and maintain a dominant patriarchal and heteronormative social order. In addition to the Irish Constitution reinforcing the family as a fundamental social unit, formal legal barriers that sought to limit married women's participation in the employment sector (such as the marriage bar),[1] national public health service campaigns that promoted stay-at-home motherhood as necessary for safeguarding children's health and general well-being, and the active role of the Catholic Church in presenting the family unit as a moral and social ideal and discrediting possible alternatives were aimed at privileging the conventional nuclear family as necessary for national stability (Mahon 1987; Nash 1993; Fahey 1995; Beaumont 1997; Wills 2001).

Those sexual identities and behaviours that disrupt familial and national stability and that challenge the dominant order must subsequently be diffused, contained or expelled. Conrad (2004) argues that homosexuality operates as a particular threat to national hegemony because the homosexual subject is unable to fit neatly within the structures of the family cell. The homosexual subject thus embodies a potential excess that threatens

---

[1] Introduced in 1932, the marriage bar banned married women from working in the public sector.

the solidity of familial and national borders and reveals the repressive nature of nationalist ideology: '[he] is unstable because he does have choice, a choice that he exercises without loyalty to the family cell and thus to the nation' (2004: 38). As a result, nationalist discourses construct gay men and lesbians 'as foreign bodies in the cell, pathological invaders threatening the very coherence of the cell' that must be controlled and contained (2004: 16).

Both *Pigs* and *The Last Bus Home* challenge this positioning of homosexuality as a threat to familial and national stability. Jimmy and Petie are central to the formation of their respective communities. Jimmy is the catalyst for the formation of his alternative family and after he is attacked the house's community begins to break down. In *The Last Bus Home*, Petie's influence in keeping his band family together only becomes fully evident once he is killed and the band falls apart.

The traditional family unit is an ideological state apparatus that works to maintain heteronormative and patriarchal structures. Within Queer Studies, scholars have developed queer theories of kinship such as 'families we choose' to redefine kinship outside of the heterosexual matrix (Weston 1991a; Freeman 2007). Specifically, Elizabeth Freeman posits kinship as a site of conflicting tensions for the queer subject. On one hand, the queer subject can seek institutional recognition and legitimation by conforming to the traditional family ideal. On the other hand, the queer subject's inability to be fully subsumed within normative kinship structures offers the subversive potential to reveal those relations as socially and culturally constructed, rather than naturally determined.

Freeman further reconsiders kinship as a fundamentally corporeal practice underpinned by relations of dependency and renewal: 'as a practice, kinship can also be viewed as the process by which bodies and the potential for physical and emotional attachment are created, transformed, and sustained over time' (2007: 298). Subsequently, she argues that queer kinship is informed by a desire to belong and to feel socially secure, as well as a desire to envision a future and longevity beyond the individual through interpersonal connections. She introduces her concept of 'queer belongings' as signifying both 'longing to belong' as well as 'being long', '[encompassing] not only the desire to impossibly extend our individual existence or to preserve relationships that will invariably end, but also to have something queer exceed its own time, even to imagine that excess as queer in ways that getting married or having children might not be' (Freeman 2007: 299).

Freeman's reconfiguration of kinship through queer belongings opens up new ways of considering how the communities in *Pigs* and *The Last*

Bus Home are formed by relations of dependency and survival and operate through promises of stability, security and protection. Yet as the films progress the limitations of these alternative families become increasingly apparent and the characters emerge as isolated individuals rather than cohesive communities. While the films begin as alternative family narratives, the ultimate failure of these family units to survive positions them within Judith Halberstam's (2005) formulation of queer subcultures. Halberstam engages with similar ideas around queer forms of relations to Freeman but she develops these ideas in opposition to kinship-based notions of community and belonging. For Halberstam, kinship-based notions of community and belonging involve creating a shared sense of unity and belonging while queer subcultures 'suggest transient, extrafamilial and oppositional modes of affiliation' and involve exploring alternative ways of being (2005: 154). Conceptualising the communities in *Pigs* and *The Last Bus Home* as queer subcultures enables a new understanding of their subversive potential to undermine the family and the nation as natural and unified formations and expose those who are excluded or marginalised within these dominant narratives.

Pigs

Pigs opens with Jimmy breaking into the abandoned townhouse and transforming it into a liveable space by prying boards off windows to let in light, fashioning curtains to hang over the windows and clearing out debris. Shortly after he moves in, there is a knock at the door and Jimmy opens it to find George, a chronically ill, middle-aged businessman, looking for a room. After Jimmy lets George into the house, he finds himself opening up the space to a host of other disparate individuals. The film offers minimal characterisation and provides little information about characters' individual histories and backgrounds. Instead, the common point of identification is their social marginalisation, and it is their exclusion from Irish society that leads them to move into the shared house. As Jim Loter states, 'the house becomes a nexus through which the marginalia of society can pass and momentarily linger outside of institutional space' (1999: 131).

Pigs sets up a strong distinction between the private space of the house, where the characters find safety and acceptance, and the public space of Dublin's city streets, where they are subject to discrimination and attack. Space within the house is divided, with inhabitants occupying and claiming ownership of their own rooms or sections which they then guard as their own private spaces. For instance, Orwell and Mary claim the basement of the house while Ronnie lives in a room on the third floor. After Tom moves in, he stands in his bedroom, which contains only a broken chair and a small suitcase, and announces 'I have to buy a lock' despite a distinct lack of belongings to steal. Sound also carries throughout the house, with the sounds of knocks at the front door, characters' footsteps as they walk through the house, and doors opening and closing echoing throughout the space and making its spatial divisions increasingly evident.

By using the space of the house to bring together these diverse individuals and by spatially and aurally setting up that space as communal and permeable, the film characterises the house's community as a type of family. In a scene that Barton terms the 'climax of this metaphor of family life', Jimmy, George, Ronnie and Tom sit down together to eat a 'family meal' (2004: 98; see Figure 3.1). Jazz music plays from a portable radio as Jimmy serves food he has prepared and Ronnie offers the others a choice of red or white wine. Jimmy asks Tom what he would like on this pizza and gently berates him when he refuses to eat vegetables. The men tease Tom, who has a severe germ phobia, by pretending to use second-hand false teeth to seal the pizza crust. When Tom becomes visibly distressed, Jimmy reassures him that they are a trick pair of teeth made of plastic. Not only does this scene suggest familial parallels, but it also solidifies Jimmy's role as the head of this alternative family.

In contrast, the city space outside of the house is set up as a space of

Figure 3.1 From left to right, George (George Shane), Ronnie (Liam Halligan), Jimmy (Jimmy Brennan) and Tom (Maurice O'Donoghue) sit down to a family dinner in *Pigs*. (*Source*: screen grab.)

danger. The distinction between the safety of the house and the vulnerability of the streets is made explicit in a scene that occurs approximately halfway through the film when Jimmy goes cruising for sex at a local pub one evening. It is night, and as Jimmy walks down the street he passes by Mary, who is standing on the street corner with two other women who also appear to be prostitutes. A car pulls up next to the women. In a close-up shot Mary glances off-screen left in the direction that Jimmy is standing and then, appearing to have caught sight of Jimmy, quickly turns away. As Jimmy stands watching, a male police officer pulls up on his motorcycle behind the car, and the women all quickly walk away from both the car and the police officer.

The film cuts to Jimmy sitting at the bar in a pub, drinking a Guinness. He is approached by a young man and they leave the bar together. The film frames them in a front tracking shot as they walk silently down the street side by side. Jimmy wears jeans and a dark-green sweater and jacket, while the younger man stands out more visibly with khakis, a white shirt, a light-green scarf and a maroon beret. They pass a group of four boys, who are customers of Ronnie that frequent the house, and the boys begin to follow Jimmy and the young man, making kissing noises, whistling and laughing. In the absence of any non-diegetic sound, the boys' voices and the amplified sounds of their footsteps, as well as the framing, which positions Jimmy and the young man in between the camera in front of them and the boys behind them, contribute to feelings of increased tension and fear of attack. The young man is visibly uncomfortable, with his hands in his pockets as he jerks his head from side to side in fear of attack. The boys pass by the two men and move off-screen. The younger man pauses and tells Jimmy: 'Some other time, okay? Look, I really like you, but I have a long way to go home. I might see you again in the pub sometime. Sorry.' He walks back in the direction they have come from, while Jimmy continues walking forward.

Throughout this entire sequence, Jimmy does not speak once. While he occupies an authoritative position within the house, in this scene he occupies a more submissive position. By opening the sequence with the exchange of looks between Mary and Jimmy, and then revealing that Jimmy is similarly prostituting himself, the film aligns these characters together; at the same time, there is no sense of a shared bond between them. They have no direct exchanges throughout the film and the hasty manner in which Mary turns away from Jimmy when they see each other suggests that she is dismissing any affiliation between them. This sequence also suggests the contested nature of public space: Mary's use of public city streets and Jimmy's use of the pub (a space normalised as homosocial and heterosexual; see Chapter 4) to market sex work temporarily shift these spaces into sites of sexual transgression. The arrival of the police officer that prompts Mary to walk away and the disruptive and fear-inducing presence of the four boys reveal how patriarchal and heteronormative structures are maintained through the social policing and regulation of sexuality within public space.

Once Jimmy has been recognised by the boys as Ronnie's housemate, they break into the house and violently attack Jimmy. The scene of them breaking into the house begins with a close-up shot of Tom's terrified face as he lies in bed, listening to the sounds of the boys frantically knocking on the front door. The sound of their knocking echoes throughout the house. While the bleeding of sounds through the house previously imbued the space with a sense of community, here the permeability of sound emphasises the house's fragility and evokes a sense of danger. Jimmy goes to the front door and opens it, but once he sees the boys outside, he quickly closes it. The boys continue kicking and punching the door, framed in an exterior shot of the house, and then the film cuts to a medium close-up shot of Jimmy on the front landing stairs, frozen with a look of fear on his face. Off-screen, there is the sound of the door being forced open and the boys running inside, and Jimmy begins to run up the stairs, framed in a tracking shot. The camera pauses at the top of the stairs as Jimmy continues running out of frame. The boys enter into and pass through the now static frame, yelling and chasing after Jimmy.

The camera cuts to Jimmy as he runs inside his room. Classical music can be heard playing from his portable radio as he reaches under his bed for a plank of wood that he arms himself with as he tries to hold his bedroom door closed. However, the boys break into the room, knock Jimmy down and begin beating him up. One of the boys also begins to break and smash objects in the room. The film cuts to Tom standing inside his room listening through his door to the sounds of the boys yelling and smashing objects. The film cuts back to Jimmy's room. The boys run out of the room and the camera cuts to a close-up of Jimmy's hand, with blood on it, clutching his bedspread. The camera cuts to a long shot of the bedroom door, with Jimmy out of frame behind the camera, as George comes running in. He runs towards the frame and looks off-screen right (presumably at Jimmy's fallen figure) before declaring 'Jesus Christ' and running back out again. Tom and Ronnie come running in and stand by the door with shocked expressions on their faces, as George returns with baking soda. George yells at them to get out and begins tending to Jimmy's injuries with the baking soda.

This attack is the climactic moment in the film, since the boys' ability to break into the house and assault the head of the family violates the space's perceived safety. Further, Jimmy's ultimate aloneness in this moment, unaided by any of the other inhabitants during the attack, shatters illusions of their community. As Jimmy is being attacked none of the other inhabitants come to his rescue, arriving only afterwards. Even after the attack when they enter his room and discover him, only George moves towards him, while Tom and Ronnie remain frozen in the doorway. The next morning Jimmy wakes up to discover George putting a lock on the front door. When he asks George whether the police have arrived to investigate the attack, George replies that the police are not interested in conflicts among squatters. Not only does this scene suggest limitations regarding the house's community, but it also points to Jimmy's marginalisation within broader Irish society and his exclusion from State protection.

Not long after Jimmy's attack Ronnie is sitting in a shop, having a coffee, when two Gardaí (Johnny Murphy and Pat Laffan) come in and take him outside to question him. They ask him about the other inhabitants of the house and Ronnie provides them with information, telling them that Tom is crazy, George is claiming unemployment benefits under the fake surname of Lestrange, and Jimmy is not married (despite claiming welfare benefits by pretending to be financially supporting his wife). Here, Ronnie is informing on the house's community, exchanging information about the inhabitants with the local Gardaí in return for him being left alone. Debbie Ging argues that the house's surrogate familial existence is threatened and dismantled 'not by internal strife but by the state authorities from outside' (2002: 182). Recalling Conrad's argument about how nationalist discourses work to position homosexual subjects as informers that threaten the coherence and survival of the family cell, in this instance it is Ronnie who is the informer, exposing the community's private workings, making it vulnerable to public interference and leading to its dissolution. Yet even as Robbie contributes to the break-down of the house's community, his informing actually works to maintain patriarchal and heteronormative structures in this film by breaking down non-normative and non-State sanctioned communities.

Ultimately it is the community's inability to forge permanent bonds that compromises its survival. The film fully reveals the house's fragile system of community as the house's inhabitants begin to leave one by one. Ronnie is the first to leave the house, telling Jimmy that he is moving back in with his mother, and is followed in quick succession by George, Tom, Orwell and Mary. As George is about to leave, he implores Jimmy to move out of the house and come live with him in a council flat. Jimmy reveals to George that he knows George has been living a lie by pretending to leave the house every morning for work but frequenting the pubs instead, telling George: 'You're like everyone else in this house, you're living a dream'. George replies:

> Listen, I survive longer than anyone in this house. . . . They're going to lock Tom up soon, forever. He's past it, too much shock treatment. Ronnie? Ronnie's a two timing little shit and if he hangs around long enough somebody will kill him. Mary has a few years left on the streets and then she's finished. Orwell will find somebody else and become a pop star . . . You have to think of yourself. Police are under this house, any of these shits would sell you out to save themselves.

Similarly to Ronnie's act of informing, George's speech shatters any remaining illusions of community that the inhabitants of the house have constructed. He points to the real severity of their circumstances, which creates a tension between their desire for community as a form of safety and belonging, and characters' own impulses towards self-preservation that prevent these shared bonds. Despite their physical proximity to each other, the inhabitants of the house evoke an overwhelming sense of isolation and aloneness. Furthermore, in opposition to Freeman's theory of how relations of queer belonging within kinship structures express 'the longing to "be long", to endure in corporeal form over time' (2007: 299), George's survival instincts suggest the individual can better survive on their own than in the group. He further expresses a deep suspicion of community as an enduring form of protection.

After all the inhabitants have left and Jimmy is the only one left, the two Gardaí who previously questioned Ronnie arrive to arrest Jimmy for false benefit claims. Jimmy initially thinks the police have arrived to investigate his attack, but they quickly inform him that they have come to question him about his absent wife. When Jimmy refuses to speak to them, one of the Gardaí admonishes him for sponging off others who work and tells him, 'why can't you be a man and own up? Be a bloody man for once, can't you?!' Jimmy sits on the bed in silence as the Gardaí continues: 'Squatters make me sick. Living off the rest of us.' They arrest him for defrauding the social welfare office and when Jimmy demands legal aid, they tell him that he will get it eventually.

One of the officers tries to elicit a confession from Jimmy by threatening him that 'I'm going to be the one in the court telling the judge what you've done, what you are' while the other officer begins to explore the rest of the house. In the light of day, devoid of human presence, the house exudes an aura of decay and neglect, with unwashed dishes, forgotten food left on the stove and broken furniture in the front hall. When the first officer leads

Jimmy towards the front door to the waiting police car, the officer that has been exploring the space announces that they 'have been living like pigs. How can you live in all this filth?!' The Gardaí, as representatives of the Irish State, first attack Jimmy's masculinity ('be a bloody man for once') and then dehumanise him by likening him to a pig, framing Jimmy as an outsider to, rather than a citizen of, Irish society.

As they lead Jimmy outside and into the police car, the camera remains frozen in the front doorway. The car drives off and out of frame, and the camera begins to pan through the now empty house accompanied by a heavy non-diegetic bass beat. There is a cut to a shot of Jimmy in the car, filmed through the car window, with images of buildings and neon lights from the street reflected against the window glass and superimposed over Jimmy's face. The film cuts to a bird's eye shot of Dublin's Liffey Bridge with crowds of people walking across it. Loter describes this final shot as a 'lingering, picture-postcard image' that 'exists as the second bookend to the film's opening shots of ruined houses, burning cars, and anachronistic horse riders' (1999: 129). This final image references a tourist vision of Ireland, and stands in stark contrast to the desperate living conditions of the house's inhabitants, who stand in for Ireland's non-visible and socially marginalised populations. Here a public/private divide is conflated with a tension surrounding a tourist representation of Ireland produced for global consumption and its disconnection from the realities of Irish contemporary life.

The Last Bus Home

The community in *Pigs* initially suggests an alternative form of kinship that offers the same protection and unity afforded by the traditional family unit; however, Jimmy's attack, Ronnie's act of informing and the inhabitants' separate departures from the house point to the community's inherent fragility and instability. Similarly to *Pigs*, *The Last Bus Home* follows the formation and ultimate dissolution of a community structured by non-normative kinship structures. While the physically peripheral space of the house is the locus for the imagined community in *Pigs*, the subcultural space of punk rock brings together the four band members in *The Last Bus Home*.

As a simultaneously musical and ideological movement, punk rock seeks to reject mainstream culture and defy convention, and is linked to youth subculture and its rebellion against establishment politics and the dominant status quo (Viegener 1993; Murphy 2003; Gosling 2004; McLoone 2000, 2008). For the band members in *The Last Bus Home*, who are all struggling against societal and familial expectations, punk rock offers a freedom from the repressive constraints of their family homes and the ideals of what they consider an outdated Irish society. Particularly for Petie, who is struggling with his sexuality, punk rock is appealing in its claims for alternative and transgressive ways of living outside of normative social codes. However, as both Murphy (2003) and McLoone (2000) note, the promises of rebellion and revolution that punk rock appears to offer are undermined in *The Last Bus Home* as punk culture is increasingly revealed to be structured by the same repressive ideologies and conservative norms as dominant Irish society. While the band members are described by Pettitt as 'Ireland's inner exiles' (2000: 272), it soon becomes apparent that Petie's marginalisation is experienced differently than that of the other three members.

The film's opening sequence sets out particular tensions surrounding community, national identity and generational conflict through which the characters' band, named the Dead Patriots, emerges as an alternate form of family. The film opens with Pope John Paul II's visit to Dublin in 1979. Irish historian Dermot Keogh's description of the Pope's visit suggests it produced, in Benedict Anderson's (1983: 6) words, 'an imagined political community': 'the occasion was converted by both church and state into a moment of national triumph. It caught the popular imagination because it was a celebration of national identity' (Keogh 1995: xv). *The Last Bus Home* ties into Keogh's description by showing Reena's family joining the rest of their suburban community to travel to Phoenix Park.

Refusing to join her family as they travel to welcome the Pope at a special Mass at Phoenix Park, Reena instead wanders through her empty and deserted suburban surroundings. All the other residents appear to have gone to the Mass, until Reena hears music in the distance and discovers Jessop in a shop. They begin to talk about their music tastes, contemplate the idea of starting a band and later have sex in Jessop's basement. As they have sex, a television in the background plays a newscast about the Pope's visit, showing a massive crowd at Phoenix Park cheering and waving Irish flags. By not taking part in the Pope's visit, Reena and Jessop not only reject Catholicism but separate themselves from a particular vision of Irish national solidarity.

By understanding the Pope's visit in 1979 as one of particular national and historical significance, Reena and Jessop's meeting and sexual coupling, which directly lead to the forming of the Dead Patriots, can be understood as a political act and form of rebellion. The film's opening sequence therefore positions the band and punk rock in direct opposition to the biological family and the idea of a national community. The band members' fractured family lives, particularly Reena's conflicted relationship with her mother, link familial and generational conflict with a rebellion against Irish society and a rejection of dominant religious and national ideologies. This link in turn allows the band to emerge as an alternative form of family, with Reena and Jessop adopting the roles of matriarch and patriarch, respectively.

Yet as the film progresses, tensions between the band's claim of offering liberation from the constraints of dominant society and the persistence of repressive and conservative ideologies break down the band's illusions of unity. These tensions emerge early on in the film in a sequence of scenes shortly after the band's first gig. The sequence begins by showing Reena and Jessop sitting in the pub, having a pint and discussing the band. Jessop tells Reena about the pressure he is facing from his father to either become financially successful with the band or else join him with a job at the local newspaper, and he suggests to Reena that they think about making a music video.

The film then cuts to a shot of Petie and Billy in a gay pub. Petie and Billy sit on stools facing each other as Petie discusses the band. Petie asks Billy about his time in London, to which Billy replies that he had to leave Ireland when he did but 'I've come back to look for something. A feeling.' When Petie presses him further on what that feeling is, Billy continues:

> I don't know exactly. But I had it for the first time in a long time at your gig the other night . . . It's the crazy thing about this place. You've got to leave it to appreciate it, but if you do leave you might never come back.

Petie tells Billy that he is afraid he may never leave and that he plans to leave Ireland once he finishes college. In response, Billy announces that 'things will change, they'll have to – we won't be outlaws forever!' He stands up and walks out of frame, while Petie stares down at his drink, deep in thought.

The conversations in these two pub scenes are significantly different. While Reena and Jessop speak about a desire to find a sense of place within Ireland, in Petie and Billy's exchange there emerges an awareness of their marginalisation within Irish society because of their sexuality and a subsequent desire to find a sense of belonging elsewhere. At the same time, Billy expresses a love for Ireland and a longing to be able to settle down and belong there, revealing the conflicted relationship he has with his home country.

The differences in these two scenes become further explicit in a scene later that night, when Reena and Jessop are walking to the bus stop and catch sight of Petie being attacked by two men in an alleyway. They are too far away to hear the men accusing Petie of being 'with those queers' in 'a homo house'. Instead, they assume the men are attacking Petie because of his association with Jessop, who knows and dislikes the attackers, and both Reena and Jessop come to Petie's aid to chase away his attackers. The film then shows all three characters boarding a city bus. Petie and Reena sit on the back seat beside each other while Jessop sits on the seat in front of them, turning to face them. Jessop tells them that Petie's attackers should stick to 'bashing old dears and queers'. Reena admonishes him for this statement, reminding him of her grandmother, and then Reena and Jessop begin to passionately make out. Because of their positioning across the two rows of seats, Reena and Jessop physically encroach on Petie's personal space as they make out, physically confining him by pushing him against the window of the bus.

Although Jessop and Reena rescue Petie, Jessop's comment of 'bashing old dears and queers' in fact aligns him with Petie's assailants, since Jessop and the attackers are both engaging in homophobic forms of social regulation. Through the characters' different occupations of space, the scene also suggests that while Jessop, Reena and Petie all may feel excluded from dominant Irish society, their experiences of marginalisation are not the same. As soon as Petie physically moves outside of the gay pub, his association with that queer space exposes him to public attack, and his vulnerability within public space points to its normalisation as heterosexual. Alternatively, Reena and Jessop are able to publicly express sexual desire without fear of repercussion, and by physically displacing Petie in doing so they further highlight how their heterosexuality gives them a privileged social position in comparison to him.

Petie's decision to keep his sexuality a secret from Jessop and Reena rather than confide in them reveals that he does not feel entirely secure with his social status within their group. One night, following another of the band's gigs, he spends the night at Billy's and on his way home the next morning he runs into Reena. Reena is also returning home from the previous night, which the film implies she spent with Steve, the London record label scout, after arguing with Jessop. Petie confides in Reena about Billy and makes her promise not to tell Jessop. In return, Reena suggests that they both say they were with each other the previous night in order to save her from having to explain to Jessop where she was. This act of conspiracy between Reena and Petie hints at inner divisions and pockets of secrecy within the band that in turn undermine the perceived solidity of their community. This act becomes the catalyst for Jessop's act of informing when he finds out that Reena and Petie have been withholding information from him.

The detrimental effect that this act of secrecy between Reena and Petie has on the band's community emerges just over half-way through the film, when Reena, Jessop, Joe, Billy and Petie all drive out into the country together to search for mushrooms in the forest. The characters disperse to search and the film cuts to Jessop, wandering down a small slope alone. He leans against a tree and then glances off-screen right at the sudden off-screen sound of voices. The film cuts to a long shot of Petie and Billy, who begin to embrace. The way that this shot is framed gives the impression of an eye, with the sloped tree trunk and the ground shaping the eye and the couple positioned as the eye's pupil. By cutting from this shot to a close up of Jessop's face, the film suggests that Petie and Billy are the subject of Jessop's stare, with the 'eye' that frames their embrace mirroring Jessop's own as he watches them. (see Figure 3.2). This, along with Jessop's shocked expression, the aural dominance of the wind and the strong swaying movements of the trees behind Jessop create a tense atmosphere.

After watching the two men embrace, Jessop turns and walks out of frame. The following scene shows him attempting to forcibly have sex with Reena in the forest. She protests and finally pushes him away, and Jessop slumps on the ground, looking away from Reena in silence. The film cuts through a series of shots from within the forest, now empty and devoid of human presence, as the sound of wind plays loudly in the background. In his aggressive sexual advance, Jessop reveals a need to reassure himself of his heterosexuality and to regain control over the situation. Jessop's violent and hypermasculine reaction to witnessing Petie and

Figure 3.2 Petie (John Cronin) and Billy (Anthony Brophy) embrace in the forest, unaware they are being watched, in *The Last Bus Home*. (*Source*: screen grab.)

Billy's embrace hints at a latent homophobia embodied within him that was previously implied in his comment of 'bashing old dears and queers'.

Following this scene, Jessop visits Petie at Petie's home in what appears to be an attempt to confront him about Billy and subsequently regain some measure of control. Petie is in his room, sitting at his desk and working on a poster for the band, when Jessop opens the bedroom door. Petie is well lit and positioned in the foreground and right-hand side of the frame, while Jessop stands slightly shadowed in the doorway in the background on the left-hand side of the frame. While Jessop directly looks at Petie as he addresses him, Petie appears nervous, avoiding eye contact and fiddling with a pen. Leaning over the desk, Jessop looks at the poster and declares, 'one big happy family!' He then sits on a chair behind and slightly to the left of Petie and begins to ask him questions. The film shifts to a close-up shot of the two characters that keeps Petie's face in the foreground and right side of the frame and Jessop in the background on the left. Jessop's control of the conversation, his positioning, slightly behind Petie and leaning forward, and Petie's visibly growing state of discomfort establish Jessop as a commanding and intimidating presence.

As he leans forward and physically moves closer to Petie, Jessop begins to ask Petie what he wants from life. Jessop appears as if he is trying to get Petie to confide in him; however, Petie steers their conversation towards his desire to go to college and his fear that his father will not financially support him. At this, Jessop leans back, looking disappointed, and then tells Petie: 'But friends are more important than family, aren't they? I mean, you choose your friends. And they don't really give a damn what you do.' Jessop positions the band members as having stronger bonds that those they share with their respective biological families ('friends are more important than family'). Yet his need to draw on family imagery in this exchange, his intimidating presence and Petie's palpable nervousness undermine the solidity of these bonds.

Jessop becomes increasingly paranoid that the band intends to replace him. His feelings of emasculation and being out of control reach a crisis point in the film's climatic scene of the band's final gig. Prior to the gig, Jessop discovers from Billy that Reena and Petie lied when they said they were together the night that Reena did not come home, and Billy further implies that Reena spent the night with Steve. After speaking with Billy and before going on-stage to perform, Jessop takes Ecstasy. As the band performs, he appears increasingly dishevelled and frenzied, and begins hallucinating that Steve is standing in the audience beside Reena. He suddenly breaks out into an explosive tirade, declaring that this performance will be the band's final performance and calling out the individual band members.

He first accuses Joe of preferring money over punk rock and selling out to capitalism. He then declares that Petie has been keeping secrets from his friends. Turning towards Petie and moving closer and closer towards him, Jessop repeatedly shouts: 'Is that any way to treat your friends?!'

The flashing lights and the rapid camera cuts between shots of the darkly lit crowd and individual close-ups of Jessop, Petie and Reena create a disorientating and claustrophobic effect. Petie continues playing the drums, his face frozen in wide-eyed fear as he anticipates that Jessop is about to 'out' him to the crowd by exposing him as gay. The loud sounds of the drums and bass, coupled with the flashing lights and the shouts of the crowd as they call out 'what secrets?!' heightens the already tense atmosphere. When Jessop suddenly shouts out 'London' (referring to Petie's desire to leave Ireland) instead of outing Petie as gay, it has the same effect of making Petie feel exposed and rejected, as evidenced when he runs out of the venue.

Similarly to Ronnie's act of informing on the house's inhabitants in *Pigs*, in this scene Jessop informs on his fellow band members by standing on-stage and exposing them to the crowd. The film suggests that through this act of informing, Jessop is attempting to regain the control and authority he feels he has lost within the band. He does not explicitly expose Petie as gay to the crowd, and yet his threat of being able to do so and the palpable fear he elicits from Petie reveal the uneven power relations embedded within their relationship. It is significant that in order to combat his feelings of being emasculated and out of control, Jessop seeks to control Petie, recalling Conrad's (2004) arguments for how nationalist discourses work to contain the perceived threat of male homosexuality. By publicly exposing his fellow band members, Jessop reveals the limitations of their band as an alternative form of family. While the traditional family unit operates as a source of security and refuge that privately works to maintain an image of stability and unity, Jessop's act of informing exposes the conflicted workings of their social unit and threatens its claims of protection.

After Petie runs out of the venue, he runs away down city streets as he is chased by Reena, who repeatedly calls out his name. Petie falls in the middle of the street and as he stands up there appears to be the white light of car headlights shining on his face. The film cuts to a close-up of Petie's face as the sound of Reena's voice calling his name is heard from off-screen. Petie closes his eyes and the film cuts to a slow motion shot of Reena as she stops running, her face registering shock and disbelief as the off-screen sounds of a car horn and skidding tires imply that Petie has been hit.

Following Petie's death, for which Reena blames Jessop, Reena breaks up with Jessop, the band dissolves and its members disperse. The film shifts forward several years later to Reena, who now lives in New York, returning to Ireland for her grandmother's funeral. She meets Jessop for coffee and when Jessop expresses his continuing feelings of guilt over Petie's death Reena reveals to him that Petie's mother told Reena that prior to the band's final performance Petie came out to his parents and that his father had threatened to have him committed to a psychiatric hospital if he ever returned home. Reena then tells Jessop that, 'he wasn't running for his bus. He wasn't running home. He had nowhere left to run.' Petie's feelings of being rejected by Jessop on-stage can be linked to this revelation that Petie felt similarly rejected by his biological father, drawing a comparison between Jessop and Petie's father rather than the stark opposition that the film, and the characters themselves, initially seem to propose. This is something acknowledged by McLoone, who argues that 'within the alternative "family" of the punk band lurk the same values of hypocrisy, prejudice and intolerance' (2000: 173).

At the end of the film, Jessop takes Reena back to the bingo hall where they used to perform as the Dead Patriots and which he now owns and has transformed into a dance club. By transforming the bingo hall into the commercialised space of the dance club, Jessop is actively participating in the consumerist culture he once so vehemently protested, and for McLoone this captures a disillusionment regarding the revolutionary ideals of punk rock: 'Not only is punk seen as a fake rebellion to the bourgeois conformity of society, its rapid recuperation by that society confirms the absence of any political alternative. There is a deep sense of sadness in the end about the thwarted hopes of the punk revolt' (2000: 174). At the club, the bartender tells Reena that homosexuality has just been decriminalised in Dublin. It is significant that Petie does not survive the film while his heterosexual band members celebrate the news of gay rights. This is something that is discussed in Chapter 5 in relation to *Cowboys & Angels*, where the queer protagonist is ultimately excluded from Irish society while his heterosexual counterpart is able to settle down and belong there. In *The Last Bus Home* it is possible for Reena, and not Petie, to come home to Ireland precisely because she is not gay.

By ending the film with the decriminalisation of homosexuality in 1993, the film links this moment with the film's opening of the Pope's visit to posit both as significant historical events in contemporary Ireland. The decriminalisation of homosexuality points to how globalisation has shifted and redefined national boundaries and citizenship, confirming Billy's previous assertion that 'we won't be outlaws forever'. Yet the film's final scene, where neither Joe nor Petie are present and where Reena and Jessop appear disconnected from each other, devoid of any strong sense of communal or national belonging within the cosmopolitan space of the dance club, stands in stark contrast to the film's opening and its strong connotations of family, community and national solidarity. The film thus questions whether the effects of globalisation on conventional understandings of community and belonging in Ireland can be seen as strictly positive or whether they have left Ireland inherently 'placeless'.

Conclusion

In both *Pigs* and *The Last Bus Home*, alternative family structures are at once presented as more liberal and inclusive alternatives to normative kinship models while also revealing the limits of such non-normative forms of kinships. Further, while nationalist discourses have historically positioned homosexuality as a particular threat to the family and, by extension, the nation, both films complicate this positioning by presenting the queer male protagonist as the catalyst for community-formation. Jimmy and Petie offer the potential to create new forms of belonging and community that operate outside of State sanctioned social structures. At the same time, Ronnie and Jessop's acts of informing, while leading to the dissolution of their communities, operate as mechanisms of social regulation and sexual repression that work to contain the queer subject and maintain a dominant patriarchal and heteronormative order. These acts of informing suggest the inability of these communities to approximate or replace traditional kinship structures, since their break-down does not signify the same threat to national stability as that of the traditional family unit would.

In both films, the instability of these alternative communities is linked to the instability of space. While initially characters seem to find a sense of community that is linked to a fixed location and a rooted form of belonging, as the films progress a tension emerges between stable placehood and unsettledness. The transformation of the house in *Pigs* from a space of safety, refuge and solidarity to a site of danger and isolation, and the successive transformations of the band members' performance space in *The Last Bus Home* from a bingo hall to a punk rock venue to a tourist dance club reveal how the communities within these spaces are similarly transient and temporary, held together by fragile social bonds. As products of 1980s Ireland, these films reflect a stagnant and 'stuck' society, unable to thrive through existing structures and formations and unable (or perhaps unwilling) to allow new ones to form.

CHAPTER 4

The Contested Space of the Irish Pub

The sustained presence of the public house ('pub') in Irish film, drama and literature indicates that it is integral to the Irish cultural imaginary. Particularly in Irish films and films about Ireland, the pub is a recurring image, from a site for rural community gatherings in *The Quiet Man* (Ford 1952) and *Ryan's Daughter* (Lean 1970), to a space where men can escape from the pressures of home and work life in *Angela's Ashes* (Parker 1999) and *Intermission* (Crowley 2003), to a target for paramilitary violence in *Resurrection Man* (Evans 1998) and *Mickybo and Me* (Loane 2004). Within these films, there is a strong tendency to highlight the importance of the Irish pub to the construction, performance and regulation of Irish ethnicity and masculinity.

Consider, for instance, the scene in *The Quiet Man* when American Sean Thornton, recently arrived in the film's fictional Irish village of Innisfree, walks into the pub that adjoins the hotel where he is staying. As he enters the darkly lit space, carefully closing the door behind him, he becomes subject to the stares of the other male patrons. The camera tracks his movement towards the bar in a medium close-up shot that emphasises the confined space and this tracking movement mirrors the silent stares of the watching patrons. Sean orders a pint and then, as he lights a cigarette and the camera cuts to a close-up shot of his face, he looks around in sudden awareness of the attention that is still focused on him. In an attempt to win over the other patrons he offers to buy them a round of drinks, at which point he is approached by an elderly man, Francis Ford, who tells him to identify himself. Once Sean has referenced the names of his father and grandfather (both former residents of the village), Francis announces: 'That being the case, it is a pleasant evening and we will have a drink!' An accordionist begins to play 'The Wild Colonial Boy', a traditional Irish ballad, and the other patrons gather around the bar, and Sean, and sing along. What this brief sequence illustrates is that not only is the pub a space populated by men, but it is a space structured by a dominant social order and strict code of conduct. There is a need for Sean, as an outsider, to establish his legitimacy within the space and a subsequent need for him to be accepted by those patrons already established within it. The Irish pub also sustains an Irish cultural identity linked to heritage, tradition and the rural imaginary.

The pub offers a unique site for interrogating competing tensions surrounding cultural nationalism, male homosociality and sexual politics in contemporary Irish cinema. Beginning in the 1980s, there emerged a trend in Irish cinema of locating queerness within the pub to challenge notions of a heteronormative Irish masculinity. In films such as *Pigs* (Black 1984), *Reefer and the Model* (Comerford 1988), *A Man of No Importance* (Krishnamma 1994), *I Went Down* (Breathnach 1997), *The Last Bus Home* (Gogan 1997) and *Garage* (Abrahamson 2007) the Irish pub is the setting for the performance of queer identities, behaviours and desires. Further, the space of the pub is central to the queering of masculinities in Neil Jordan's films *The Crying Game* (1992) and *Breakfast on Pluto* (2005). By revealing how gender, sexuality and power relations inform social and spatial structures and produce queer identities in relation to those structures, these films expose the ways in which the pub encodes queer relations even as it operates within the sex/gender system to sustain a patriarchal order and heterosexual privilege.

This chapter focuses on *A Man of No Importance* and *Garage* as indicative of this trend. The male protagonists in these films are produced as queer not only in their performance of non-normative masculinity, but in terms of their social status as outcasts. Both films make it difficult to understand these characters in terms of easy social categories, and instead each character embodies multiple and competing forms of identity that reach a crisis within their respective pub scenes. The films' representations of queer Irish masculinity are part of a broader trend in contemporary Irish cinema of showcasing non-normative Irish men onscreen. Ed Madden argues that 'a number of Irish texts and films of the late 1990s were exploring the boundaries of intimacy, gender and sexuality in lives of gay and straight Irish men' and that 'these texts are very much part of a cultural moment obsessed with the nature of masculinity and its possibilities for crisis, interrogation and transformation' (2011: 78, 79). In a similar vein, Debbie Ging notes a tendency in recent Irish films of displacing the heroic, patriotic and successful Irish male figure 'in favour of male subjects who are socially marginalised, criminal and underclass, depressed, suicidal, abused, forced into exile, gay, queer or transsexual, violent and variously conflicted or in crisis' (2013: 16).

Both Madden and Ging suggest that these representations can be read in relation to growing critical and public debate in the 1990s and 2000s surrounding traditional Irish masculinity and men's roles in contemporary Irish society. Chapter 5 explores how this debate is reflected in Irish queer cinema through the cinematic figure of the hip, urban and sexually liberated queer Irish man who represents a 'new Ireland' that embraces economic and social change and is liberated from the constraints of the past. Yet neither *A Man of No Importance* nor *Garage* fit comfortably within this cosmopolitan construction, and the characters' queerness emerges precisely through their association with (rather than disavowal of) traditional markers of Irishness. Analysed together, these films use queerness to critique the impact of socio-economic change on Irish society and to complicate dominant cultural narratives of forward national progress. *A Man of No Importance* is set in 1960s Dublin and was released in 1994 when Ireland was on the cusp of the Celtic Tiger economic boom, with both periods marked by extreme optimism for economic prosperity and social progress. Alternatively, *Garage* emerged at the beginning of the Celtic Tiger's dissolution, when inflated economic and social statistics began to burst to reveal real lived destitution. Alfred (Albert Finney) in *A Man of No Importance* and Josie (Pat Shortt) in *Garage* both struggle with how to negotiate broader societal change in relation to their own social lives and sexual desires, with their struggles taking place primarily within the space of the Irish pub.

The Male Homosocial Space of the Irish Pub

As a historically and culturally significant space in Ireland that is central to the performance of gender and ethnicity, the Irish pub is a locus for examining how Irish masculinities are produced and regulated. It operates as a microcosm for Irish society and yet even as it reflects dominant society it contests it, operating as what Michel Foucault (1986) terms a 'heterotopia'. By examining the historical and cultural significance of the Irish pub and then suggesting the potential of queer bodies to reveal it as a heterotopic and contested space, this essay examines how the queer body is shaped by regulatory systems and forms of normativity embedded within the pub.

In exploring the particular formation of Irish drinking practices, it becomes evident that the pub has a particular cultural and ideological significance in Irish history that renders it unique as a national institution. In one of the few historical discourses on the social history of Irish drinking, Richard Stivers (2000) argues that in the eighteenth and nineteenth centuries there was a common practice of occupational drinking in

England, Scotland and Ireland (see also Inglis 1998). However, from the mid-nineteenth century onwards, Irish drinking practices began to differ significantly and Stivers attributes this variation to a shift in economic development. As England and Scotland became increasingly industrialised, old patterns of occupational drinking became incompatible with the growing rationalisation of economic life. The need for a well-disciplined and reliable work force, the emergence of other public social spaces such as coffee houses and amusement centres, and stricter government regulations that enforced licensing laws and limited hours of operation undermined the central role of the pub within the community. Industrialisation was also linked to the emergence of the temperance movement and a new moral system that denounced and restricted drinking practices more generally (Stivers 2000; see also Lloyd 2011).

In contrast, until the mid-twentieth century, Ireland remained largely agrarian and plagued by extreme poverty. The Great Famine and its aftermath shifted social structures, with an increase in late marriages, fewer marriages overall, and a stronger connection with the Catholic Church and its doctrine of celibacy and the segregation of the sexes. These conditions led to the formation of the 'avunculate' bachelor drinking group: an all-male group that 'functioned to make palatable the system of single inheritance, few and late marriages, and chastity to young males' (Stivers 2000: 74). Stivers characterises this group by intense male homosocial bonding that provided for the emotional, recreational and social needs of its members. Through this group, male 'hard drinking' became central to the cultural definition of masculinity in Ireland, preserving 'a culturally demanded link between drinking and male identity' (2000: 31). It also emerged as a form of cultural remission for men in Ireland. In Ireland, the priest in the community and the mother in the home personified the moral system, enforcing strict moral codes particularly around sexuality and sexual practices. Irish drinking practices, and their performance within the pub, offered 'a release from the difficulty of adhering to the dominant symbolic of culture by which personality is socially constructed [and] a release from sexual puritanism' (2000: 90).

The relationship between alcohol consumption and the performance of masculinity is not distinct to Ireland; however, the Irish example is unique in degree due to Ireland's complex colonial relations with Britain. David Lloyd argues that a key means through which nationalist movements articulate their difference from the colonising body is through the 'transvaluation of values': inversing those stereotypes that have been marked by the coloniser as signs of the colonised subject's cultural difference and inferiority (2011: 94). Yet he argues that arguably the most common and perdurable stereotype of the Irish as having a propensity for alcohol and drunkenness is a difficult stereotype to reverse or eradicate. Because drinking practices in Ireland are considered as an effect of colonialism as well as an ingrained ethnic trait, 'any national movement that attempted to overlook this phenomenon would have been obliged to disavow a profoundly significant popular mode of articulating cultural difference' (2011: 95). Lloyd further suggests that Irish drinking can be understood in relation to Irish nationalism since, 'like nationalism, drinking represents the imbrications of resistance with dependence . . . it is at once the cause and effect of an individual and national lack of autonomy' (2011: 96). Therefore, even in the potential self-destructiveness of Irish drinking, it has historically operated as a form of rebellion against British rule and the civilising process it imposed. Lloyd suggests that the Irish nationalist movement and its partner, the Catholic Church, sought to reconstitute Irish masculinity: 'nationalism at once accepted the colonial stereotype of "turbulent" Irish masculinity and sought to respond by transforming Irish masculinity into "governable" forms that would found an independent state formation' (2011: 97). One of the means through which masculinity was transformed into a 'governable' form was by institutionalising male drinking practices within the pub.

Male drinking practices within the pub therefore constitute a profoundly gendered national expression that is deeply imbricated within a struggle for power. As Stivers notes, the pub became a space in which men exercised their power outside of the home and the Church and, as Lloyd further suggests, it also became a space where colonial structures where at once integrated and resisted. Such power relations are mapped out in *A Man of No Importance* and *Garage* in terms of the relationship between masculinity and cinematic space. Steve Neale argues that 'current ideologies of masculinity involve so centrally notions and attitudes to do with aggression, power, and control,' and film theorists have used the Western and the road movie to examine how these ideologies are frequently expressed through masculine desires to possess and dominate the landscape (and those bodies within it) (Neale 1983: 11; Roberts 1997). Power is considered to be embodied within a hegemonic masculine ideal, and exercises of power operate through that male subject's social and diegetic control of space. Subsequently, the exercise of male power is not simply a matter of physical constraint or violence, but is about space and who controls it. In both films, the pub acts as a cinematic space for the performance of masculinity, where male fantasies of control and power are played out to maintain a dominant patriarchal and heteronormative order. Alfred and Josie's performances of queer masculinity within the pub challenge the dominant order and reveal concepts of identity and space to be fundamentally unstable.

The pub is an ostensibly public space that is structured by private features. The term 'public house' connotes an open and inclusive space. As already highlighted, the pub offers a space where individuals can congregate outside of domestic and work spaces, and outside of the social norms that underscore those spaces. Yet despite claims of being public, it operates along its own system of binaries and exclusion to maintain a dominant male homosocial order. In this respect, the pub functions as what Foucault terms a 'heterotopia': 'juxtaposing in a single place several spaces, several sites that are in themselves incompatible' (1986: 25). Foucault differentiates between heavily structured modern space (defined by oppositions such as private/public space, family/social space, leisure/work space) and more broadly the 'other' spaces of heterotopia that disrupt the continuity and normality of common everyday places by breaking down boundaries within and between places. Like utopias, heterotopias relate to other spaces by both representing and at the same time inverting or distorting them. Therefore, heterotopias simultaneously reflect and contest the space we live in: they 'suspect, neutralise, or invert the set of relations that they happen to designate, mirror, or reflect' (Foucault 1986: 24). Foucault outlines a number of these 'other' spaces, including cinemas, cemeteries, prisons and asylums, and argues that modern heterotopias often relate to containing some sort of deviation, enclosing 'individuals whose behaviour is deviant in relation to the required mean or norm' (1986: 25).

Foucault's heterotopia can be productively aligned with Jean-Ulrick Désert's (1997) 'queer space'. Désert develops his concept of 'queer space' to theorise how queer bodies can disrupt the perceived homogeneity and unity of space by revealing it as contested and contradictory. Rather than perceiving certain spaces as straight and others as queer, Désert suggests that all space has the potential to double as queer space, and that space remains latent until activated by a queer presence, a presence 'where queerness, at a few brief points and for some fleeting moments, dominates the (heterocentric) norm, the dominant social narrative of the landscape' (1997: 11). To the extent that queer space is structurally dependent on heteronormative space, its very existence is defined by an opposition to and an exclusion from the heteronormative.

Like 'heterotopia', 'queer space' exists within and beyond the demarcations of public/private space. Both are disorganising concepts that question normative social and spatial structures by revealing space as multiple, fluid and contested. By arguing for the Irish pub as a heterotopic and queer space, it is characterised as an inherently unstable and conflicted space that embodies multiple spatial orders and contradictory social relations. It is a space that exists in relation to dominant Irish society even as it operates as a counter-site where that society is 'represented, contested, and inverted' (Foucault 1986: 24). The disruptive potential of queer bodies to reveal the pub as a contested space is made evident in Elspeth Probyn's (1995: 81) account of two women kissing in a bar filled with men:

> While their kiss cannot undo the historicity of the ways in which men produce their space as the site of the production of a gender (Woman) for another (men), the fact that a woman materialises another woman as her object of desire does go some way in rearticulating that space . . . the desire of one woman for another produces a small opening in the male gendered, or more precisely, a male homosocial space; a crack though which we may see the possibility of a sexed space . . . one articulation of desire that bends and queers a masculine place allowing for a momentarily sexed lesbian space.

Similarly to Désert's claim for how queer presence can temporarily upset the heterocentric norm, here Probyn suggests that this act of female same-sex desire can restructure what is a fundamentally male and homosocial space.

This incident suggests the anxieties that emerge when the pub's normalisation as male and heterosexual is undermined, and yet it remains frozen in action. This chapter uses *A Man of No Importance* and *Garage* to expand on Probyn's account, examining what occurs in the aftermath of such a queer act and considering the broader implications that these consequences may signal with regards to traditional forms of belonging and community in contemporary Ireland. The pub is a central setting in both films where queer identity is shaped and contested. As Alfred and Josie move into the pub, their action 'bends and queers a masculine place' to result in a tension between their profound desire to belong to that space and its connoted community, and a fundamental inability to do so. They are unable to fit within the social and spatial structures of the pub and are consequently produced as queer and identified as threats that must be removed. For both characters, their ultimate exclusion from the pub community has significant and tragic consequences that affect the course of their lives.

A Man of No Importance

A Man of No Importance is set in 1960s Dublin and follows Alfred, an eccentric middle-aged bus conductor who is unmarried and lives with his sister Lily (Brenda Fricker). Alfred is passionate about Oscar Wilde and he often quotes passages from Wilde's work to bus passengers. One day he meets a beautiful young woman named Adele (Tara Fitzgerald) who inspires him to stage a community production of Wilde's *Salome* with Adele as the lead. At the same time that he is staging *Salome*, Alfred is struggling with his secret desire for Robbie (Rufus Sewell), the young bus driver with whom Alfred works. Afraid to openly express his feelings for Robbie, Alfred tries to find another outlet for his desires by approaching a group of young men in what is revealed as a gay pub. Alfred's attempt at gay cruising results in him being violently attacked by the young men and his transgression becoming public knowledge. The local butcher, Mr Carney (Michael Gambon), demands Alfred's resignation but Alfred is ultimately supported by his bus passengers, who defend his character and dismiss allegations about his personal life. The film ends with Alfred retaining his job but with no further resolution made on how to express his private sexual desires within his tolerant but nevertheless conservative community. *A Man of No Importance* was directed by British director Suri Krishnamma and written by Irish screenwriter Barry Devlin. Reviews of the film were generally not positive, ranging from criticising it for being overly sentimental to labelling it a 'seriously inept movie' (*The Irish Independent*), and the film itself has been largely underrepresented within Irish film criticism.

The film contains two significant pub scenes. Early in the film, Alfred sits in the pub watching a group of young men sitting by the bar. This scene plays out through a relay of looks between Alfred and the young men, particularly Breton-Beret (Joe Savino) and Kitty (Paudge Behan). While the pub and the young men are not explicitly identified as queer, this series of looks implicates the men and the space within a sexually dissident identity that Alfred appears aware of. In the pub, Alfred sits partially obscured behind a partition by the pub entrance, peeking out around the partition to look at Breton-Beret and the other young men (see Figure 4.1). These men are singled out within the pub space. They are younger and are dressed in a more stylish fashion than the other patrons. The shot of Breton-Beret is framed in a medium shot, restricting the pub space to him and the men surrounding him. Their central positioning within the space (sitting by the bar, which all patrons must approach to order drinks) further connotes a position of power and authority.

As Breton-Beret glances off-screen right, the eye-line match of this shot with the previous shot of Alfred implies that Breton-Beret has caught sight of Alfred looking at him. Breton-Beret gestures to Kitty and nods in Alfred's direction. Kitty turns to look and there is a cut to Alfred quickly looking away and ducking behind the partition. As the camera slowly moves towards Alfred in a tracking shot, closing in the space around

Figure 4.1 Alfred (Albert Finney) peeks out from behind the partition in the pub in *A Man of No Importance*. (*Source*: screen grab.)

him, he begins to peek once again around the partition. Appearing visibly uncomfortable, Alfred abruptly gets up to leave. On his way out of the door he turns to look back at Kitty and the film cuts to a close-up of Kitty's face as he puckers a kiss. The film then cuts back to Alfred rushing out of the entrance door.

In contrast to the authoritative position held by Breton-Beret and Kitty, Alfred has a peripheral status within the pub. He is physically peripheral, sitting by the pub entrance. He does not command the space but rather observes it from behind the partition. The partition itself can be seen as symbolic of the closet, whereby Alfred is emerging from behind it ('outing' himself) and then fearfully retreating back behind it (back into the closet). The use of close-ups and the camera's movement in this scene suggest Alfred's own increasing discomfort as the space closes down around him and he becomes the target of the young men's stares. His hasty exit out of the space indicates his discomfort and awareness of his social marginality.

Alfred returns to the same pub later in the film. His return is motivated by two events happening in quick succession: he walks in on Adele having sex with her boyfriend and then witnesses Robbie kissing a woman on the street. Both of these events bring Alfred face to face with the physical articulation of sexual desire and solidify his resolve to find a means of expressing his own desires, which he attempts to do by returning to the pub and approaching the young men. When Alfred returns to the pub, he does so in full costume reminiscent of the camp style of Wilde, with a cape, wide-brimmed hat, scarf and make-up (eyeliner and rouge). This second pub scene begins with a shot of Alfred's shadow on the pavement. As Alfred's feet enter into the frame, the film cuts to a medium tracking shot of him walking along the street. Dramatic non-diegetic orchestral music plays.

Prior to entering the pub, Alfred is framed standing behind the entrance door, visible but slightly distorted through the door's mottled glass. His pause posits the door as a threshold, a physical demarcation between the city streets and the space of the pub. He opens the door and walks inside, standing tall and in full view by the entrance. As he enters, the orchestral music fades out and the diegetic music of the pub fades in. This shift from non-diegetic to diegetic music further emphasises that Alfred has entered into a different and insular space. There is a shot of the pub interior as various patrons turn to look at Alfred. Unlike the previous pub scene where the view of the inside of the pub was restricted to a medium shot of the young men, in this wider shot the space has opened up. Alfred walks towards the centre of the pub (and the young men) and the pub space begins to close down around him as he becomes framed by more close-up shots. He also becomes physically closed in as the young men surround him.

In a close-up shot, Alfred leans forward and whispers in Kitty's ear. Kitty then relays Alfred's request to the surrounding patrons: 'You want a what? A cuddle?' Kitty nods at Alfred and leads him out of the frame by pulling on his shirt. The film then cuts to a shot of two bartenders as one leans over to the other and says: 'He's a queer looking tulip.' Alfred's conspicuous entrance and the way he moves towards the centre of the pub indicate his refusal of a peripheral position. At the same time, the bartender's comment suggests Alfred's inability to belong; he is produced as queer in relation to this already 'queered' space.

The film cuts to a shot of Kitty leading Alfred down the alleyway beside the pub. As they move down the alleyway (and towards the camera), Breton-Beret and his men are visible in the background, following them unbeknownst to Alfred. The music from the pub fades out and only Alfred's heavy breathing can be heard. Kitty removes Alfred's hat and unties his scarf, and then puts one hand behind Alfred's head, appearing as if he is about to embrace him. In the same motion, Kitty turns Alfred slightly so that Alfred's back is to Breton-Beret and the other young men. Kitty suddenly steps back and punches Alfred in the face. As Alfred falls, groaning in pain, the men surround him and begin to punch and kick him. Kitty also robs Alfred. Finally Breton-Beret tells them to stop, and the men turn away and walk back towards the pub (and away from the camera). The camera pulls back into a longer shot and the same orchestral music from the beginning of the scene, but more slow-paced and melancholy, floods in. The young men exit out of the frame, leaving Alfred alone and lying on the ground in the foreground of the shot.

The entire scene in the alleyway is filmed in one long take with a mobile camera. The control has shifted from when Alfred entered the pub, with his increased vulnerability and more submissive position made evident in how Kitty removes his costume and in the sound of his heavy breathing. As the men leave the alleyway, the repeat of the orchestral music juxtaposes the image of Alfred striding along the street at the beginning of the scene, propelled forwards by a particular fantasy of being accepted into the pub community, with the image of him lying bruised and bloodied on the ground, contrasting his fantasy with the harsh reality of his circumstances.

In this scene, Alfred's fantasy and performance operate in the service of his desire to belong. It is significant that Kitty leads Alfred out of the pub, encouraging and continuing his performance rather than publicly ejecting him from the space. After the young men beat up Alfred and return, unchallenged, into the pub, it becomes evident that not only is Alfred excluded from this group of men but he is excluded from the pub itself. To unpack the complicated relations of power in this scene, it can be argued that by appropriating the figure of Wilde, Alfred inadvertently engages with a complex web of contradictory and historically contingent discourses. The figure of Wilde embodies paradoxical ways of being, and he has subsequently historically operated as a disruptive presence within Irish cultural discourses, particularly in terms of how to reconcile his nationality with his sexuality.[1] During his period of public prominence, Wilde was frequently associated with a camp sensibility both in terms of his personal character and his writings. Yet, as historical considerations of Wilde reveal, this association with camp did not necessarily correlate to an association with homosexuality. In his historical mapping of shifting social attitudes to homosexuality through the cultural figure of Wilde, Alan Sinfield argues that prior to Wilde's arrest he and his literary characters were perceived as effeminate rather than homosexual precisely because they so explicitly manifested camp behaviour which had not yet been linked to public perceptions of homosexuality (1994: 3–4). However,

---

[1] Born in Dublin to Anglo-Irish parents and gaining notoriety and fame in London as a playwright, Wilde actively chose to see himself as both Irish and English. His personal life was similarly contradictory: while married with children, he also had affairs with many young men. Wilde's ability to upset binary logics of identity and challenge coherent identity categories have made him a difficult figure to incorporate within Irish public and cultural discourse. For further study see Sinfield (1994), Lapointe (2006) and Walsh (2010).

Michael Patrick Lapointe notes that after his trials and his subsequent 'outing', 'Wilde became the stereotypical paradigm of the modern homosexual who combined decadence and aestheticism with sexual "deviance" and effeminacy, which until his trials in 1895 had not been widely linked in the public's perception' (2006: 89).

By appropriating the figure of Wilde in his performance, Alfred references an association between homosexuality and camp effeminacy that, while largely tolerated during Wilde's life, has since shifted to become an increasingly negative and pernicious stereotype. Both Maria Pramaggiore (2006) and Éibhear Walshe (2009) claim that Alfred's appropriation of Wilde makes his homosexuality visible, with Pramaggiore suggesting that 'by literally assuming the mantle of gayness in his performance of Wilde, Alfie's desires have become public property' (2006: 125). I further argue that through his performance, Alfred not only makes visible his sexual dissidence but also that of the other young men and of the pub space itself. The young men's hypermasculine and violent reactions can then be framed as attempts to undermine this visibility. Their actions suggest their own anxieties regarding the marginalised position of sexual minorities within Irish society, since the ongoing persecution of gay men in Ireland during the 1960s meant that social spaces for these communities occupied a precarious position and relied on strategies of secrecy and façade to resist visibility. As Probyn argues, the normalisation of the pub as male, heterosexual and homosocial relies on sexual dissidence resisting visibility (1995: 80–1). Alfred's actions present the possibility for the pub to double as queer space, where queerness briefly 'dominates the (heterocentric) norm' (Désert 1997: 11), only for this possibility to be immediately denied when the young men identify Alfred as a threat and lead him outside the space.

It is significant that while Alfred is marginalised within the pub, his discomfort within that space does not hold true for public space in general. In particular, he commands the space of the bus: he holds the attention of the passengers as he stands in front of them quoting Wilde, he makes the bus wait for Adele one morning when she is running late, and he physically ejects Mr Carney from the bus at the end of the film when Mr Carney publicly denounces Alfred. Unlike in the pub, where he hides behind the partition or later uses masquerade to propel himself forward into the space, in the bus Alfred stands in full view, appearing confident and in control. Those qualities that help to produce Alfred as queer, such as his flamboyant mannerisms and embodiment of Wilde, are not only tolerated within the bus but contribute to his claims of authority and ownership over the space. Alfred's increased comfort on the bus in comparison to the pub can be attributed to the bus's mobility: it is both physically mobile, and a space not clearly defined or determined (in contrast to the complex historical and cultural structures embedded within the pub).

Garage

Like *A Man of No Importance*, *Garage* is a film about male isolation and exclusion that is linked to the protagonist's inability to perform a socially normalised form of masculinity within the space of the pub. The film is set in an unidentified rural town in contemporary Ireland and is centred on Josie, the town misfit who works and lives in the local garage. He is characterised as dim-witted, with an inability to empathise and connect emotionally with other characters, and he is largely regarded by the other townspeople as the town simpleton. Josie's characterisation as different is linked to his physicality: he has a limping gait, a habit of nervously nodding, and often wears a hat that has 'Australia' written across it.

One day the owner of the garage, Mr Gallagher (John Keogh), brings his girlfriend's fifteen-year-old son David (Conor Ryan) to the garage to work alongside Josie. A friendship gradually develops between David and Josie, and Josie begins inviting David to stay later after work and drink ciders with him outside the garage. When Josie is given a pornographic video by one of the truck drivers that frequently passes by the garage, he decides to show it to David in an attempt at further homosocial bonding. David is visibly disturbed by the video and tells his parents about it, resulting in Josie being arrested and questioned by the town police chief for providing a minor with alcohol and indecent material. Josie is later fired from the garage by Mr Gallagher, losing both his job and his home in the process since his home is built as an extension onto the back of the garage. The film ends with Josie wading into the town river in an apparent attempt to drown himself. *Garage* was directed by Lenny Abrahamson and written by Mark O'Halloran, and is the Irish duo's third collaboration. The film was a fixture on the festival circuit, has received considerable praise from film critics and has been strongly represented as a subject of inquiry within Irish film scholarship.

Both Alfred and Josie are characterised by an inability to belong which is most clearly evidenced in their interactions within their respective pubs. However, whereas the pub in *A Man of No Importance* produces Alfred as queer through his failed performance of homosexuality, the pub in *Garage* produces Josie as queer through his inability to belong to the male, homosocial community, with Josie emerging more generally as a form of failed masculinity.[2] Male homosocial spaces such as the pub work to neutralise forms of male bonding and to justify the act of men congregating together and excluding women. Yet, as Eve Kosofsky Sedgwick (1992) has shown, even as homosocial relations are frequently articulated through homophobic and misogynistic expressions, these expressions reveal how forms of desire and identification that structure men's relations with other men operate in multiple and complex ways beyond the simple binary of homosexual/heterosexual. Rather than conceiving of homosociality in opposition to homosexuality, Sedgwick argues for a 'continuum of male "homosocial desire"' that considers social bonds between men to be more fluid and flexible. Josie's failed attempts to approximate a male homosocial ideal in *Garage* opens up queer possibility by undermining the normalisation of masculinity as unproblematically heterosexual and homosocial. Fintan Walsh has similarly positioned *Garage* as a queer text in how it situates its protagonist within a web of complex and unresolved tensions surrounding desire and otherness. Analysing *Garage* alongside Lenny Abrahamson and Mark O'Halloran's earlier collaboration *Adam and Paul* (2004), Walsh argues that in these films, 'non-normative relationships between men negotiate hostile social milieus, and queerness saturates the cinematic landscape as a mark of loss and exclusion, but also as a force of possibility in the face of a precarious present and an uncertain future' (2013: 218). The pub in *Garage* acts as a 'hostile social milieu' that simultaneously produces Josie as queer and frames such queerness as an untolerated social transgression.

There are two significant pub scenes in the film that produce Josie as a form of failed, and subsequently queer, masculinity. Early in the film Josie goes to the town pub after work. The first shot of the pub interior is a medium long shot from the pub entrance that shows two male patrons, Breffni (Don Wycherley) and Bon (Brian Doherty), sitting at the far end of the bar with Josie sitting slightly apart from them in the middle of the bar. Val (Gary Lilburn), the barman, stands across from Josie on the other side of the bar. As the men converse, the film cuts between shots of Josie (who is framed alone) and Breffni and Bon (who are framed together).

[2] In his seminal work on masculinities, R. W. Connell (2005) argues that heterosexual masculinity has historically been defined as the 'authentic' masculinity to in turn produce homosexuality as a form of 'failed' masculinity. If we were to reverse this dialectic to argue that a form of 'failed' masculinity does not correspond to normalised heterosexual masculinity, then while it would be difficult (and unhelpful) to make the claim that Josie is homosexual, it is possible to argue that his deviation from this masculine ideal queers him. The argument for viewing Josie as queer is further substantiated when Josie's actions with David result in him being labelled a social and sexual deviant.

Josie attempts to act as the voice of authority on the illness behind the recent death of a local townswoman, but his comments are quickly undercut by the other men. There is no music playing and the only sound is the men's conversation.

Breffni asks Josie how work is going at the garage and Josie tells the men that business is picking up with 'houses flying up around the lake'. Josie uses 'we' as he speaks about the garage and Breffni immediately interrupts him to call into question his claim of ownership over the garage since Mr Gallagher owns it while Josie only works there. As he challenges Josie, Breffni stares at him while Josie alternates between glancing over at Breffni and staring down at his pint, nodding nervously. Another townsman, Sully (Andrew Bennett), enters the pub and sits between Josie and Bon. Up until Sully's entrance, the shots of Josie have been framed from Val's position; however, once Sully sits down next to Bon (and becomes included within Bon and Breffni's frame), shots of Josie shift to be more angled from the three men's position. Through this framing, Josie becomes more visually focalised as the subject of the men's attention. Breffni continues mocking Josie, asking:

> Have you heard Tom Gallagher's plan yet Josie? . . . Get some fucking idiot to look after your garage way . . . Sit on it, don't invest, like not a fucking dime. Then, when the time is right, knock it down and start building apartments. And just fuck you out on your ear.

As Breffni speaks, Josie becomes more physically agitated, staring down at his pint, nervously nodding and laughing uncomfortably. Breffni watches Josie while the other men watch Breffni and these dynamics, along with Breffni's command over the conversation, indicate Breffni's full social and diegetic control over the pub space. Breffni openly shames Josie to undermine Josie's claims of authority, implementing a type of 'ritual putdown' that Tom Inglis (1998: 171) argues is common practice within male drinking groups and is a strategy by which members strengthen their male alliance and reinforce their group's boundaries. In doing so, Breffni presents himself as a dominant form of masculinity whilst reminding Josie of his more subordinate status. This scene also situates the film at the beginning stage of Ireland's Celtic Tiger economic boom by hinting at its early impact and emerging forces of capitalism with Josie's observation of new housing developments ('houses flying up around the lake') and Breffni's suggestion that Mr Gallagher will capitalise on these new development opportunities.

Josie goes outside for a cigarette and this movement out of the pub, while voluntary, suggests an escape from Breffni's taunting. It is dark outside and the pub windows behind Josie are brightly lit. Sully comes out of the pub to join Josie and the two men are included within the same frame. Their framing together indicates a shared sense of equilibrium, especially since Josie appears more at ease. The shift from the close-up shots used inside the pub to the longer shot framing Josie and Sully further connotes a sense of 'breathing space' outside the confined space of the pub. When Sully asks Josie why he continues to come to the pub, implying that Breffni's taunting is ongoing, Josie's innocuous reply of 'few pints' reveals his desire to belong to that social space. Yet as the target of the men's ridicule, Josie is unable to form strong homosocial bonds with them and instead he remains on the margins of that male community.

In a later scene, Josie returns to the pub. The pub is populated by a broader range of patrons that includes women and children, and there is a band playing Irish folk songs. Carmel (Anne-Marie Duff), a woman with whom Josie is infatuated, and her sister Pauline (Una Kavanagh) sit on benches along the back of the pub while the male patrons congregate on bar stools. The men discuss the women while the band plays a popular Irish folksong, 'Black Velvet Band', that cautions men to beware of women who are pretty and conniving. This song, along with the topic of the men's discussion and the spatial separation of the two genders, reveal a gendered hierarchy and clear allocation of space within the pub. Josie's inclusion within the men's conversation and their framing together also suggest his elevated social status in the presence of the women.

Later in the scene, a heavily inebriated Carmel asks Josie to dance with her. As they dance, turning on the spot, the film cuts from a medium shot to a close-up of their faces, closing down the space around them so that their interactions appear more private and intimate. Light casts unevenly over their faces. Carmel pulls Josie in close to her and puts her head on his shoulder, telling him: 'You're pure soft Josie.' Josie responds by putting his head on her shoulder and rubbing her back. The film cuts back to a medium shot of them dancing, opening up the space around them so that other patrons are visible in the background. Josie's hand travels up past Carmel's covered lowered back to her bare upper back and she suddenly pulls back and pushes him away from her, berating herself out loud for being too drunk and yelling at Josie to go home. After Carmel pushes him away, Josie stands with his mouth open and appears full-faced under the bright pub lights. He takes a few steps towards her and in doing so draws attention to the return of his limping gait. Breffni is visible in the background of the frame behind Josie, watching the events unfold (see Figure 4.2).

As Carmel and Josie dance together within the close-up frame, they

Figure 4.2 After being pushed away by Carmel (Anne-Marie Duff), Josie (Pat Shortt) stands confused and alone as Breffni (Don Wycherley) watches in the background in *Garage*. (*Source*: screen grab.)

create a private space that appears insular from the rest of the pub. However, once the camera pulls back into a longer shot, their interactions no longer appear private. The watching figure of Breffni behind them draws attention to the regulatory processes at work within the pub space. The film implies that Josie has an erection as he and Carmel dance together, both in the abrupt way that Carmel pushes herself away from him and in how she glances downwards at his trousers after doing so. For Carmel, Josie's physical reaction to their intimacy is a form of transgression since it refutes her image of him as 'pure soft' and makes her anxious about how her interactions with the town simpleton might appear to the other patrons. Carmel's public rejection of Josie once again excludes him from the community he so desires to belong to.

In both of these pub scenes, Josie's marginality and exclusion are evident. He is unable to engage with the men's banter or pursuit of women that are the foundation for male homosociality, and emerges instead as a form of failed masculinity. His inability to belong to the space of the town pub propels him to create a social space outside the garage for him and David to drink ciders after work. However, when Josie then takes David into his home to show him the pornographic video, he transgresses normative social codes of conduct. David tells his parents and this results in Josie being criminalised and labelled a social and sexual deviant. Unlike Alfred, who is able to command the space of the bus, Josie's social discomfort is not limited to the pub but applies to the town as a whole.

Conclusion

Returning to *The Quiet Man*, Sean initially transgresses the social hierarchies within the pub by brazenly entering into the space and moving towards the centre of the bar without first establishing his legitimacy; however, he is quickly accepted into the space and its male homosocial community. Sean is able to endure within the pub because he can align himself with those ethnic and gender norms that structure the space. In contrast, Alfred and Josie's actions within the pub are framed as untolerated transgressions that destabilise the relations of power and regulatory systems ontologically embedded within the space, and their removal from the space becomes necessary to preserve the dominant order. Alfred identifies the pub as a queer site that offers him a space within which he can express his own sexuality and a place of belonging outside the norms of dominant Irish society. Yet his performance of a highly visible form of camp and his refusal of a peripheral position within the pub destabilise the social and spatial relations embedded within that space that must then be restabilised through Alfred's removal from the pub. Alfred's performance not only points to sexuality as plural (differentiating his 'queerness' from that of the other pub patrons) but also characterises it as historically contingent. His appropriation of a form of camp associated with Oscar Wilde reveals it to have evolved into a pernicious and untolerated homosexual stereotype that subsequently results in him being attacked and rejected by the young men. He is therefore out of place within the pub as well as 1960s Dublin society, and is produced as queer through his inability to conform to normative heterosexual or homosexual identities.

In *Garage*, Josie attempts to approximate a male homosocial ideal through male banter and his pursuit of Carmel. When he is belittled by Breffni and the other men and rejected by Carmel, he emerges instead as a queer form of masculinity. He is unable to belong to the community of the town pub and this propels him to create his own improvised drinking space outside the garage where he and David can socialise after work. However, Josie's actions with David, providing him with alcohol and pornography, label him as a social and sexual deviant and result in him being exiled from his town community. Josie's queerness is linked to his inability to keep up with the changing complexities of modern Irish rural life; as Abrahamson describes him in a press release for the film, Josie is 'a contemporary village idiot character but the Irish village doesn't have any place for him anymore' ('Garage'). Josie is thus positioned as queer not only in terms of his (failed) performance of gender but in terms of his spatial and temporal dislocation, fundamentally out of place within an Irish society caught between 'a precarious present and an uncertain future' (Walsh 2013: 218).

Alfred and Josie are characterised by a sense of placelessness, with their queerness emerging more broadly in terms of their shared status as social outcasts. Their positions on the margins of Irish society can be productively analysed by contextualising them in relation to recent social and economic developments in Ireland. *A Man of No Importance* evokes multiple temporalities through its reference to Wilde, the film's setting of 1960s Dublin and its time of production in the early 1990s to re-imagine the national narrative in light of the gay rights movement in Ireland, notably the decriminalisation of homosexuality in 1993. The film projects a type of retrospective liberalism around Alfred's homosexuality, characterising most of the heterosexual characters as sympathetic and tolerant despite their conservatism and vilifying Mr Carney and the young men. At the same time, by using the space of the pub to characterise Alfred as out of place within both heterosexual and homosexual communities, the film reveals the persistence of underlying conservative values and social inequalities that continue to shape contemporary Irish society.

Similar tensions emerge in *Garage*, a film that can be interpreted as a cautionary tale of the Celtic Tiger by identifying its narrative as taking place during the economic boom and then interpreting the text through a post-Celtic Tiger lens. Colin Coulter argues that while the Celtic Tiger has been heralded as an era of unprecedented growth and progress that should be celebrated, 'it has also marked a time of disadvantage and disruption for a great many others . . . that are all but absent from the official narratives of the recent social history of the Irish Republic' (2003: 17). By using the space of the pub to show Josie's inability to fit within existing social structures as well as his inability to modify or recreate them, the film offers a bleak and pessimistic image of contemporary Irish society that counters utopian illusions of the Celtic Tiger. Queerness functions in *A Man of No Importance* and *Garage* to represent identities and life modes caught between competing social and cultural relations surrounding tradition and modernity, and the local and the global. As a result, both films move beyond stereotypical representations and cosmopolitan constructions of queer Irish masculinity to engage with more complex configurations of gender and sexuality, and to enable new forms of what Fintan Walsh (2013) terms 'non-normative imaginings' within a specifically Irish context.

CHAPTER 5

Compartmentalised Cosmopolitans and Rigid Fluidity

Moving outward from the spaces of the family and the pub, this chapter focuses on the more broadly constituted space of the city. Beginning in the late 1990s there emerged a new urban sensibility in Irish cinema that celebrated the city as a cosmopolitan and utopian space. Films such as *About Adam* (Stembridge 2000), *When Brendan Met Trudy* (Walsh 2001), *Intermission* (Crowley 2003) and *Inside I'm Dancing* (O'Connell 2004) express a desire to move away from traditional narratives and iconography by disavowing the past and projecting a utopian and liberal Ireland free from political and sectarian conflict. Martin McLoone has characterised these films as promoting a brand of 'hip hedonism', claiming that they 'epitomise a kind of transglobal "cool"' (2007: 212), while Ruth Barton has described this filmmaking practice as 'the culturally specific desire not to be culturally specific' (2004: 112). Whilst this re-imagining of Ireland through a re-imagining of urban space can be seen as an attempt to escape traditional markers of Irish cinematic identity, particularly those related to placehood and the rural imagery, this representational strategy has also been criticised for its failure to offer a clear sense of local identity. Thus, while the desire to not be culturally specific may be a strategy of avoiding a representational history steeped in issues around the nation and national identity, it also signals a potential inability to engage with contemporary political and social realities.

This becomes a particularly significant issue when considering the politics of queer representation. The majority of Irish queer films are structured by urban narratives, reinforcing a commonly held association of the city with the queer imaginary. The city is often theorised as a catalyst for the increased visibility (often conflated with a perceived increased tolerance) of minority groups. With regards to sexual minorities, David Bell and Jon Binnie claim that the city 'is the primary site both for the materialization of sexual identity, community and politics, and for conflicts and struggles around sexual identity, community and politics'

(2000: 83). Because of the lack of resources available to queer citizens in rural areas and resulting feelings of isolation, the city is constructed in the queer imaginary as a beacon of tolerance and community, and Bell and Binnie cite Henning Bech's (1997) claim that the city is 'the home of the homosexual' (Bell and Binnie 2000: 84). At the same time, there is a large body of work proving that even as LGBTQ populations seek to establish a sense of placehood in cities, they are still policed, restricted and 'Othered' through, for instance, law enforcement systems, heteronormative urban planning policies and tourism strategies.

Urban space thus constitutes a space where sexual identity is both produced and contested. The modern city's utopian and dystopian qualities draw McLoone to align it with Michel Foucault's 'heterotopia', a 'simultaneously mythic and real contestation of the space in which we live' (1986: 24) that was examined in Chapter 4 in relation to the Irish pub. Characterising the city as a heterotopic space allows it to be analysed as a conflicted space that embodies various spatial contradictions and different forms of social relations and modes of belonging. As McLoone argues, the city represents 'progress, modernity, education, culture, and opportunity and at the same time, [represents] disharmony, individualism, materialism, alienation, and conflict' (2007: 215). While other Irish queer films such as *Pigs* (Black 1984) and *The Last Bus Home* (Gogan 1997) use queer identity to draw out the heterotopic qualities of the city and to present Ireland as a conflicted space, *Cowboys and Angels* and *Goldfish Memory* present an Irish urbanity reclaimed by the LGBT groups that have been historically discriminated against and excluded by the Irish State, instead aligning the city with heterotopia's inverse, the utopia: '[presenting] society itself in a perfected form' (Foucault 1986: 24). In their re-imagined visions of a 'New Ireland', these two films create a new sexual cityscape that appears void of homophobia or prejudice.

Reviews of these two films frequently highlight their representations of urban space, particularly in terms of their aesthetic and utopian qualities. In a review for *Goldfish Memory*, Ronnie Scheib considers the pleasures of watching the film as stemming largely from its aesthetic qualities rather than what he sees as a limited narrative that relies heavily on stereotypes: 'Besides the luminous footage of Dublin's streets, rivers and bridges, bars glow with warmth, apartments look welcoming, high-ceilinged libraries and classrooms are bathed in light. Even the most tired of visual clichés are dusted off, gussied up and trotted out good as new' (2003: 24). In a similar vein, McLoone argues that the film's postproduction effects provide 'an almost impossibly attractive contemporary milieu for the film's daring sexual politics . . . turning the old premodernist city into a postmodernist playground' (2007: 213). The title of a review for *Cowboys and Angels* proclaims 'Hit film turns Stab City into Fab City' (McElroy 2003), while Gerry McCarthy claims that the film counters Limerick's violent reputation by presenting the city as 'a stylish, modern city free from mindless violence and provincial piety' that has been shot to great aesthetic and stylish effect (2004a: 10). While McCarthy admits that 'Gleeson never really achieves a true sense of place', he maintains that 'with its clubs and fashion schools, the city portrayed in the film looks like a promising gay destination' and that this 'gay mecca is a great improvement over Stab City' (2004a: 10).

However, these films' projections of an already achieved liberal and tolerant Ireland are juxtaposed with a depoliticised and desexualised image of male homosexuality that reinforces stereotypes and sexual binaries, lacks political and historical ties to the lived realities of LGBT populations in Ireland and ultimately subordinates homosexuality to heterosexuality. Rather than using queerness to destabilise existing cultural and social codes of conduct and behaviour, these films produce Irish queer masculinity as a highly visible and recognisable form of homosexuality that reinforces rather than challenges the heteronormative order. Further, this chapter considers how such representational strategies influence constructions of urban space on-screen. Specifically, it argues for understanding these films' constructions of urban space in terms of 'compartmentalisation'. Here, compartmentalisation refers to a disconnect between identity and place, both visually (the division and separation of spaces within the urban fabric) and in terms of embodiment (how bodies move in and out of spaces and define themselves within those spaces). *Cowboys and Angels* and *Goldfish Memory* visually compartmentalise space by marking a divide between public and private spaces, by structuring places around systems of exclusion and belonging, by repeating anchoring shots as geographical and ideological references, and by framing public space as heteronormative.

Cowboys and Angels

Beginning with *Cowboys and Angels*, the film is a coming-of-age tale about a young man named Shane (Michael Legge) who moves away from his rural home town to Limerick to find work and live independently from his overprotective mother (Angela Harding). He moves into a flat with Vincent (Allen Leech), an openly gay art school student, when he and Vincent both reply to an advertisement and end up being paired together by the letting agency. At first Shane finds Limerick to be intimidating and alienating. In an attempt to explore an alternative lifestyle he briefly becomes involved with two drug dealers, Keith (David Murray) and Budgie (Colm Coogan), helping them to push and distribute drugs. However, through his developing friendship with Vincent, who gives him fashion advice and helps him win over the affections of his art school friend Gemma (Amy Shiels), Shane becomes more settled and self-confident. The film ends with Shane himself enrolling in art school, becoming romantically involved with Gemma, and finding a stronger sense of place in Limerick. Meanwhile Vincent, after helping Shane in his journey of self-discovery, leaves Ireland to travel to America.

Within the film, Vincent and Shane are shown to occupy space differently, and it is through this differing occupation of space that the film reinforces uneven power relations along a homosexual/heterosexual binary. *Cowboys and Angels* opens with Shane's voice-over, immediately framing the film within the perspective of its self-identifying heterosexual protagonist, as he searches for a flat to rent in Limerick. When Shane first arrives to move into the flat, he climbs up the stairs of the building to find a brightly dressed mannequin wearing a sparkly purple cowboy hat in front of the flat's front door. Opening the front door, he walks in, framed in a medium close-up shot, and stares in surprise past the camera. He moves closer to the static camera so that his face becomes framed in a close-up shot, and this movement forward mirrors his increasing incredulity as he states 'Jesus...'. The film then cuts to a shot of the living room, set up as Shane's point of view, filled with plants, and boxes and bags of Vincent's belongings. Shane moves cautiously into the shot as his mother, following him, tells him that Vincent 'puts you to shame anyway with all his stuff'. Later that day, as Shane attempts to put away some of his toiletries in the men's shared bathroom, the film shows him reacting again with surprise and confusion as he opens all of the cabinets to discover them already filled up with Vincent's many toiletries. Shane's reactions in both of these instances frame Vincent as strange and enigmatic, a perspective which the viewer is positioned to share.

However, Vincent's occupation of space, his ability (in Sara Ahmed's words) to embody and extend into space, 'becoming part of a space where one has expanded one's body' (2006a: 11), reflects a subsequent comfort moving through and settling into different spaces. In contrast, Shane appears uncomfortable in most public spaces and is often shown sitting alone in his bare-walled, sparsely decorated room, drawing. The way the two men inhabit space differently is best exemplified in a scene shortly after the two men have moved into the flat together in which Shane decides to go to the local nightclub. The scene begins with Shane walking up to the front doors of the club, outside of which two tall male bouncers

Figure 5.1 Shane (Michael Legge), left, is refused entry to the nightclub while Vincent (Allen Leech), right, is inside dancing on the middle of the dance floor in *Cowboys & Angels*. (*Source*: screen grab.)

stand. As he tries to walk inside, they physically push him back, telling him that it is for members only. The film shifts between framing Shane from behind, facing the bouncers, and framing him in a medium high angle shot from in front, with the two bouncers' heads slightly visible in the foreground. In both framing techniques, the bouncers are positioned as barriers to Shane's access to the club space. After several protests and subsequent refusals, Shane turns away from the door and begins to walk away. The film then cuts to a shot of Vincent inside the club, dancing in the middle of the dance floor (see Figure 5.1). While Shane's night ends up with him going to the chip shop and taking his takeaway back to his room, Vincent ends up picking up a man from the club and having sex with him, linking his ability to inhabit space with an increased sociability.

The men's differing occupation of space is also linked to a difference in representational strategy. Shane and Vincent are presented as embodiments of opposing male characteristics. Shane has poor fashion sense (with a vast collection of patterned sweater vests that Vincent declares are 'naff'), low self-confidence when speaking to women, and no strong social ties. Furthermore, he works for the Department of Agriculture and carries around a pendant of St Christopher that his mother gave him, linking him with traditional Irish rural and Catholic ideologies. In contrast, Vincent exemplifies an established male homosexual stereotype: he often goes to nightclubs, he is a fashion designer, he gets along easily with women, he has a groomed appearance and wears colourful and trendy clothing, and he has camp mannerisms that include exaggerated eye rolling and hand gestures.

By positioning Vincent within this stereotype, the film offers an easily recognisable and consequently 'safe' image of male homosexuality. As Richard Dyer argues, stereotypes function to fix and locate identity 'into recognisable categories in order to gain a measure of control over it'

(2002: 97). Because gay men and women do not have the same visibility as an ethnic minority, for example, 'queer stereotypes are posited on the assumption that there is a grounding, an essential being which is queer, but since this is not immediately available to perception, they have to work all the harder to demonstrate that queers can be perceived' (Dyer 2002: 97). Queer stereotyping in *Cowboys and Angels* functions to assign a visible difference to Vincent by setting him up in clear contrast to Shane. The film explicitly addresses the visibility of Vincent's homosexuality to both Shane and the viewer in a scene in the men's flat the day after Shane's attempted visit to the nightclub. As Shane stands in Vincent's doorway, watching him unpack, he asks Vincent about his sexuality:

> Shane: Are you gay?
> Vincent: Why'd you ask? (pause) Yes, I am. It's the fashion thing, isn't it?
> Shane: It's everything. I'm not by the way.
> Vincent: I figured.
> Shane: It's the hair thing, isn't it?
> Vincent: It's everything.

In this exchange, Shane displays a need to categorise Vincent's sexuality and to immediately affirm his own heterosexuality. The scene reinforces homosexuality as 'Other' by having Vincent define himself as gay whilst Shane defines himself as 'not-gay', highlighting the absence of a need for a similar label for Shane's sexuality ('heterosexual' or 'straight'). Homosexuality and heterosexuality are set up here as opposing forms of desire, in a manner which strictly compartmentalises sexuality rather than allowing for any fluid form of desire that moves between the two poles.

The film does attempt to dislocate sexual identity from its rigidly imposed binary in a later scene where Keith and Gemma try to seduce Shane and Vincent, respectively; however this attempt is unsuccessful since it ultimately reinforces compartmentalised sexuality. After Shane's elderly co-worker and surrogate father figure Jerry (Frank Kelly) dies unexpectedly, Shane goes to the nightclub with Keith and Budgie and attempts to self-medicate by taking Ecstasy. However, he has a bad reaction to the drug and when he sees Vincent and Gemma dancing together he punches Vincent and gets kicked out of the club. He heads home, followed by Keith who is worried about him. Meanwhile, Gemma and Vincent have also returned to the flat and are lying in Vincent's bed as Gemma attempts to console Vincent. As Shane cries, lying on the floor of the living room, Keith leans over him, telling him 'It's hard to keep it all inside – we all pretend to be something we're not' and begins to make advances, kissing Shane's neck and undoing his trousers. Meanwhile,

Gemma begins to kiss Vincent in Vincent's bed, mounting him as she pulls off her shirt. As she begins to climax, Vincent pushes her off of him, crying out 'No! Stop!' and the film quickly cuts to Shane pushing Keith away with a similar cry of 'No! Don't!' As Keith stands up and begins to walk out of the flat, Shane calls out to him, telling him that 'I'm not like you'. The film then cuts to Vincent and Gemma lying in Vincent's bed, with Vincent turned away from her as she stares up at the ceiling, crying.

In this scene, the film invokes queer desire only to immediately disavow it. Keith embodies the archetype of the hard-bodied drug dealer, with long greasy hair, a sullen attitude and a criminal past, and Shane's interactions with him take place within the film's thriller sub-plot. Because the film has not adequately developed Keith's character, his advances on Shane are conflated with Shane's feelings of being overwhelmed and out of control. Shane's rejection of Keith then becomes a rejection of both Keith's sexual advances and the drug lifestyle, aligning homosexuality with criminality and signifying Shane getting his life back on (the 'straight') track. While Gemma's character is given more complexity early on in the film when Vincent reveals to Shane that she has had past sexual relationships with women and while her attempt to seduce Vincent suggests queer desire, the film hints at lesbianism and subversive sexual desire only to ultimately disavow these and reinforce normative sexual binary systems through Gemma and Shane's romantic relationship which ends the film. Both Shane and Vincent remain rooted within their dichotomised sexual orientations.

Not only does the film set up Vincent and Shane in terms of a homo/hetero dichotomy, it also presents a highly commodified vision of homosexuality. This is especially apparent in a scene in which Vincent offers to give Shane a makeover. The scene begins with Vincent leaning over Shane, who is sitting on a chair, as he tells him suggestively that 'I'm going to give you something you desperately need, something I've wanted to do to you since I first laid eyes on you, and you're going to love it!' Shane sits with his arms crossed, an expression of wide-eyed fear passing across his face. As an up-tempo pop music track begins to play ('The Rhythm is Always Inside' by Dreamcatcher), the film cuts through a series of montage shots that includes Vincent cutting Shane's hair, teaching him about moisturiser and taking him clothes shopping.

Throughout this montage the film plays out certain homophobic fears of the homosexual under the guise of a playful (but ultimately derisive) humour. For instance, as Vincent adjusts Shane's jacket, framed in a medium close-up shot of the two boys with Shane facing towards the camera and Vincent facing away, Vincent suddenly ducks downwards and out of frame. The camera stays frozen on Shane's face, which momentarily registers an expression of fear at what Vincent might be doing, before tilting downwards (mirroring Shane's own gaze as he glances down) to reveal Vincent adjusting the cuffs of Shane's trousers. The camera tilts back upwards as Vincent stands upright and Shane offers a relieved smile as the two put their arms around each other and stare at each other in jubilation: the transformation is complete! The film then cuts to the two men going to the nightclub, framed from behind them in a mobile shot as they walk towards the front doors. As they approach the nightclub, a group of men clustered by the front door (perhaps being prevented from entering similarly to Shane) turn to watch them walk by. Shane and Vincent pass by the same bouncers that previously rejected Shane with no hesitation or incident. Inside the club Shane orders two glasses of sparkling wine, informing Vincent that 'this is a special occasion' and the two men salute each other with their champagne glasses.

Rather than challenging the sexual binary which previous scenes have set up, the comic tensions in the interactions between Shane and Vincent in this makeover scene reinforce the homo/hetero dichotomy and underline the uneven power relations embedded in it. The scene presents the gay male lifestyle in a commodified form that allows Shane to safely perform elements of it without destabilising his own heterosexuality. Here it is useful to draw from the work of Dereka Rushbrook, who claims that the emergence of 'world cities' went hand in hand with a strategy of marketing themselves as cosmopolitan through the promotion of 'ethnic spaces': 'appropriately bounded neighbourhoods that present an "authentic" other or others in consumable, commodified forms' (2002: 188). She argues that increasingly 'queer space' can be aligned with these ethnic spaces since 'Queer space is one more place in which cultural capital can be displayed by the ability to negotiate different identities, to be at ease in multiple milieus, to manoeuver in exoticised surroundings' (2002: 189).

The key term here is 'exoticised surroundings': even as Shane participates in queer culture, he remains distanced from it, linking back to Rushbrook's argument that 'the consumption of queerness depends on interaction, or at least on a proximity that allows for (safe) observation, a gaze from a distance' (2002: 198). Shane's access to the previously banned space of the nightclub shifts him from the periphery into the social centre, and the film attributes this shift to his changed ('queered') appearance. At the same time, Shane marks this participation in queer culture as temporary by describing it as a 'special occasion', retaining a firm grip on his heterosexuality.

The film's strategy of having the straight man discover and perform elements of a homosexual lifestyle while ultimately distancing himself from it has been acknowledged by Debbie Ging, who argues that this makeover scene relies on a contemporary trend of television makeover programmes (such as *Queer Eye for the Straight Guy*) to 'suggest that gay culture has much to offer straight men when it comes to attracting women' (2008: 5). However, for Ging this appearance of fluidity with regards to gender and sexuality fails to challenge the limitations of traditional masculinity: 'In this new consumerist guise [homosexuality] is made available to all: not so much as a means of destabilising heteronormative masculinity as a way of reforming it to comply with a more liberal consensus' (2008: 5). Even as this on-screen Limerick celebrates queer space it commodifies it, subsequently producing a desexualised and depoliticised form of male homosexuality.

While the film seems to depict Shane's move away from a masculine identity framed within the parameters of traditional Irish institutions, in its closing sequence *Cowboys and Angels* promotes a sense of personal identity which remains delimited by an institutional framework. The sequence begins with a medium shot of Shane standing in front of a large window in his flat, framed from behind with him contained within the frame of the window. The camera zooms in quickly on Shane as ambient instrumental music floods in and the shot dissolves into mobile aerial shots of Limerick. The film cuts to various city street shots and then to a slow-motion shot of Shane walking through the crowd, towards the camera, as the camera moves backwards to contain Shane within the shot. As Shane's voice-over begins, reading through the personal essay he has submitted in his application for art school ('In 200 words or less state why you would like to study art'), the camera cuts through a series of images: Shane filling out his application, neatly containing his answers within the boxed sections provided, a close up of a plaque reading 'Limerick College of Art and Design', a close-up shot panning a series of framed photographs that show Shane with his deceased father and Shane with Vincent, a shot of Shane drawing Gemma as she lies asleep on the bed. The final shot is a close-up of Shane's face, as he looks out beyond the frame whilst his voice-over states: 'I've found my voice, show me how to use it.'

In this closing sequence, there is a closing down of space, from aerial city shots to progressively smaller and more intimate and private spaces. Throughout the sequence there is a theme of structure and containment: Shane is contained within the frame of the window as he stands in the flat and contained within the camera frame as he walks in slow motion along the street. The shots of the framed photographs and Shane drawing in his room further reiterate this theme of containment. Shots are also structured visually through the straight angles of the boxed sections in the application form, the photo frames, windows, Gemma lying horizontally in bed, the mattress.

The final message of *Cowboys and Angels* suggests tensions surrounding individualism and assimilation. Shane is speaking about finding a sense of self (expressing an individuality and personal agency that would seem to go hand in hand with progressive identity politics), yet this sense of self is one that emerges through an institution. Earlier in the film Vincent tries to convince Shane against applying to art school, telling him that it is soul destroying. Yet Shane's final line ('I've found my voice, show me how to use it') implies that this voice will be expressed within the parameters of existing social institutions rather than in some radically queer space.

This institutionalised form of identity is also one that is resolutely heterosexual. Vincent is the catalyst for Shane's transformation into a more hip, modern version of himself, and this not only makes Shane more self-confident but is also later suggested as one of the reasons for his ability to attract Gemma. The men's relationship borders on parasitic, with Shane in a position of clear advantage, and this reinforces the uneven power relations embedded in their relationship. While *Cowboys and Angels* begins by emphasising Vincent's inhabitation of space and Shane's placelessness, by the end this has been reversed and taken to a further extreme. Shane becomes settled in Limerick, in a relationship with Gemma and in a new career path; he moves from the periphery into the social centre. Meanwhile, Vincent leaves Ireland to travel to America, shifting beyond the periphery and out of Irish society altogether. This suggests an intrinsic incompatibility between the heterosexual and homosexual subject, and posits the film's re-imagined 'New Ireland' as one that is inherently straight.

Goldfish Memory

Shifting to a consideration of *Goldfish Memory*, the film is a romantic comedy which cross-cuts between the various inter-related stories of a group of young men and women dealing with their love lives in contemporary Dublin. Red (Keith McErlean) is an openly gay man who falls in love with David (Peter Gaynor), who leaves his girlfriend Rosie (Lise Hearns) to be with Red. However, their relationship is jeopardised when David discovers that Red has accidentally impregnated Red's best friend Angie (Flora Montgomery) in a drunken encounter before Red and David began dating. Meanwhile Angie, an openly lesbian woman, has been dating Clara

(Flora O'Shaughnessy) but Clara, unwilling to concede to Angie's request to be monogamous, breaks up with Angie and starts casually dating Isolde (Fiona Glascott), the ex-girlfriend of Clara's ex-boyfriend, Tom (Sean Campion). The characters' movements around Dublin reflect this circularity, with the same locations often reappearing and characters constantly running into each other. When characters fall in love, gender or sexual preference are not defining factors; instead, the film promotes a more fluid attitude to love and sexuality.

Goldfish Memory depicts a queer community that exists both outside of and in relation to the heteronormative public sphere. In this re-imagined Dublin, lesbian, gay and bisexual characters move freely through the city's public spaces without fear of social exclusion or discrimination. Not only are public spaces reclaimed by queer subjects, but these spaces actively propel characters towards each other to facilitate their various couplings. Angie meets Clara as she films a live news report on the St Patrick's Day parade. Red and David meet when David accidentally locks his bike to Red's on the street, and then meet again by chance in a pub. Clara runs into Isolde in the local café. Furthermore, these public spaces allow for same-sex displays of desire with no real sense of social repercussion. Red and David first kiss as they walk down the street late at night. Angie and Clara kiss on the street outside Angie's house, and Clara and Isolde kiss in full view as they sit in front of the main window of the café. The film constructs Dublin as a place of possibility and opportunity, with chance meetings and run-ins often jump-starting a new relationship and narrative; at the same time, this narrative approach obscures character motivations and limits character development. Instead, characters are produced as two-dimensional stereotypes, minimising the subversive potential of having queer subjects reclaim the city. As Ging argues, 'Sexuality is portrayed as a matter of choice, and the choices characters make have little or no impact on their rights or on issues of social inclusion and exclusion ... There is arguably little in *Goldfish Memory* which genuinely challenges received views of existing gender structures or relations' (Ging 2008: 5).

The film's re-imagined Dublin could stand in for any cosmopolitan space. Apart from the characters' accents and the use of anchoring shots of recognisable Dublin landmarks, *Goldfish Memory* refrains from explicitly identifying its setting. The film begins with a series of exterior shots of Dublin that include the Millennium and Ha'penney footbridges, Trinity College and the Liffey canal, and these shots are referred back to throughout the film, often used as transition shots when the film moves between different narratives. These shots act as anchors for Dublin's identity and yet limit its real sense of place by not showing characters within these spaces. As Conn Holohan argues, 'The relationship of these representational spaces to the lived spaces of the city, where the film's action takes place, is never articulated' (2010a: 106)

These anchoring shots also carry particular ideological significance since they locate the film and its characters within Dublin's more affluent spaces. These are educated characters, who frequent the university, libraries and art galleries, and who for the most part are implied to live in the city centre (for instance, Clara follows Isolde and Tom on foot from centrally located Trinity College as Tom walks Isolde back to her flat). Coffee shops, restaurants and nightclubs are heavily featured, and this focus on and celebration of visible consumption spaces ties these characters to the discursive myth of the 'pink economy,' whereby LGBTQ subjects' claims to citizenship are articulated through consumer spending and buying power. These queer citizens are produced as respectable and contributing members of Irish society, conforming into the normalising model of the 'good gay citizen' and assimilating into heteronormative structures and institutions rather than challenging them.

Where *Goldfish Memory* arguably shows more radical potential than *Cowboys and Angels* is through its lesbian characters. Through Gemma, *Cowboys and Angels* hints at lesbianism and subversive sexual desire only to ultimately disavow these and reinforce normative sexual binary systems. In contrast, *Goldfish Memory* features openly lesbian characters and explicit sexual encounters between women, as well as a lesbian social space (Miss Julie's Ladies Club). Yet as Holohan has already remarked, the film often positions lesbian displays of desire as humorous rather than subversive by framing them through the perspective of the male (assumed heterosexual) onlooker. For instance, as Clara and Isolde kiss in the café window, Tom, their shared ex-boyfriend, passes by the window and stares in amazement (see Figure 5.2). For Holohan (2009: 143), the reactions of male onlookers position the viewer

> to react to lesbian desire as incongruous, as out of place, as other. It is as if the film does not have the confidence to simply represent lesbian sexuality without immediately positioning it in relation to the patriarchal norms which it disrupts, and then reinforcing those norms by playing the scene for comedic effect.

Goldfish Memory therefore constructs and maintains public space as male and heteronormative.

While the film's cast includes gay, lesbian, bisexual and straight characters, the film does not mark heterosexual desire in the same way as queer desire. Whereas displays of desire between Angie and Clara, and Clara

COMPARTMENTALISED COSMOPOLITANS AND RIGID FLUIDITY 79

Figure 5.2 Clara (Fiona O'Shaughnessy) and Isolde's (Fiona Glascott) kiss in *Goldfish Memory* is watched by Tom (Sean Campion), who stands outside. (*Source*: screen grab.)

and Isolde are remarked on through the presence of the male heterosexual onlooker, this does not hold true for their heterosexual counterparts (for instance when Tom and his new girlfriend Renee – Jean Butler – kiss as they walk along the coast or when Rosie and her new boyfriend Larry – Stuart Graham – kiss on the doorstep outside Rosie's flat), which go largely unremarked. Furthermore, none of these characters emphatically state 'I'm straight!' in the same way that Clara announces to Angie that she is bisexual, or that Red and David constantly define their sexualities to each other.

Similarly to Shane and Vincent, Red and David need to define their sexual orientations to each other in order to stabilise their relationship. However, unlike Shane and Vincent, Red and David undermine these self-definitions through their actions. As they kiss for the first time, David repeatedly tells Red that he is not gay and later, after Red tells David about Angie's pregnancy, they have the following exchange:

> David: If I wanted a wife and kids, I could've just stayed with Rosie. You said you were gay.
> Red: Yeah, well you said you weren't.
> David: Well, I'm not.
> Red: Well, I am.

David defines himself as 'not gay' whilst being intimate with another man, whilst Red defines himself unambiguously as gay despite having just slept with a woman. Subsequently even as the film implies a need for queer characters to define their sexualities and undermines public displays of same-sex desire, it suggests that these forms of identity and desire are not as fixed as they try to claim.

Goldfish Memory ends with Angie and her new girlfriend Kate (Justine Mitchell) deciding to raise Angie's child together with Red and David, with the added implication that Kate and David will attempt to produce a child together to give all four adults a claim on the family they are creating. Monogamy and the institution of the family (albeit in an alternative form) are firmly established, with the men assuming fatherhood roles and the women assuming motherhood roles. Thus even as the film imagines a future Ireland where same-sex couples can raise children, it is still an Ireland that privileges monogamous relationships and the conventional family structure of mother and father, reaffirming the centrality of conservative family values to contemporary Irish society.

By implying fluidity through queer sexuality, but compartmentalising that fluidity within rigid and non-fluid spatial structures and representational strategies, both *Cowboys and Angels* and *Goldfish Memory* ultimately reinforce heteronormative structures and binary understandings of sexuality. While neither film offers a fluid representation of male sexuality, the lesbian characters in *Goldfish Memory* offer a slightly more fluid (although still limited) conception of queer desire. Of the two films, *Goldfish Memory* also offers more radical potential in allowing its queer characters to find a sense of placehood and belonging in Ireland, unlike Vincent in *Cowboys and Angels* who is excluded from Irish society altogether.

Situating Irish Lesbianism within Urban Space

This section focuses specifically on representations of Irish lesbianism, and the relationship between queer femininity and urban space in *Snakes and Ladders* (McAdam 1996), *Crush Proof* (Tickell 1998) and *A Date for Mad Mary* (Thornton 2016). Along with *Cowboys & Angels* and *Goldfish Memory*, these are the only feature-length Irish queer films in this study that showcase explicitly lesbian characters on-screen. They are also all urban narratives, suggesting that the emergence of a new urban sensibility in Irish cinema has not only been accompanied by more overt representations of queer sexuality on-screen but has also been integral to the cinematic representation of queer women.

The relative absence of Irish queer women on-screen is indicative of the more general invisibility of lesbians in Irish society and culture, an occurrence which is 'rooted in pervasive gendered societal attitudes to Irish women and their sexuality' (Connolly and O'Toole 2005: 173). The previous discussions of *Cowboys & Angels* and *Goldfish Memory* reveal ways in which queer subjects' negotiations of urban space are implicitly gendered. In *Cowboys & Angels*, Shane first meets Gemma at the chip shop where she works after he is refused entry to the nightclub. In this scene she teases him and he becomes flustered, with his inability to speak with her mirroring his discomfort within public space. However, in the film's ending, where Shane articulates his new found confidence, this articulation is linked to Gemma's containment, spatially within the bedroom and narratively as the heterosexual object of male desire. Similarly, *Goldfish Memory* positions female experience within masculinist structures, characterising public space as not only heteronormative but also patriarchal in its framing of female same-sex displays of desire through the perspectives of male characters.

Both films reveal how queer women on-screen are subject to containment as both women and queers. Such containment can be contextualised in relation to woman's ideological role within the Irish nationalist movement. Images of Cathleen ni Houlihan and Mother Ireland at once idealised women's place in the private sphere and limited their public visibility to the inspirational and iconographic, in turn reinforcing a passive, submissive and desexualised femininity against which an active, hypermasculine and virile male militant ideal could emerge. As metaphors for the Irish nation, women were 'the body acted upon as well as acted for' (Conrad 2004: 56), and this gendering of the Irish nation as female became an ideological system of control that sought to contain women through material practices. In particular, this system sought to uphold the morality of the nation by regulating female sexuality through the institution of marriage and domesticity. As the Irish feminist movement sought to challenge women's containment within the home and to assert women's rights, their aims aligned with lesbians' own experiences of gendered oppression. Yet this movement, like many second-wave feminist movements across America and Europe, was inherently heterocentric, with the result that 'the question of lesbian feminism became one of the points of dissonance within the Irish women's movement' (Connolly and O'Toole 2005: 176).

Lesbian issues and experiences have been similarly subordinated within the Irish gay rights movement. Gay and lesbian activism in Ireland in the 1970s and 1980s was mainly centred on the HIV/AIDS crisis and the campaign to decriminalise male homosexuality, with the result that lesbian issues did not gain the same public exposure as those issues affecting gay men (Connolly and O'Toole 2005). As discussed in Chapter 1, the absence of legislation directly addressing lesbianism has not equated with greater sexual freedom for Irish queer women; rather, as Joni Crone asserts, the 'taboo status of lesbianism functions as an unwritten law, suppressing not only the practice of lesbian sexuality but the awareness of its very existence' (1988: 346). This lack of a public identity for Irish lesbians further suggests a difference between queer men and women in their relationships to space. In particular, despite the characterisation of the city as 'the home of the homosexual' (Bech quoted in Bell and Binnie 2000: 84), many early studies on geographies of sexuality focused on the lives of gay men and ignored gender differences. Subsequently, territorial practices of lesbians in city spaces have not often been subject to rigorous interrogation. Yet through their different representational strategies, both *Snakes and Ladders* and *Crush Proof* posit queer women as central to their urban re-imaginings of Ireland and, in doing so, reveal specifically gendered relationships to city space. Whereas *Snakes and Ladders* uses queer femininity to reinforce its depiction of Dublin as a cosmopolitan, and largely feminist, space, *Crush Proof* presents Irish urbanity as a conflicted and chaotic space and frames queer femininity as a form of social deviance that works to support this representation.

Beginning with *Snakes and Ladders*, the film focuses on the friendship and relationship struggles of two friends, Jean (Pom Boyd) and Kate (Gina Moxley), who work as street performers in Dublin. When Jean's boyfriend Martin (Sean Hughes) proposes to her, she accepts but remains hesitant about her desire to marry. As Jean's uncertainty grows, she begins to flirt with ladies' man and rebel Dan (Paudge Behan), ultimately breaking up with Martin. After Martin and Kate have a drunken night of sex together, Kate discovers she is pregnant but refuses to tell anyone who the father is. Jean and Martin reunite and the film ends with them getting married, with some ambiguity around whether or not they know that Martin is the father of Kate's baby.

The film has three queer female characters in largely supporting roles: Orla (Catherine White), the manager of Martin's band; Maureen (Stella McCusker), a friend of Jean's mother Nora (Rosaleen Linehan); and Sybille (Anne-Sophie Briest), Orla's German girlfriend who appears only at the end of the film. As in *Cowboys and Angels* and *Goldfish Memory*, the film's queer characters are key to its urban re-imagining. In particular, both Orla and Maureen are positioned centrally within their respective social groups and occupy positions of authority within these groups. Orla is not only the band's manager, but also gives Kate advice on how to improve her performance piece when Kate goes to the Edinburgh Fringe Festival. Orla is frequently shown with a camera taking pictures, reversing the 'gaze' (Mulvey 1975) that is traditionally attributed to the male figure and suggesting Orla's more active and privileged position as bearer, rather than subject, of the look. As with the queer characters in *Goldfish Memory* and *Cowboys & Angels*, Orla does not appear to experience any social struggle or discrimination on the basis of her sexuality. In one scene Jean is in her room and, hearing someone approach her bedroom door, thinks Nora has arrived to speak to her about wedding plans and hides in her closet. When Orla comes into the room instead, she looks in surprise at Jean standing in the closet and asks, 'What are you doing in there?' Here it is Jean, who is suppressing her uncertainties about marriage, who is in the closet rather than Orla.

Similarly to Orla, Maureen appears open and confident about her sexuality. Among Maureen and Nora's group of friends, nicknamed by Jean as 'The Dead Husbands Club', Maureen exudes confidence. Her confidence sets her apart from the other women, who express anxieties about their children and relationships with men, and is emphasised spatially in one scene where the women exercise in the backyard. As Nora leads the sweating women through a series of calisthenics in the hot sun, Maureen reclines on a chair in the shade. At the end of the film, the Dead Husbands Club sits in a circle knitting items for Kate's baby. Nora expresses disappointment in Jean not seeming to have a strong desire to have children, to which Nora drily comments: 'And having fun without children is a sin I suppose?' Spatially and through dialogue, Maureen's difference is emphasised in relation to the other women.

At the same time, like Orla, Maureen does not explicitly face any discrimination. In a scene where all the women go to a Joe Dolan concert, Orla and Maureen are shown dancing together on the dance floor as Dolan sings. Yet rather than destabilising the surrounding space, as occurs in Alfred's act of approaching the young men in the pub in *A Man of No Importance* (Krishnamma Comerford 1994) or when the sergeant interrupts Badger and the soldier's dance in the pub in *Reefer and the Model* (1988), the women's dance is left unremarked on by the other characters in the space. Further, while in these two other films the men's transgressive actions are emphasised by the camera's focus on them, in this the women's act is not the main focus of the camera but instead occurs in the background.

The differences here can perhaps be attributed to a gendered difference that Sedgwick (1992) identifies in her theory of 'male homosocial desire'. Eve Kosofsky Sedgwick argues that the homosocial and the homosexual have been rigidly dichotomised in terms of men's relations with other men, while women's relations with other women tend to be rendered in more comparable terms. Subsequently, 'women loving women' and 'women promoting the interests of women' often appear as congruous and closely related rather than in strict opposition (1992: 2–3). Through this lens, the interactions between Orla and Maureen in the dance hall do not signify the same homoerotic threat as those between men, and are therefore not subject to the same regulation.

While Orla and Maureen do not appear closeted, their lesbianism is not explicitly addressed by the other characters. Instead, non-normative female sexuality is aligned with a range of other female-centric identities and experiences that include motherhood, female friendship, sexual relationships, out-of-wedlock pregnancy and marriage. In doing so, the film recalls Adrienne Rich's (1980) 'lesbian continuum', a theory which, using the concept of compulsory heterosexuality re-envisions women's solidarity by arguing for a continuous history of women's individual and collective experiences of resisting patriarchal forces. The female characters in *Snakes and Ladders* express strong individualistic sentiments and assert control over their own bodies and lives. Jean's obvious hesitation about marriage after Martin's proposal, Kate's open contemplation of whether to have an abortion, the Dead Husbands Club members' reliance on each other in place of their deceased male partners and Orla's visible disappointment seeing Maureen with new girlfriend Sybille reflect fundamental issues facing Irish women in the 1990s. At the same time, even as the film's portrayal of a broad spectrum of female relations foregrounds female-centric relations and experiences in ways rarely found in Irish cinema, it simultaneously risks marginalising or desexualising the specificities of Irish lesbianism by characterising lesbianism as just another type of female relationship.

As with *Snakes and Ladders*, *Crush Proof*'s queer women are found in supporting roles. However, whereas *Snakes and Ladders* uses queer femininity to characterise Dublin as a cosmopolitan, liberal and feminist space, *Crush Proof* uses its queer female characters to reinforce a depiction of Dublin as a conflicted and chaotic space. *Crush Proof* follows Neal (Darren Healy), a young man recently released from prison, as he rejoins his old gang of friends and tries to reconnect with his ex-girlfriend and his newborn son. In a scene over halfway through the film he sneaks into his mother's house to visit his younger sister Suki (Lisa Fleming), and the film reveals that Neal's mother is living with another woman. The appearance of Ma (Charlotte Bradley) and her partner (uncredited) in their dressing gowns with dishevelled hair in the kitchen as Neal and Suki cook breakfast invites the suggestion that they have been in bed together. Ma's partner gives Neal the middle finger upon seeing him and shortly after Ma demands that Neal leave.

By having a queer woman operating as the maternal figure, the film challenges the myths of maternity associated with Mother Ireland and the Virgin Mother: Ma neither protects and nurtures her son nor embodies a virginal ideal. Yet in its subversion of such traditional iconography, the film offers a limited and ultimately misogynist image of Irish femininity that associates queerness with social deviance. In the kitchen, Neal presses his mother to acknowledge him as her son. She tells him: 'Oh I had a son. But I don't know where he is. That was all a long time ago though. I was somebody else then.' Rather than characterising Ma within a more fluid sexuality, attracted to both men and women, her admission to Neal that 'I was somebody else then' suggests more rigid sexual development, from (straight) mother to queer. Neal later reveals to Suki that Ma has three children by three different men, solidifying her characterisation as a sexual deviant.

Thus while *Goldfish Memory* ends with a celebration of the family that shows lesbian characters replicating traditional kinship structures, *Crush Proof* enables a queering of the family only to frame this subversion as a destructive form of social deviance. The film explicitly links lesbianism to social chaos later in the film when it cuts from a violent confrontation between police officers and the residents of Ma's housing development to show Ma and her partner being intimate inside the home. This scene occurs shortly after Neal leaves Ma's house. After a series of shots showing the police officers and residents in violent confrontation (a burning car, a masked man running), the film cuts to show Ma and her lover being intimate, kissing and undressing.

In a medium close-up shot, Neal's mother and her partner kiss. They are only visible from the shoulders up; however, their bare shoulders imply their state of undress. The film cuts to a shot of four men (three of which are uniformed Gardaí) who have suddenly appeared in the home. The film cuts from the men looking in surprise off-screen right to show the two women stopping as they look in surprise off-screen left. In this sequence of shots, the intimate interaction between the two women is linked to the chaos outside through the cross-cutting of these spaces, and the interruption caused by the four men signifies the male and heterosexist regulation of female sexual desire. Even as this domestic space is initially set up as a matriarchal space, it becomes, like public space in *Goldfish Memory*, framed as male and heteronormative by positioning queer female desire in relation to patriarchal norms. While the male Gardaí are rendered impotent and unable to intervene in the chaos outside, within the home they are rendered more powerful in their ability to interrupt the women's actions. Further, while Ma and her partner are not shown outside the house, the Gardaí's ability to move easily between the public and private divide, and to invade the home without Ma's knowledge, imbue them with a greater sense of mobility.

The queer women's limited characterisation is made explicitly evident in the film's ending credits, which leave the characters unnamed. Neal's mother is listed simply as 'Ma' while her partner is not included. Ma and her partner are only shown in three brief scenes, all of which take place within the space of the home. The film therefore not only spatially contains the women within the private domestic sphere but contains Ma within her maternal role by only identifying her as Neal's mother, despite her own expression that she no longer views herself as his mother. This containment of Ma within domestic terms is reflected spatially, with Ma and her partner only shown within the space of the home. While the queer women in *Goldfish Memory*, *Cowboys & Angels* and *Snakes and Ladders* are able to move within public space, in *Crush Proof* they remain confined to the domestic sphere and lesbianism is reinforced as belonging to the private realm.

Ultimately, *Snakes and Ladders* is a feminist text that places female experience at the centre of its narrative. In an interview with *Film West*, Trish McAdam described her inspiration for the film stemming from films like '*All About Eve* and *Whatever Happened to Baby Jane*, films about the tensions between women' (McAdam quoted in White 2001: 222). Whereas the metaphoric relation of the female body to the Irish land within nationalist discourses has produced a narrative of Irish liberation in which women are denied agency, in *Snakes and Ladders* the city is constructed as a feminist space. Its urban representation thus not only contributes to the development of a new urban sensibility in Irish cinema but suggests the potential of city space to offer new opportunities for female agency and empowerment, particularly with regards to female sexuality.

Just as lesbian specificity in *Snakes and Ladders* is conflated with other forms of female relationships and experiences, issues surrounding lesbian representation in *Crush Proof* can be linked to the film's treatment of female characters more generally. Critics have characterised the film as inherently sexist (Barton 1999; Flanagan 2001; Maher 1999). Barton describes the depiction of women in the film as 'miserable', arguing that 'they're either nagging, negligent, over-sized and/or queer' (1999: 37), while Martin Flanagan states that female characters 'are given little independent existence save for the purpose of eluding or frustrating Neal in various ways' (2001: 333). For Kevin Maher (1999), female sexuality in the film operates in service of male fantasy: 'the movie's women, all lipgloss and negligées, seem to have come straight out of a particularly bad soft-porn film . . . Neal's mother and her lesbian lover indulge in a kitchen romp that is "accidentally" interrupted by the police'. By representing female sexuality in terms of sexual deviance or for the purpose of male pleasure, *Crush Proof* constructs a conservative conceptualisation of the female body in need of social regulation and control.

Finally, post-Celtic Tiger queer film *A Date for Mad Mary* (Butler 2016) challenges the trend of compartmentalisation found in *Cowboys & Angels* and *Goldfish Memory* as well as the strategies of queer female representation found in *Snakes and Ladders* and *Crush Proof*. The film is set in Drogheda, the sixth largest town in Ireland. It opens with Mary (Seána Kerslake) leaving prison, where she was imprisoned for violent assault, and transitioning into life after jail: repairing relationships with her best friend Charlene (Charleigh Bailey) and her family, finding a job, carrying out bridesmaid responsibilities for Charlene's impending wedding, and coming to terms with her temper and drinking that led to her imprisonment in the first place.

Against this backdrop, Mary also seeks love and companionship, particularly as she becomes increasingly aware that Charlene is spending more time with her soon-to-be husband and their friends and distancing herself from Mary. Mary's quest to find a date for Charlene's wedding leads her on a series of unsuccessful dates with various men. When a friendship she sparks up with Charlene's wedding videographer Jess (Tara Lee) turns into a romantic relationship, both women are initially surprised and hesitant about how to proceed. Mary is also struggling with feeling that her friendship with Charlene has changed, and Jess begins to feel as if Mary is using her to get even with Charlene. In the film's ending, Mary, having accepted her changed relationship with Charlene, leaves Jess a heartfelt voicemail. Jess then calls Mary back and the film ends with Mary picking up the call, with the implication that there may be a reconciliation between them.

Whereas the previous case studies suggest a tendency in Irish queer cinema of compartmentalising identities and spaces on-screen, in *A Date for Mad Mary* spatial compartmentalisation works to emphasise Mary's uneasy negotiation of her surroundings. Its filming style is defined by the heavy use of close-up and medium close-up shots of Mary that position the viewer in close proximity to the character. According to director Darren Thornton, this shooting style was a deliberate attempt to '[be] able to watch Mary try to process everything that's happening to her. To spend the time staying close, even to feel her boredom . . . so a lot of what we were doing with the camera was basically chasing that stillness' (Johnston 2017). The film begins with Mary leaving prison, a space defined as one of control and regulation, to suggest she is leaving a state of physical containment. Yet, through the film the visual style works to emphasise her spatial containment, in turn mirroring her psychological and social containment. Thus, while spatial compartmentalisation works to reinforce stereotyped representations in *Cowboys & Angels* and *Goldfish Memory*, in this film it strengthens the queer character's complexity to provide a more multi-faceted characterisation.

Further, *A Date for Mad Mary* avoids compartmentalising Mary's sexuality within a defined sexual binary. Even as the film traces Mary's personal process of sexual self-discovery and her evolving relationship with Jess, it avoids labelling either woman as unambiguously lesbian. Both are shown being intimate with men, with Jess in particular shown the morning after a sexual encounter with a man. Even after Mary's relationship with Jess becomes sexual in nature, the women's sexualities are left somewhat ambiguous. For example, after witnessing Mary kissing Jess, Charlene asks her: 'So you're into girls now?' Mary replies, 'maybe'.

This reluctance to label Mary's sexuality along a sexual binary does not mean that the film delimits Mary and Jess's relationship by rendering queer female desire into subplot, as found in *Cowboys & Angels* and *Crush Proof*. Instead, queer female desire figures into a broader narrative of Mary feeling different and alone. Further, Mary's romance with Jess and friendship with Charlene are interwoven throughout the film. The film opens with Mary's voice-over stating, 'The things you need to know about Charlene', emphasising the women's relationship as central to the film narrative. Yet by the end, it is evident that Mary and Charlene's friendship has become less close and that Mary and Jess's relationship is beginning to take precedence. Rather than compartmentalising Mary's experience of sexual self-discovery, the film links it to other parts of Mary's life, in turn providing a more fluid conception of how different facets of identity and personal relationships inform one another.

Conclusion

This chapter argues that the emergence of a new urban imaginary within Irish cinema created the preconditions for a new representational strategy surrounding the sexually liberated queer Irish man. In both *Cowboys and Angels* and *Goldfish Memory*, queer identities are centrally positioned within the cities' social structures. At the same time, stereotyping, sexual labels and commodification strategies limits these representations by normalising queer identity, evacuating it of its historical context and diffusing its radical political potential. Rather than using queerness to destabilise essentialised gender and sexual identities and complicate heteronormative practices and institutions in Ireland, queer male identity instead becomes largely figurative for a new, modern and liberal Irish nation.

Yet despite such critique of these films, they should be recognised as historical products that are inseparable from a broader interrogation of traditional forms of identification and ways of belonging in Ireland that was taking place in the wake of the Celtic Tiger. David Gleeson positions *Cowboys and Angels* in contrast to what he argues are the three main categories of Irish films (IRA films, rural dramas and 'inner-city downer films'), claiming that these categories are becoming less relevant to those living in contemporary Ireland (Clarke 2004: 12). In a similar vein, Liz Gill has stated with regards to *Goldfish Memory* that 'I wasn't as focused on exploring the depiction of Dublin as I was the new side of Irish life that I think is present across Ireland – young, free, single, and independent in a way that the previous generation would never have imagined' (Gill quoted in Knell 2010: 225). These films therefore represent a fleeting celebratory moment during Ireland's Celtic Tiger that promised progress and change, and a release from past preoccupations and constraints. However they, like the Celtic Tiger, are deceptive, with illusions of social liberalism and progressive identity politics obscuring real-life social inequalities and the persistence of conservative ideologies.

At the same time that representations of Irish urbanity emphasised the centrality of sexuality to the portrayal of the modern and cosmopolitan city, they were also accompanied by more reductive gender representations regarding non-normative female identities: evident in *Cowboys & Angels*, *Goldfish Memory*, *Snakes & Ladders* and *Crush Proof* with queer women primarily operating as narrative devices or objects of male pleasure.

The urban setting of *Snakes and Ladders* aligns with the cosmopolitan images of urbanity perpetuated in *Goldfish Memory* and *Cowboys & Angels*. McAdam stated that 'I was conscious that I wanted to make a film that didn't look like a conventional Irish film' (McAdam quoted in Barton 2001: 196), and in this aim the film begins to encounter some of the pitfalls of urban depiction faced by the later films. Michael Patrick Gillespie notes that through the film's focus on middle-class and bohemian lifestyles and spaces, 'it projects a world seemingly detached from the lives of most of the people who live in that city' (2008: 67). At the same time, Gillespie suggests that the film uses the dissolution of local cultural markers to emphasise the social alienation and generational conflict emerging from Ireland's transition into a cosmopolitan society. As such, *Snakes and Ladders* operates as a precursor to the utopian urbanities in *Cowboys & Angels* and *Goldfish Memory*, where the absence of cultural identity becomes a cause for celebration rather than critique.

Like *Snakes and Ladders*, *Crush Proof* has been criticised for its lack of cultural specificity. For Ging (2008; 2013), *Crush Proof*, along with a number of Irish films released in the 1990s and early 2000s, can be linked to a similar cycle of 'lad' films emerging out of Britain. She characterises these films as largely apolitical and ahistorical products that frame social exclusion in exclusively male terms as a subcultural lifestyle rather than a social problem. The film embraces male criminality and disenfranchisement, with the result that it perpetuates misogynist representations of women. Rather than queer femininity working in the service of a cosmopolitan and neoliberal image of Irish urban society, the film aligns non-normative female sexuality with broader social disorder and conflict characterising its dystopian city setting.

Snakes & Ladders and *Crush Proof* further demonstrate how the queer woman operates as national allegory. Recalling Fintan Walsh's assertion that the homosexual subject tends to be evacuated of his sexuality to mark 'the outermost limits of social degradation . . . and future possibility' (2008: 17), in these films the queer female figure becomes a symbol of national utopia (*Snakes & Ladders*) and dystopia (*Crush Proof*). In this sense, these films continue the historical tradition of reducing women to emblems, as exemplified by the figures of Cathleen ni Houlihan and Mother Ireland.

Finally, *A Date for Mad Mary* represents a more fluid representation of queer female identity, emphasised through the spatialities and socialities shown on-screen. As a post-Celtic Tiger film, it can be seen as allegory for a contemporary Ireland trying to break out of preconceived notions about what it means to be Irish. In an interview, actress Seána Kerslake describes the character of Mary: 'even in a small town you can't escape that [label], so for her to escape she has to get out to transform herself . . . she needs to break away to become a new person' (Barry 2016). Mary's struggle to come to terms with her past and move ahead into the future can thus be understood as representative of a contemporary Ireland attempting to redefine itself in the aftermath of the economic boom.

CHAPTER 6

The Queerly Productive Constraints of Rural Space

The previous chapter revealed that as queer identities have become more visible in Irish cinema, they are frequently incorporated within urban narratives. These urban queer narratives reinforce the centrality of the city to the queer imaginary whilst also signalling Irish filmmakers' attempts to introduce new urban sensibilities that shift away from traditional rural narratives and reflect a more modern and urbanised Irish society. Much of queer theory 'unquestionably posits an urbanised subject' (Creed and Ching 1997: 7), with the result that the relationship between rurality and queer sexuality is often rendered insignificant or non-existent and remains under-theorised. This chapter confronts this gap by considering the queer potential of rural space, focusing on how the rural narratives of *Reefer and the Model* and *Clash of the Ash* re-imagine rural space as a queer space whilst challenging dominant cultural modes of representation linked to the Irish rural imaginary.

In Irish films and films about Ireland, the landscape has persisted as a metaphor for Irish identity. As Luke Gibbons contends, the 'landscape has tended to play a leading role in Irish cinema, often upstaging both the main characters and narrative themes in the construction of Ireland on the screen' (Rockett *et al.* 1987: 203). The metaphorical function of the Irish landscape in film can be traced back to the central role it has occupied in romantic nationalist rhetoric as the location of authentic Irishness. As Irish nationalists sought to construct an Irish identity distinct from Britain, they reclaimed and often reinvented a native Gaelic culture that existed prior to British rule. In addition to Catholicism, the Gaelic language and aspects of Gaelic culture (such as sport and music) were embraced as key markers of Irish difference in opposition to Britain. The west of Ireland, as the most distanced from the colonial capital, became representative of the purest form of Gaelic Ireland, a form uncorrupted by colonial influences and processes of modernisation and industrialisation (McLoone 2010: 137). It thus operated as a powerful national symbol within the nationalist cultural imaginary, perpetuated by Irish artists and writers for whom it signified 'the source for the revitalising of Ireland, a landscape of both personal and national regeneration' (Nash 1993: 91). Shaped by nationalist and Catholic ideologies, cultural representations romanticised Irish rurality as a vibrant space defined by traditional communities, normative gender roles and simple, idyllic lifestyles.

From the early films produced by American film company Kalem, to the outsider representations of rural Ireland found in *Man of Aran* (Flaherty 1934), *The Quiet Man* (Ford 1952) and *Ryan's Daughter* (Lean 1970), to the tourist visions of Ireland promoted by the Bord Fáilte, Ireland's history of cinematic representation is steeped in images of the Irish countryside and the simple traditions of rural life. More recent indigenous productions, such as *Into the West* (Newell 1992) and *Circle of Friends* (O'Connor 1995) further reveal how the romanticised and nostalgic pastoral image of Ireland remains a dominant mode of cultural representation. With the emergence of the First Wave, there also emerged new strategies for deconstructing and revisualising the Irish rural imaginary, including adopting a realist gaze, addressing social issues plaguing rural communities and 'peopling the familiar landscape of Ireland differently' through a focus on outsider characters (McLoone 1999: 51).

Reefer and the Model and *Clash of the Ash* are both First Wave films and their queering of rural space can therefore be understood in relation to the aesthetics and political critique characterising this film movement. By locating queerness within the rural, both films further challenge the common 'coming out' migration narrative that posits the city as 'the home of the homosexual' (Bech quoted in Bell and Binnie 2000: 84). Within this narrative, the construction of queer subjectivity is frequently embedded within a story of rural to urban migration which maps the psychological journey of 'coming out' onto a physical journey to the city. In contrast to the queer subject's rural beginnings, the city is framed as 'a beacon of tolerance and gay community' (Weston 1991b: 262). Mary L. Gray suggests that this opposition between the rural and the urban works to reinforce contrasting characteristics of each, so that 'the specific symbolisation of urban spaces (like modernity itself) as dynamic, forward-thinking, brimming with potential requires a rural (other) that is static, traditional, and inadequate' (2007: 8). Here, the rural operates as the devalued term, and renders rural queers as out of place or somehow 'stuck' in a place they would rather not be (Halberstam 2005: 36).

Consequently, there is a tendency within queer narratives to represent rural space as inherently oppressive and characterised by traditional gender roles and compulsory heterosexuality. As 'a locus of persecution and gay absence' (Weston 1991b: 262) associated with sexual repression, isolation and discrimination, the rural tends to be framed as an inherently heteronormative and anti-queer space devoid of the city's sexual possibilities and liberatory potential. Yet, as Chris Gibson suggests, 'Some of the more profound tensions at work in rural places – between conservatism and rebellion, between ruggedness and intimacy, between isolation and estrangement and community and belonging – reveal themselves vividly in sexual practices and identities' (2013: 201). In the recent rural turn within Queer Studies, scholars consider the specificities of what Detamore (2012) terms 'rural queerness', exploring the social and spatial processes that emerge at the intersection of queer place-making practices and rural sensibilities. As Judith Halberstam (2005) reminds us, not all rural queers leave home to become queer. It is therefore necessary to consider the alternate possibilities that 'the condition of "staying put"' may offer in the production of queer subjectivities. Rather than conceiving of rurality as always being a detriment to or in conflict with queer identity, rural queerness is more productively conceptualised as the complex negotiation of queerness within and through rural norms.

Previous chapters began to explore tensions surrounding rurality and queerness. The rural town in *Garage* and the forest scene in *The Last Bus Home* suggest the potential of rural space to make queerness visible even as such queer visibility is framed as potentially threatening. In *Garage* Josie is produced as queer in relation to the small-town community where he lives and works. Embodying a naiveté and simpleness that is unable to be sustained within a changing Ireland, Josie is ultimately framed as a sexual deviant when he transgresses normative social codes. The rural setting of *Garage* is far removed from the traditional rural idyll, and instead the film reconstructs Irish rurality in the 2000s as alienating, repressive and lonely. In *The Last Bus Home*, Petie and Billy embrace in the forest as they collect mushrooms, implying the liberatory potential of the countryside where queer desires can be freely expressed. The only other scene in the film where the men are openly intimate is in the private space of Billy's bedroom, and therefore their embrace in the forest constitutes the film's only public expression of same-sex desire between the two characters. Yet this same act becomes dangerous when Jessop witnesses their embrace and later confronts Petie on-stage, contributing to Petie's panicked flight and ensuing death. Even as the film implies the queer potential of rural space, it simultaneously reveals how that space continues to be policed by heteronormative structures. Thus, in both *Garage* and *The Last Bus Home*, rural space operates as contested space where queerness can be at once expressed and yet not sustained.

Similar tensions surrounding rurality and sexuality emerge in *Reefer and the Model* and *Clash of the Ash*. In *Reefer and the Model* the west of Ireland is represented as a contested space where competing identities and ideologies collide and where the concept of the national in 1980s Ireland is exposed as a complex web of unresolved tensions. The film is about four outsider characters who come together to form a transient community: Reefer (Ian McElhinney), a petty criminal and former IRA member; Teresa – 'the Model' – (Carol Scanlan), a reformed heroin addict and prostitute who is pregnant; Spider (Sean Lawlor), a former IRA member on the run from Northern Ireland, where his family still remains; and Badger (Ray McBride), a gay man. In the film, a rural pub operates as the setting for Ireland's first on-screen kiss between two men to not only complicate the common characterisation of the rural as inherently anti-queer but to undermine nationalist constructions of the west of Ireland as an idealised site of Irish cultural identity. The film further suggests the queer potential of rural space through its use of a rural setting for the formation of an alternative form of family, recalling previous discussion in Chapter 3 surrounding queer kinship.

Clash of the Ash also complicates dominant rural imagery by positing the rural as a space of crisis. The film is set in the small town of Fermoy and follows school boy and local hurling star Phil Kelly (William Heffernan) as he struggles against the high aspirations that his parents, teacher and coach have for his future. The film is not an explicitly queer text; however, it can be productively reread as queer in terms of Phil's ambiguous sexuality and his failure to conform to the expectations of his town's society. In particular, Phil's conflicted relationship to his home town, presented as a claustrophobic space with limited opportunity, reflects his own crisis of identity. Through such a reading, this chapter aligns *Clash of the Ash* with *Reefer and the Model* to argue for both films as queer narratives that reveal contradictory pressures shaping non-normative identities in rural Ireland.

Reefer and the Model

Reefer and the Model opens with Teresa standing on the side of the road. She is picked up by Reefer and his mother (Eve Watkinson), who are driving by, and later joins Reefer, Spider and Badger on their dilapidated trawler, which they use to ferry goods between the Galway coast and the islands. When the trawler breaks down, they decide to rob a bank to pay for the parts to repair it. However the robbery goes awry and the characters become separated. Badger and Spider take refuge in an underground hideout. They are surrounded by police and when Spider attempts to shoot his way out he is killed, while Badger is captured and imprisoned. Meanwhile Teresa manages to start the trawler and takes off as Reefer tries to catch up with her in a rowboat. Teresa suddenly begins to go into labour and becomes incapacitated with contractions. As she slumps behind the wheel of the trawler, she unintentionally sets the boat in Reefer's path. Reefer is forced to jump out of the rowboat and the film ends with him swimming behind the trawler, desperately calling out Teresa's name.

The contested nature of rural space is made explicit in a scene that takes place approximately halfway through the film when the characters arrive at Kilronan on the island of Inis Mor. In this scene, a rural pub becomes the setting for Ireland's first on-screen kiss between two men in what Martin McLoone (2000: 136) describes as the film's 'most subversive aspect'. After arriving at Kilronan, Reefer, Spider and Badger dock the trawler and go to the local pub, leaving Teresa asleep on the boat. In the pub, town locals play folk music and dance, creating a lively and upbeat atmosphere. The three men walk into the space and sit down at a table, with Badger describing to the others how he picks up men: 'Sometimes I give them the dukey treatment, sometimes I give them the macho treatment. Some kids need it so badly it's easy to pick them up.' Badger speaks openly despite the other patrons visible around him, suggesting an ease with discussing his sexuality in this space.

In a scene implied to take place later that night, the film cuts to a close-up shot of Badger as he glances off-screen right. It then cuts to a shot of a soldier sitting across the room, with Badger's head visible on the left in the foreground of the shot. The soldier looks towards Badger as dancing couples move in between the two men, and then stands up, walks towards Badger and then moves off-screen right. Badger immediately stands up and follows him off-screen. Shortly after, the soldier's sergeant is shown approaching the men's washroom. He stands outside the cubicle, listening with his ear against the door. He then moves back and kicks the door open to reveal the young solider with his trousers undone and Badger inside. This reveal of the men inside the cubicle is framed from the sergeant's point of view, with both men looking at the camera as they each leave the cubicle. The three men are shown reappearing in the pub, where they disperse in different directions. The film tracks Badger as he moves around the dance floor, watching the dancing couples, and then walks over to where the young solider is now sitting. The young soldier stands, looking nervously at another solider sitting at the table, and then he and Badger move onto the dance floor and begin to dance among the other couples. Badger kisses the top of the soldier's head and both men smile and begin to dance more enthusiastically around the room. Suddenly the sergeant appears from off-screen and interrupts the men's intimate moment by pulling Badger away and throwing him to the ground.

In this scene, the men's act of queer desire exposes the rural pub doubling as a 'queer space', where the men's 'queerness, at a few brief points and for some fleeting moments, dominates the (heterocentric) norm' (Désert 1997: 21). Yet, unlike Alfred's act of transgression in the pub in *A Man of No Importance*, the men's act in this scene does not appear to destabilise the pub space; rather, their act seems largely tolerated by the surrounding locals. As the men begin to dance with one another, they become almost indistinguishable from the other dancing couples around them, who do not pay any particular attention to the dancing men. Further, it is significant that it is an outsider (the sergeant) who disrupts the men's interaction, instead of one of the locals. This scene implies a politics of queer visibility that operates through rural norms and challenges the assumption of rural queerness as necessarily closeted. As Debbie Ging notes, the locals' acceptance of the men's sexual intimacy suggests 'a more pluralistic, pre-Christian moral code or "radical memory" which is contrary to conventional understandings of the rural as regressive and modernity as necessarily progressive' (2013: 191). Rather than being represented as a homophobic and repressive space, the rural is reconfigured in more complex terms as the catalyst for the articulation of queerness.

At the same time, the film does not mythologise the west of Ireland as an idyllic queer utopia. Even as Badger is publicly intimate with the soldier, the men's encounter ends when they are interrupted by the sergeant. Badger's narrative is left unresolved, with no further mention of his sexuality and with this imprisonment at the end of the film. *Reefer and the Model* thus reconfigures the rural as a postmodern space: fragmented and unstable, encompassing multiple and conflicting spatial and social relations.

Whereas the west of Ireland has traditionally operated as a powerful symbol for Irish national identity, the film uses this setting to portray the loss of such an identity. Shortly after first meeting Teresa, Reefer takes her to a golf club for dinner which he tells her is an Ascendancy space, populated with newly wealthy Irish. As Badger and Spider load the trawler, they discuss the hunger strikes and Spider's inability to return to Northern Ireland to see his family. While Reefer's mother criticises him for leaving the IRA and being a coward, he tells Teresa he always wanted to be a criminal but his mother's politics got in the way. Reefer and his mother's relationship is representative of a generational disconnect between post-nationalist and nationalist positions, as Reefer rejects any strong affiliation to the idea of nation and instead lives his life in largely individualistic terms. Ruth Barton (2004) also notes that through the film's marginalised outsiders the issues of homelessness, drug addiction, poverty and prostitution that are commonly characterised as urban problems become situated within the rural. The rural is thus not presented as an insular space, untouched by the vestiges of modern urban life, but is instead presented as a space operating in complex negotiation with the traditional and the modern, the rural and the urban, the local and the global.

The representation of rural Ireland as a contested site is further reinforced by the film's emulation and subversion of traditional kinship structures, recalling Chapter 3's discussion of *Pigs* and *The Last Bus Home*. In Ireland, links between the rural, family and the nation have reinforced heteronormative and patriarchal assumptions underlying these constructs. The gendering of the nation through national allegory and the role of the Irish State and the Catholic Church in promoting social and moral norms as integral to national stability in turn solidified the 'family's place in the moral economy of rurality and nation' (Whatmore *et al.* 1994: 3).

Whereas the dominant rural imaginary is inherently tied to familial stability, in *Reefer and the Model* family, like rural Ireland, becomes a contested site. Teresa is pregnant, and no mention is made of who the father of her child is. Reefer's mother expresses disappointment in him, taunting him in front of Teresa for leaving the IRA and telling Teresa that she was once proud of him. Spider reveals that he escaped Northern Ireland without saying goodbye to his family, and has not seen his wife or kids because there is an outstanding warrant for his arrest there in connection with IRA activities.

In place of the security and support offered by traditional kinship relations, an alternative form of family emerges between Reefer, Teresa, Spider and Badger. After Reefer picks up Teresa, they drive through Galway and he asks a photographer to take a 'family portrait'. In a later scene, as the four characters sail out to the islands, they dress up and pose for a photograph. Looking at the Polaroid afterwards, Teresa exclaims: 'Look, we're like a family in this!' When Reefer proposes robbing a bank to pay for their boat repairs, Teresa asks if he means breaking the law. He replies that it is in order to 'protect the family'. The characters' repeated reference to family tropes suggests an inherent craving for kinship. Yet this alternative family does not survive at the end of the film. Instead of becoming representative of a unified national whole, this queer family experiences a breakdown of communal structures that ultimately leaves individuals isolated and alone against the harsh landscape.

Clash of the Ash

Clash of the Ash similarly presents the rural as an inherently contested space characterised by competing tensions. Phil Kelly struggles against his growing frustration with the expectations others have for his future. While his hurling coach dreams of Phil qualifying for the county minors and establishing a career in the Gaelic Athletic Association (GAA), Phil's mother (Kay Rae Malone) is more concerned with his Leaving Certification and both of his parents expect him to work at the local garage. When his friend Martin's (Vincent Murphy) girlfriend Mary (Gina Moxley), who is also a former resident of the town, returns from London, Phil begins to romanticise London as an avenue of escape. Mary is glamorous and exciting, and represents new opportunities outside of Ireland. After Phil attacks an opposing player on the field during a hurling match and is kicked off the team, he announces to his parents that he is leaving for London. The film ends with Phil on a bus bound for England.

Phil's sexuality is not explicitly addressed in the film, apart from Martin's comment that he should 'try with Rosie', one of their friends, since 'she's mad about you'. While Phil appears fascinated by Mary, this fascination does not emerge as an obvious form of sexual attraction but rather appears as more of a captivation with her perceived worldliness and experiences living in London. However, the most poignant scene that opens up the text to a queer interpretation occurs near the end of the film, after Phil runs off the hurling pitch following his violent attack on an opposing player during a big match.

After Phil leaves the hurling field, the film cuts to a tracking shot of him as he runs frantically through the forest, pushing past branches. The film cuts to a shot of Rosie (Marian Dowley) walking along the town road. She slows down and then stops, looking off-screen, and the film cuts to show Phil, looking off-screen and then stopping. The eyeline match between these shots implies the characters have seen one another. Phil moves off-screen and there is a cut to Rosie also moving off-screen. The next shot shows Phil in what appears to be a livestock market space, climbing over gates, and then there is a cut to Rosie also moving past similar looking gates. While the characters have not yet been included within the same frame, the cross-cutting between these shots and their spatial similarities suggest they are in proximity to one another. The shots of the characters are also framed in medium close-ups, contributing to feelings of claustrophobia and containment that are further emphasised by the gates around them, which act as obstacles to their movements.

In a longer shot, Phil is shown approaching a gate when Rosie runs into

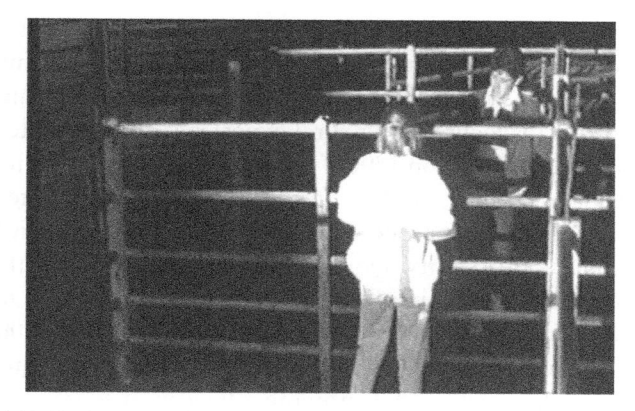

Figure 6.1 Phil's (Liam Heffernan) confession to Rosie (Marian Dowley) about feeling trapped is reflected by his fenced-in surroundings in *Clash of the Ash*. (*Source*: screen grab.)

the frame and stands on the other side of the gate (see Figure 6.1). Phil asks her what she is doing there and tells her to leave him alone, and she replies that he is bleeding and should have his cut looked at. Phil moves under the gate to stand next to Rosie. He leans against the gate and begins to sob: 'Look Rosie. It's not just you it's fucking everything, everything in this fucking – everyone!' Rosie moves towards Phil and looks at the cut on the back of his head. As she tells him 'it's okay', he turns to her and there is a pause as they look into each other's eyes. Phil then leans into her shoulder and they hug.

The pause in this scene is loaded; whereas its inclusion following Phil's emotional admission appears at first to signify a moment of romantic realisation that will result in a kiss between the two characters, that possibility is only introduced to be immediately denied. It is also significant that it is Phil's movement that denies this possibility, since his act of leaning against Rosie's shoulder becomes a continuation of his previous rebuffs against her advances. In reading this disavowal in terms of a disavowal of heterosexuality, Phil's declaration that 'it's everything' opens up a new reading of those social pressures he is struggling against to include feelings of sexual repression. When Phil attacks the hurling player, he does so after he sees Mary and Martin leaving the pitch and walking away together. His feelings of aloneness in this moment contribute to his frustration with his rural life, and emerge through his violent attack.

By reading Phil's undefined sexuality as queer, this chapter begins to unpack how queerness might emerge in unique ways in relation to the rural community. Through such a queer reading, rural space does not operate as an anti-queer space but one structured by conflicting terrains of social and spatial belonging and exclusion. Rather than emerging in opposition to rural structures, queerness emerges through and within these structures. In documenting rural experiences of non-heterosexuals in America, Angelica Wilson (2000) emphasises that the key to survival for many revolves around social conformity and community interdependence. She suggests that the influence of small-town loyalty and familial ties on discourses of identity should not be overlooked, and that rather than sexuality being a defining feature of one's identity it may instead be located within a complex web of 'multiple social belongings' (2000: 214).

In a similar vein, Gray argues that rural communities operate through an insider/outsider politics that promote a lexicon of legitimation based on family and community ties. Through what she terms a 'politics of rural recognition', Gray considers how rural queers use these ties to promote a sense of familiarity and sameness that allows them to be seen as 'just another local' (2009: 37). She demonstrates how in many cases queer difference was tolerated as long as it did not interfere with one's commitments to family and community. Therefore, in contrast to the 'out and proud' stance that characterises many contemporary LGBTQ social movements and cultural representations, rural queers may articulate their queerness through the norms of their local communities.

Both Wilson and Gray challenge the assumption that rural places are 'endemically hostile' towards queer difference by considering how rural queers foster belonging and visibility in rural areas by working within local structures (Gray 2009: 30). Rather than queerness operating as the defining core of one's identity, it becomes imbricated within a broader web of identifications linked to family, community and rural life. In *Clash of the Ash* the recognition of 'multiple social belongings' is key to understanding the film as a queer text. Phil's queerness does not emerge in opposition to rural structures, but rather through his uneasy negotiation of those key institutions of traditional rural Ireland: namely, family and organised sport.

Dominant strains of Irish nationalism position the nuclear family as the central model of social and community organisation, particularly in rural areas. While *Reefer and the Model* re-imagines the family through the queering of traditional kinship structures, *Clash of the Ash* emphasises the continuing centrality of the family to Irish rural life. Even as Phil's parents pressure him to think about his future, they demonstrate unwavering support and love for their son. One evening Phil comes home to discover his parents hosting a party to celebrate their twenty-fifth wedding anniversary. The atmosphere is warm and jovial, as the guests gather around the piano singing and drinking. Phil's friend Willy (Myles Breen) works for his father at the family shop, and in one scene he sells Phil's parents a newspaper as they ask him about his parents. Familial ties and domestic relations thus remain a central mode of belonging within the town.

At the same time, the film comments on shifting rural practices and generational differences that are redefining these traditional social relations. As Phil helps his father (Michael McAuliffe) with the gardening one morning, his father tells him that when he was his age he and his brother were running their family farm: 'Up at six every morning and you wouldn't get the breakfast until you had the cows milked and the pigs fed – ah, that was the days . . . we didn't even think of it as work.' In Ireland's shift from being primarily an agricultural economy to becoming an industrial one, there was a subsequent renegotiation of traditional gender and social roles. As studies by Catríona Ní Laoire (2002; 2005) have shown, this shift has undermined traditional constructions of rural masculinity based on values of hard physical work, responsibility and family values. This scene locates the film within this shift, alluding to how it has led to a disassociation from traditional markers of identity and generational disconnect. Whereas Phil's father's recollection emphasises a male rural identity based on work ethic and a duty to the family and the farm, Phil's general laziness and his desire to leave the town put him at odds with that identity.

Phil's crisis of identity is made more visible in his relationship to hurling. Chapter 4 explores the significant role played by the Irish pub in the formation of identity and community, as a space for the expression and performance of male homosocial bonding and national culture. Sport, particularly in rural Ireland, can be similarly conceptualised as central to the production of hegemonic masculinity and nationalist expression. The GAA was founded in 1884 to aid in the preservation of Irish indigenous culture through the promotion of Gaelic sport. The organisation was a key cornerstone in the dominant strain of cultural nationalism that emerged at the end of the nineteenth century, with the practice and popularity of the Gaelic games linked to a wider political struggle for independence from colonial rule and an Irish cultural renaissance.

The GAA and the growing popularity of Gaelic sport were instrumental in the restructuring of an Irish nationalist masculinity (McDevitt 2004). The GAA marketed male Gaelic Games, specifically football and hurling, as being pre-colonial and mythological warrior sports and the permeation of GAA factions across each of Ireland's thirty-two counties provided a locus for an anti-colonial battle in rural culture beyond urban colonial control. Stating that 'The GAA produced nothing less than a social revolution in parts of rural Ireland' (2004: 23), Patrick F. McDevitt notes how the organisation forged strong rural networks that encouraged young Irish men to become strong athletes and fostered strong nationalist sentiment.

In *Clash of the Ash*, Phil's identity within the town is closely tied to his status as a star hurling player. At the same time, he fails to embody the masculine ideal promoted by the GAA. As described in a 1907 GGA annual, 'the ideal Gael is a matchless athlete, sober, pure of mind, speech and deed, self-possessed, self-reliant, self-respecting, loving his religion and his country with a deep restless love, earnest in thought and effective in action' (quoted in McDevitt 2004: 22). However, as Séan Crosson has similarly noted, Phil consistently falls short of this 'ideal Gael' and its values of bravery, nationality and masculinity: he emerges instead as 'a poor student, temperamental, violent and prone to binge drinking and drug abuse' (2009: 117).

Phil further expresses an individuality that is at odds with the social bonding promoted by the GAA. The team nature of the sport and the coach's assertion that the GAA 'looks after its own' implicate hurling, and the GAA, within a community model. Tom Inglis (2009) notes the role of the GAA in the construction of community, describing sport in Ireland as the 'language of the community' that 'replaced institutional religion as the main form of identity and social bonding'. He further suggests the contribution that the GAA player can make to their local community: 'Participation in the GAA has not only become a major source of local identity and pride, it has also become a source of local cultural capital. There is enormous value in being involved with and playing for the local parish or, better still, the county' (Inglis 2008: 136). Through his participation in hurling, Phil contributes to the reputation of the town. However, Phil shows up late for practice and expresses a generally ambivalent attitude towards his coach.

At the same time, there are two separate sequences in the film where Phil is shown training on his own: doing chin ups, dribbling the ball, jogging and practicing his strokes by hitting the ball against a cement wall. In these sequences Phil displays a greater sense of freedom and pleasure, unencumbered by the coach and team dynamic as well as the rigidity of organised practices. Further, in both of these sequences traditional Celtic music plays. Outside the confines of organised sport, Phil is able to express his true passion for the game, invoking a desire to be without strong affiliation or responsibility that links him with Reefer's post-nationalist position in *Reefer and the Model*.

A similar expression of individual liberation via sport can be found in the recent Irish queer film *Handsome Devil* (Butler 2016). Set in a boarding school where 'rugby [is] a religion', the film initially sets up the school's rugby team as a heteronormative and oppressive community that persecutes forms of difference. The musically oriented Ned (Fionn O'Shea) becomes the subject of the team's homophobic taunting when they associate his artistic nature with homosexuality. For Ned's roommate and new student Conor (Nicholas Galitzine), who is a talented rugby player but is also struggling with coming to terms with his homosexuality, rugby becomes a contested site.

Like Phil in *Clash of the Ash*, Conor displays unbridled pleasure and ease as he plays sport. The first time he plays with the school rugby team, the film cuts through a series of slow motion shots that show Conor running, catching and throwing the ball with ease. Big Star's 'Thirteen', a ballad about the innocence of adolescence, plays in the background. Yet as the rugby coach places increasing pressure on Conor he begins to lose his passion for rugby, telling his coach that it makes him feel like a robot at times. Conor is also pressured by the coach and other players to stop hanging out with Ned because of his presumed homosexuality. After witnessing Conor going to a gay bar and upset at Conor for deserting him for the rugby team, Ned outs Conor at a school assembly. Conor runs away from school and it appears he will miss competing in the school rugby final. However, Ned finds Conor and convinces him to play in the final rugby game.

Despite harbouring a deep hatred of rugby, Ned tells Conor that he will support the school rugby team if Conor plays on it. When Conor tells him that 'I'm not sure I can play for them,' Ned replies, 'you're not playing for them, you're playing for us.' Here, Ned underscores the significance of Conor playing in the match. As Ed Madden argues, 'if sports culture is impelled by and structured around the regulation and production of hegemonic gender norms, it is also contested from within and without' (2013: 249–50). Conor's decision to play in the school rugby final even after being publically outed as gay becomes a subversive act that undermines the myths of athletes as necessarily heterosexual and of gay men as effeminate. This act in turn begins to break down binary divisions, reinforcing Ned's assertion to Conor that 'you don't have to be one thing or the other'.

Further, while the rugby coach's own homophobic attitudes lead him to initially refuse to allow Conor to play in the final, his decision is overridden by the other players as one by one they go and stand by Conor. Again, rugby is framed as a contested site where homophobic and liberal attitudes collide and where tensions surrounding the individual and the collective play out. Subsequently, both *Clash of the Ash* and *Handsome*

Devil complicate normative constructions of masculinity by using sport as the vehicle for the expression of individualism and liberation. Returning to *Clash of the Ash*, the film's framing of hurling as both a source of liberation and constraint for Phil reflects the heterotopic quality of Phil's home town, which operates simultaneously as a space of belonging and alienation. Such paradoxical characteristics underline Phil's own personal crisis of identity.

Yet while the film presents the town as a claustrophobic space with limited opportunity, it also reveals the conflicted relationship that the young protagonists have to their home town. Even as Phil expresses the need to leave, his emotional goodbyes to his parents reveal his underlying fears in doing so. While Martin, who is unemployed and drinks heavily to pass the time, appears to be a product of the town's limitations, he also nostalgically recounts a memory of flattening 'ha'pennies' on the train tracks as a child and tricking the almost blind shopkeeper into accepting them as payment for penny sweets. Although Mary has been living in London, she tells Phil she returned to the town for 'a break'. Her lingering attachments to the space are further revealed when she remains in the town at the end of the film rather than returning to London with Phil.

The film therefore comments on a continuing tension around how to reconcile rural life within contemporary modes of living. Further, in its framing of *Clash of the Ash* as a queer text this chapter considers how it operates as a queer migration narrative, with Phil's feelings of frustration and of not fully belonging to his rural surroundings becoming the impetus for his emigration to the urban hub of London. High levels of emigration in Ireland in the 1970s and 1980s, particularly in rural areas, have been linked to the country's desperate economic conditions as well as its conservative social and moral climate. Particularly for those sexual bodies, including sexual minorities, unmarried mothers and women seeking abortions, that were unable to fit neatly within institutionalised patriarchal and heteronormative structures and that were deemed deviant, emigration out of Ireland was necessary to avoid discrimination and persecution.

The Stag

A more recent reconfiguration of the queer potential of rurality is found in John Butler's 2013 film *The Stag*. In *The Stag*, self-professed metrosexual Fionnan (Hugh O'Conor) reluctantly agrees to go on a stag camping weekend after the persistent insistence of his fiancé Ruth (Amy Huberman) and his best friend Davin (Andrew Scott). Along with Fionnan and Davin, the stag group consists of Simon (Brian Gleeson), Fionnan's friend who is heavily in debt; Fionnan's brother Kevin, who is nicknamed 'Little Kevin' (Michael Legge); Kevin's boyfriend 'Big Kevin' (Andrew Bennett); and Ruth's brother, referred to simply as 'The Machine' (Peter McDonald).

Like in *Reefer and the Model* and *Clash of the Ash*, *The Stag* represents the rural as a complex and contradictory space. Initially the setting works to emphasise the men's stereotypical representation. The group represents a broad spectrum of Irish male stereotypes, including the macho man, the metrosexual and the gay man. In particular, The Machine at first appears to embody an alpha male, hypermasculine archetype: he is loud, outspoken, aggressive and muscular, and he confronts his natural surroundings with a rugged determination (jumping into a freezing cold lake, challenging a bull in a field, attempting to leap over an electric fence). He also does not talk easily about his feelings, and is unable to apologise. The Machine's embodiment of hypermasculinity is made more apparent by his contrast to the other more reserved, metrosexual men.

However, as the film progresses the rural setting becomes the site for dismantling these stereotypes and revealing Irish masculinity as a shifting and complex construct. Davin and Fionnan assume they will be able to deter The Machine from coming on the trip by lying and telling him that two transsexual friends are coming, and they later hesitate when introducing him to Little Kevin and Big Kevin. Yet their assumptions that his hypermasculine persona is necessarily coupled with transphobic and homophobic attitudes are undermined when The Machine welcomes both Kevins without question. After hearing that Fionnan and Little Kevin's father will not support Little Kevin bringing his boyfriend of six years to the wedding, The Machine declares that 'Fionnan needs to man up' and immediately confronts him about not standing up to his father on Kevin's behalf. Here, the milder mannered Fionnan is viewed in more critical terms because of his reluctance to stand up for his brother. Not 'manning up' becomes equated with inaction against inequality.

The men's rural surroundings act as the catalyst for helping them to share and resolve their personal issues: Davin is secretly in love with Ruth, Simon is hiding his business debts, Little Kevin is struggling with how to reconcile his relationship with his father, who disapproves of his homosexuality, and The Machine is unsure how to repair his relationship with his estranged wife. Filmmaker John Butler describes his interest in male bonding narratives:

> Men rely on and cherish their friendships with men so much, and at the same time, very often, they don't talk about anything to those friends. That's fascinating to me — the distance that's kept between men is what men cherish, which is such a weird, paradoxical feature. (McCarthy 2017)

Subsequently, in *The Stag* the rural becomes the vehicle for the expression of new forms of male intimacy and vulnerability.

In this sense, *The Stag* recalls the role that rural imagery has historically played within the nationalist cultural imaginary as 'the source for the revitalising of Ireland, a landscape of both personal and national regeneration' (Nash 1993: 91). At the same time that the rural operates as the setting for the men to work through their personal issues, it simultaneously signals the forming of a new 'imagined community' that is composed of a plethora of different masculinities. This new 'imagined community' is visualised at the end of the film in a speech that The Machine gives at Fionnan and Ruth's wedding:

> In recent times, we've taken a hell of a beating – what with the economy, Europe tearing us a new one and the Church being total assholes about everything. And we've got to forgive ourselves, forgive each other, and learn to love ourselves again. Cause the thing is: we're Ireland. And that, my friends, is deadly.

He then breaks out into a rendition of 'One' by U2.

As a product of post-Celtic Tiger Ireland, *The Stag* can be understood as a film that is trying to deal with the aftermath of the economic boom. O'Connell argues that a number of post-Celtic Tiger films reflect the 'breaking open of secrets and admissions of mistakes, cover ups and bad treatment of fellow citizens, particularly those less privileged' (2016: 166). In contrast to Celtic Tiger Ireland's promises of producing a more egalitarian and progressive society, post-Celtic Tiger Ireland has '[ushered] in a questioning of authority in some shadowy zones of society, a willingness to admit to scandal and an attempt to redress' (2016: 166). Through the men's different experiences of male struggle, the film begins to expose issues facing men in contemporary Ireland that gained public exposure in the aftermath of the Celtic Tiger: depression, financial stress, emotional intimacy and homophobia. In addition to reconfiguring Irish rurality, *The Stag* also implies the liberatory potential of mobility, with the men's journey outside of the city becoming a catalyst for self-discovery and the exposure of a more complex spectrum of Irish masculinities. The trope of mobility in Irish queer cinema is explored in more detail in the following chapter.

Conclusion

Neither *Reefer and the Model* nor *Clash of the Ash* adheres to the romanticised stereotype of rural Ireland; instead, in both films the pastoral emerges as a site for exploring the contradictions and complexities of contemporary

Irish life. In *Reefer and the Model*, the west of Ireland is represented as a contested space, where competing identities and ideologies collide and where the concept of the national in 1980s Ireland is exposed as a complex web of unresolved tensions. Rather than operating as a national site of memory, community and identity, the rural landscape is characterised as an isolating, alienating and conflicted space devoid of any strong cultural markers. For McLoone, the film's bleak imagining of Ireland can be attributed to Comerford's own views of 'the unfulfilled idealism of Irish nationalist rhetoric' (2000: 135). He suggests that the ambiguity and contradictions surrounding the characters' motivations are indicative of an Irish identity crisis surrounding 'the lack of idealism in conventional society' (2000: 136). Both McLoone (2000) and Barton (2004) have also noted how the film departs from dominant cultural representations of rurality through its postmodern aesthetics and its play with Hollywood conventions and a European art film sensibility.

The rural town in *Clash of the Ash* also complicates the traditional romantic imagery of rural Ireland. The town is represented as a stifling and claustrophobic space, with limited opportunities available for its young residents. A review in *The Irish Times* describes the film as offering 'a portrait of a still largely uncharted part of contemporary Irish society – small town life and the struggle of the young to resist its stifling conformity' ('Video Releases' 2000). The town contrasts with de Valera's idealised rural Ireland as described in his 1943 St Patrick's Day speech as 'a land whose countryside would be bright with cosy homesteads, whose fields and villages would be joyous with the sounds of industry'. Instead, it is a space characterised by unemployment, alcohol abuse and emigration. In the film, the institutions of the family, community and organised sport are presented as pillars of Irish rural life and central to rural belonging; at the same time, the film reveals how these institutions produce strong social pressures that, for Phil, become unbearably restrictive. The realist aesthetics of *Clash of the Ash* further counter the dominant cultural tradition of romanticising the Irish landscape; as Kevin Rockett describes: 'Using a self-conscious "art" form and photographic style, the film succeeds in evoking an atmosphere which contrasts sharply with the ways in which so much realist writing has traditionally dealt with the Irish Provincial town' (Rockett *et al.* 1987: 268).

By evoking queer possibility inherent within the pastoral, both *Reefer and the Model* and *Clash of the Ash* challenge the common characterisation of the rural as anti-queer space. At the same time, neither film presents a utopian queer rurality associated with the 'gay pastoral' and cultural representations of queer Arcadias where same-sex desire can be freely expressed. Instead, in these films the rural operates simultaneously as a space of belonging and alienation. In these films, the articulation of queerness within rural surroundings temporarily destabilise those social and sexual norms embedded within the space, whilst simultaneously making visible those hegemonic processes of regulation that continue to work to police and regulate non-normative identities and behaviours.

Finally, *The Stag* provides a post-Celtic Tiger representation of Irish rurality as a space for simultaneous expressions of masculinity and vulnerability. Its reliance on gender stereotypes and sometimes over-the-top humour recalls Jenny Murphy's (2003) claim for the subversive potential of humour to elicit new self-awareness and self-reflexivity amongst Irish audiences. Therefore, although the film appears to operate through homosocial norms, it somewhat undermines these by showing male bonding across a spectrum of different masculinities. In contrast to the other two First Wave independent films, *The Stag* articulates queerness via mainstream conventions, aligning queerness with other male identities and utilising comedy to portray male intimacy and vulnerability.

CHAPTER 7

Queer Mobilities and Disassociated Masculinities

Globalisation and a changing European socio-geographical space have produced new spatialities and subjectivities associated with deterritorialisation, delocalisation and transnational mobility. Within the Irish cultural imagination, national identity has historically been defined in relation to placehood and landscape, with a rooted sense of place and control over land representing Ireland's evolution from an experience of colonial oppression to a post-colonial assertion of independence. Yet the increasing global mobility of people, information and capital and the emergence of transnational organisations such as the European Union (EU) have created new geographies of belonging and exclusion that work to redefine the national and put into flux the idea of Ireland itself. These new mobilities have been accompanied by a postmodern identity politics that privileges fluidity: 'if the modern "problem of identity" was how to construct an identity and keep it solid and stable, the postmodern "problem of identity" is primary how to avoid fixation and keep the options open' (Bauman 1996: 17).

This chapter explores how *I Went Down* (Breathnach 1997), *The Disappearance of Finbar* (Clayton 1996) and *Breakfast on Pluto* (Jordan 2005) construct such a postmodern 'problem of identity' through tropes of mobility. All three films are structured by journey narratives that trace the queer characters' movements as they negotiate their identities in relation to shifting social and spatial structures. As 'being is replaced by becoming' (Aitken and Lukinbeal 1997: 353), the mobile queer subject experiences a crisis of identity linked to their physical and psychic disassociation from stable referents of identity associated with placehood. Through such crises of identity these films reveal the liberatory potential of mobility to release the queer subject from the social and spatial restraints of placehood and to reconfigure Irish identity outside of national paradigms. Here, queer mobility operates as a disruptive position of alterity that challenges hegemonic structures and social norms, and reveals identity to be in flux and fundamentally unstable.

All three films posit movement and mobility as central to the constitution of sexual and gender subjectivities. Increased mobility within and between nations has been cited as key to the social and political mobilisation of LGBTQ communities by fostering connections across borders and within urban centres. Scholars such as Larry Knopp (2004; 2007), Jon Binnie (2004) and Kevin Hannam, Mimi Sheller and John Urry (2006) explore how circuits of queer mobility, including travel, tourism and migration, enable the queer subject to break away from codes of signification determined by dominant systems of family, community and nationhood. Such conceptualisations of queer mobility emphasise its potential to produce new discourses of identity and life modes outside of normative models. For instance, Knopp argues for how the journeys of queer individuals often involve 'quests for identity' that are 'about testing, exploring, and experimenting with alternative ways of being' (2004: 123). As a result, queer subjects may be attached to movement as a life mode, with their spatial displacement motivated by a psychic search for wholeness; by a search for physical, emotional and ontological security within a heterosexist world.

Such quests for identity inform the journey narratives of *I Went Down*, *The Disappearance of Finbar* and *Breakfast on Pluto*. Yet as queer bodies move through space, their negotiations of shifting spatialities reveal the ways in which places are inscribed with socio-cultural meaning and suggest mobility is a question of both 'mobilities and moorings' (Hannam *et al.* 2006: 2). Although these films are structured by journey narratives, they tend to emphasise moments when the characters' movements are halted. The queer subjects' experiences of self-transformation subsequently occur in relation to their movements as well as their temporary states of immobility.

In his reconfiguration of Knopp's 'quests for identity', Andrew Gorman-Murray argues that Knopp's model risks eroticising mobility and instead 'attachment to movement simultaneously signifies a need queer people often feel to find somewhere – some place – to explore alternative ways of being' (2007: 113). For Gorman-Murray, the queer subject's attachment to mobility co-exists with a desire for (at least temporary) emplacement, with migration as 'the spatialisation of an ongoing process of coming out, where each site of attachment along a migratory path momentarily grounds who one is, or was, in this process of becoming' (2007: 113).

Gorman-Murray's formulation of queer migration at once challenges its conception as a linear process as well as its romanticisation of the nomadic queer subject. Instead, he proposes understanding queer migration in terms of multi-directional, start-and-stop and ongoing movements whereby queerness is negotiated in relation to constant processes of displacement and emplacement. Such tensions between placelessness and placehood are key to understanding how queer mobility operates in *I Went Down, The Disappearance of Finbar* and *Breakfast on Pluto*. In these films, the queer characters' movements are propelled by simultaneous attachments to mobility and place to suggest the potential liberation as well as anxiety from 'riding at the edge of self-identity' (Aitken and Lukinbeal 1997: 358). This chapter begins by analysing *I Went Down* as an Irish queer road movie that reconfigures cultural conventions associated with the American road movie within a distinctly Irish setting. It then shifts to examine how queer mobility is linked to a coming-of-age narrative in both *The Disappearance of Finbar* and *Breakfast on Pluto*, with the films' protagonists emerging as 'queer wanderers' that disrupt stable forms of identity and space.

I Went Down

I Went Down follows Irish ex-cons Git (Peter McDonald) and Bunny (Brendan Gleeson) as they travel from Dublin to Cork and then back to Dublin on a mission to kidnap a man named Frank Grogan (Peter Caffrey) under the orders of Dublin mob boss Tom French (Tony Doyle). This film does not emerge explicitly as a queer text. Yet, by using the road movie as an analytical framework, this chapter seeks to productively reread the film as queer in order to examine how mobility acts as a disruptive and catalytic force by subverting and transforming stable forms of identity and space. In its adaptation of the American road movie's narrative structure and conventions within an Irish context, *I Went Down* reveals how movement along the road liberates the Irish queer male subject from rigidly defined social identities and gendered roles. Both Git and Bunny are initially characterised within a hard-bodied hypermasculine ideal. However, as the men move forward along their journey, this characterisation is undermined by the characters' increasing lack of agency and control over their mode of transportation and their surroundings.

The film's subversion of the men's masculinities reaches a climax point approximately halfway through the film in a scene where Bunny reveals to Git that he had a not entirely unwelcomed sexual encounter with a man while he was in prison. The scene begins with Git and Bunny stopping at a roadside motel for the night. They head to the motel pub for a pint, and the first shot of the two men inside the pub is of them framed side by side, smoking cigarettes and drinking their Guinness in unison. Bunny begins to tell Git his theory on women, differentiating between good looking and ugly women and theorising how their looks influence their attitudes about life. Throughout Bunny's speech, the men are framed together. Bunny's theory prompts Git to ask him about his marriage. Bunny tells him that he has been married for twelve years, but also admits that his wife has changed the locks on the house they share and will not allow him inside. As Bunny tells Git that he was imprisoned for over six years for attempted armed robbery, the characters are framed individually, with cross-cuts between close-up shots of Bunny and Git. Bunny reveals that in jail, 'there was a man I shared a cell with for two or three months. And what went down – it wasn't full – I'm not a queer you know. Me wife doesn't know.' He then tells Git that French knows about Bunny's sexual indiscretion and is blackmailing Bunny by threatening to tell his wife about it unless Bunny keeps working for French.

In this confession, Bunny does not frame his sexual encounter as an attack or rape, leaving it unclear whether it was consensual. Instead, he appears more anxious about it becoming public knowledge. By leaving it ambiguous as to whether it was a welcomed or unwelcomed experience, and whether Bunny was a willing participant, the film undermines Bunny's hypermasculine gangster persona and makes it difficult to view him as unambiguously heterosexual. At the same time, when Bunny reveals that his motivation for pursuing Grogan is to prevent his sexual dissidence from being publicly exposed, the film suggests that the men's journey is Bunny's attempt to reinscribe himself back into the patriarchal status quo. Thus, even as Bunny's journey is the catalyst for his queer confession, this same mobility is fuelled by a desire to reassimilate into dominant patriarchal structures by conforming to the ideals of the Irish male hard-bodied gangster.

This tension between deviance and conformity becomes further evident when immediately following Bunny's confession two women walk into the pub and the film works to restabilise the men (and the pub space) as heterosexual and homosocial. As Git turns to look at the women, the background music becomes louder and the film returns to framing the two men together. The pub shifts from operating as a site for Bunny's queer confession to a space that facilitates the men's sexual pursuit of the two women as Bunny gets up from his seat to approach them. This doubling of the pub space as simultaneously queer and homosocial recalls Jean-Ulrick Désert's 'queer space', where 'queerness, at a few brief points and for some fleeting moments, dominates the (heterocentric) norm, the dominant social narrative of the landscape' (1997: 21). The tension in this scene between Bunny's sexuality and his negotiation of the public and private divide within the pub (shifting from a secretive confession to a public pursuit of the women) undermines stable forms of identity and space.

Yet even as the film works to restabilise homosocial norms through the presence of the two women, it continues to develop queer undertones with regard to Bunny's character. Later that night, as Git and Bunny pee side by side at the urinals in the pub washroom, Bunny looks down at Git's penis with interest and comments on its size. After Git takes one of the women from the pub to his motel room and they begin to have sex, they are interrupted by the sound of Bunny listening voyeuristically outside the room door, with Git even momentarily breaking away from the woman to go and try to catch Bunny in the act. Although the film shifts away from any explicit engagement with Bunny's queer sexuality, this scene still suggests particular anxieties surrounding Bunny's masculinity; as Michael Patrick Gillespie points out, Bunny 'suffers quite self-consciously from sexual ambivalence in an environment intolerant of that kind of ambiguity' (2008: 92).

The complicated relationship between the liberatory potential of queer mobility and the ongoing pressures of hegemonic patriarchal impulses is further evidenced in the film's adaptation of the road movie genre. While Irish film scholars such as Luke Gibbons (2005) and Díóg O'Connell (2010) have characterised *I Went Down* as a road movie, they have not fully addressed how the film uses the iconography and conventions of the road movie to produce a queer form of masculinity. As a masculinist film genre with particular historical and cultural ties to 1960s American counterculture, the road movie has since evolved and been adapted within different national and cultural contexts. At the same time, Laura Rascaroli claims that at the genre's core is the use of 'journey as cultural critique, as exploration both of society and of one's self', that is preserved amidst shifts in cinematic style, narrative structure, thematic concerns and representational strategies (2003: 72). Even as *I Went Down* retains this generic core, its specifically Irish context sets it apart from the traditional American road movie. Replacing the boundless American highways and expansive landscapes with the by-ways of the Irish midlands, and emphasising its protagonists' discomfort with technology and mechanised transport rather than the harmonious relationship between machine and man that is central to the traditional road movie, *I Went Down* not only evokes a strong sense of local particularity but uses these points of difference to suggest a crisis of masculinity.

Git and Bunny's initial movements along the road are motivated by French's orders. Whereas the traditional American road movie tends to frame the protagonist's journey as a form of escape or rebellion, as scholars such as Timothy Corrigan (1992) and David Laderman (2002) have suggested, *I Went Down* frames Git and Bunny's journey as an act of compliance, with their movements dictated by French's instructions. The conforming nature of their journey is further evidenced by its circularity. The men travel from Dublin to Cork and then back toward Dublin. They are not moving through space into the unknown but instead remain on a circular course that will return them to their origin, implying character regression rather than development.

The film emphasises the circularity of their journey in a scene shortly after they have kidnapped Grogan in Cork and begin heading back towards Dublin. Their car is stopped by a Gardaí who is helping to tow a broken car off the road. After a short exchange with the officer, they pass through the police barricade unchallenged and a long shot shows the car driving away from the barricade and towards the camera. In the shot, the road forms a U shape so that as the car moves towards the camera it follows the curve of the road and begins to head back in the same direction the characters came from (see Figure 7.1). Not only does this shot reference the small size of Ireland, since Git and Bunny have been able to cross from one side of the country to the other in two days, but it stands in stark contrast to the more conventional landscape shots used in American road movies, such as *Easy Rider* (Hopper 1969), where the highway stretches out to disappear into the distant horizon. Such an explicit reformulation of the American road movie is not found in other Irish queer journey films, such as *The Disappearance of Finbar* and *Breakfast on Pluto*. This more direct reference to the road movie in *I Went Down* therefore signifies the film's self-reflexive play with film genre, acknowledging the influence of American culture on Irish cinema even as it attempts to shape a specifically Irish cultural product.

Figure 7.1 A circular journey in *I Went Down*: Bunny (Brendan Gleeson) and Git (Peter McDonald) begin heading back towards Dublin. (*Source*: screen grab.)

I Went Down further distinguishes itself from the traditional American road movie by not evoking the same joys of mobility and exploring space. Rather than travelling along a highway that borders expansive landscapes, Git and Bunny travel along by-ways that border the bogland. There are very few long shots in the film that emphasise the characters moving across the landscape. Instead, their movements along the road follow a start-and-stop pattern whereby a shot showing them driving away down the road is often followed by a shot of them stopping for some reason. For example, when Bunny steals a second car after having to ditch the first one, there is a shot of Git waiting by the side of the road in a small town and then Bunny pulling up to the curb. Git gets into the car and Bunny drives off down the road. The film then cuts to a bird's eye shot of an idyllic Irish landscape with lush green fields and a picturesque farmhouse in the distance, before tilting downward to reveal Bunny leaning over the front hood of the stationary car, which has broken down. Throughout the film, the characters' movements through space are halted by bouts of immobility and frustration.

Git and Bunny's stunted mobility is largely the result of their inharmonious relationship with their mode of transport, which acts as an impediment to their journey. Whereas Corrigan argues that the vehicle in the American road movie becomes 'the only promise of self in a culture of mechanical reproduction' (1992: 146), this symbiotic relationship between self and technology is undermined in *I Went Down*. Git and Bunny initially set off to Cork in a stolen car, but their inability to open the car's petrol cap at the gas station alerts the attendant's suspicions. Bunny ditches the car as a precaution, forcing the men to walk through country fields to the next town. Bunny steals a second car, which becomes increasingly unreliable as the heater malfunctions, the radio refuses to work and the car finally breaks down completely on the side of the road. After Git and Bunny abandon the second car and are forced to continue their journey on foot, the Irish landscape offers a further source of defeat. The rain begins to pour down and Git falls, gets stuck in the bog and needs to be rescued by Bunny.

While the landscape impedes the men's forward movement, Ruth Barton suggests that the film's setting in the Irish midlands operates as a liminal space that offers the potential to redefine Irish masculinity outside traditional paradigms. Because the 'Irish midlands represents one of Ireland's least colonised regions, subject neither to the Romantic gaze of tourism nor the physical hallmarks of colonial architecture', Git and Bunny are freed 'from the kind of inorganic cultural identities imposed on other areas of Ireland and thus more able to explore the alternatives'

(Barton 2001: 198, 199). The men's antagonistic relationship to their vehicle and their environment undermines claims to conventionally masculine traits of agency and control, and their physical displacement from dominant Irish society suggests that hegemonic concepts of masculinity are becoming unhinged. The liberatory potential of such disassociation then emerges explicitly in the pub scene with Bunny's queer confession. This scene also suggests the significant role played by sites of attachment along the journey; as Gorman-Murray argues, 'Each site of attachment becomes a context for experimenting with and exploring sexual desires, and each relocation can be, to a greater or less extent, informed by the quest for new bodies and new pleasures' (2007: 115). Along with the men's experiences of mobility, their temporary emplacement at the roadside pub and motel offers the transformative potential to reconstitute sexual subjectivities.

As Git and Bunny move along their journey, tensions emerge as their place-bound sense of self is destabilised and they become increasingly disassociated from rigidly defined gender identities and social roles. Yet even as the film begins to use queer mobility to subvert and transform dominant social norms produced by national paradigms, it fails to engage directly with Bunny's non-normative sexuality and ultimately frames his sexual ambiguity more broadly as a form of confused masculinity. The film's closing shot, which shows Git and Bunny driving down the highway towards Dublin airport, further emphasises a continued hold on the linear 'straight' path.

By ending the film with Git and Bunny leaving Ireland, *I Went Down* links queer mobility to the imagining of a future elsewhere that offers greater freedoms and opportunities than Ireland. Yet the film's final shot also emphasises the ultimately linear nature of Git and Bunny's journey and implies a continued hold on heteronormative ('straight') structures. In doing so, the film undermines the disruptive potential of queerness to de-naturalise social norms and challenge heterosexual privilege. In this closing shot, *I Went Down* once again engages with the tension between the liberatory potential of queer mobility and the forces of hegemonic patriarchal logic. The men's liberation (and smooth movement forward) is achieved through their act of conforming to the linear road. Therefore, even as *I Went Down* makes evident the reconstruction of Irish identity within global parameters, it promotes a sense of personal identity which remains delimited by a heteronormative framework; as Bunny emphatically asserts to Grit in the pub, 'I'm not a queer you know'.

The Disappearance of Finbar and Breakfast on Pluto

Those tensions between conformity and deviance that structure the narrative of *I Went Down* similarly shape the journeys in *The Disappearance of Finbar* and *Breakfast on Pluto*. Yet whereas queer mobility emerges in *I Went Down* through the film's appropriation of the road movie, the queer journeys of Finbar (Jonathan Rhys Meyers) and Kitten (Cillian Murphy), respectively, are structured around coming-of-age narratives that link mobility to the experience of growing up and trying to make sense of the world. Both films begin in Ireland, where the central protagonists are framed as outsiders within their local contexts. Within these home spaces, Finbar and Kitten are produced as 'queer children': children who feel out of sync with their peers or who reject the futures mapped out for them, and who 'may prefer growing sideways in relations that are not the standard connections to peers' (Stockton 2009: 52). Their queerness is not rooted solely in a dissident sexuality but is produced through their process of growing up at odds with the social norms that structure their home towns and their embrace of mobility as a life mode. Their feelings of unbelonging and being out of place propel them on their journeys out of their home towns and, ultimately, out of Ireland.

The Disappearance of Finbar is about two childhood friends, Finbar and Danny (Luke Griffin), who grow up in Aachen Close, a low-income housing estate in Dublin. At the beginning of the film, Finbar leaves to play football in Switzerland on a scholarship but returns home after being kicked off the team for bad behaviour. Upon returning, Finbar is no longer seen as the home-town hero and becomes increasingly frustrated with what he considers mundane everyday life. Further, to his annoyance, Danny appears largely satisfied with life in Aachen Close. To disrupt his friend's complacency, Finbar seduces Danny's crush Katie (Lorraine Pilkington) and makes sure that Danny sees them together.

In this scene of discovery Danny walks by a derelict building where he sees Finbar and Katie leaning on a wall as Katie kisses Finbar's neck. Finbar looks bored and unengaged; however, when he sees Danny watching them he begins to grope Katie while maintaining eye contact with Danny (see Figure 7.2). The interactions between the characters in this scene recalls Eve Kosofsky Sedgwick's (1992) 'triangulated desire', whereby Katie operates as an object of desire that mediates bonds of power and desire between the two men by disguising them as bonds of rivalry. Rather than Finbar's seduction of Katie operating solely as an expression of heterosexual desire, it hints at more complex, and queer, configurations

Figure 7.2 Finbar (Jonathan Rys Meyer) maintains eye contact with Danny (Luke Griffin), off-screen, as he gropes Katie (Lorraine Pilkington) in *The Disappearance of Finbar*. (*Source*: screen grab.)

of desire and power that structure Finbar and Danny's relationship, with these configurations emerging more explicitly over the course of the film.

When Danny later confronts Finbar, Finbar tells him that he did him a favour by freeing him of Katie since otherwise 'you get married and move in and in no time at all you'll be pushing buggies'. In his outburst, Finbar associates the act of settling down and staying in place with conforming to societal expectations and the heterosexual narrative. Immediately afterwards he stages a dramatic disappearance by jumping off an unfinished highway flyover in front of his friends. Over the next three years his disappearance becomes international news and the subject of a pop song, 'So Long Finbar Flynn'. One night Danny receives a phone call from Finbar telling him he is in Stockholm, and Danny travels there in search of his friend. The film follows Danny as he traces Finbar's movements from Stockholm into the north of Lapland, only to arrive at a dead end at a tango bar called Finn-bar in a small Lapp village. Danny meets Abbi (Fanny Risberg), a former girlfriend of Finbar's, and begins to settle down with her when Finbar suddenly reappears and tries to convince Danny to leave with him. Danny refuses and the film ends with Finbar once again disappearing.

In *The Disappearance of Finbar*, tensions between displacement and attachment are articulated through the relationship between Finbar and Danny, with this relationship propelling Danny along his journey in his search for Finbar. Neither Finbar nor Danny expresses a strong attachment to Ireland; rather, their negotiations of space reflect the men's attachments to one another. Near the beginning of the film, when Finbar returns home from Switzerland, he jokingly tells Danny that it is because he missed him too much. Finbar's phone call to Danny in the middle of the night and his later appearance in the Lapp village imply his continued attachment to his friend. For Danny, Finbar's disappearance results in him being unable to develop his own sense of self. From Finbar's mother wandering the streets in search of her son, to the music video playing on television, to Katie setting up a shrine to Finbar by the flyover, Danny's everyday life is structured in relation to Finbar's absence. When Finbar calls Danny in the middle of the night from Stockholm, Danny travels there immediately, suggesting Finbar, rather than family or Ireland, is his primary attachment.

Danny's movements around Stockholm and into Lapland are similarly motivated by his attachment to Finbar, with his journey shaped by tips he receives about Finbar from those he meets. Yet as his questions about Finbar are met with growing confusion and miscommunication and when he is ultimately led to a dead-end at Finn-bar, his spatial displacement from Ireland and psychic displacement from Finbar become the preconditions for a new subjectivity and agency to emerge. For Danny, Finbar (and Ireland) no longer operate as a stable source of identification. Once Danny stops looking for Finbar, there is a shift from Finbar to Abbi as his primary attachment. Both Katie and Abbi operate as objects of desire within their respective love triangles with Danny and Finbar. Through his initial act of seducing Katie Finbar is able to destroy her relationship with Danny so that the men's relationship remains Danny's primary relationship. When Finbar reappears in Lapland and attempts to cause similar disruption with Abbi, Danny ultimately chooses Abbi over Finbar. This final decision results in a divergence in the men's narratives. Until this point, Danny's narrative has largely been mapped onto Finbar's, with his movements tracing Finbar's assumed journey. However, the film ends with Danny remaining in Lapland with Abbi and Finbar once again disappearing into the unknown, but this time with no one following him.

The queer undertones in the men's relationship, signalled by such configurations of triangulated desire and by their attachments to one another, are ultimately denied when Danny conforms to what can be conceived as a heteronormative life path characterised by stasis and monogamy. In contrast, Finbar's attitudes towards community and home remain deeply ambivalent, producing him as an outsider both in and outside of Ireland. He is a disturbing presence in Aachen Close and the Lapp village, refusing to settle down and become part of these communities, and he also actively attempts to prevent Danny from settling down. The catalytic quality of Finbar's mobility characterises him as what Todd Barry, working within the context of Irish drama, terms a 'queer wanderer': a queer subject whose movement through space disrupts its perceived solidity and calls into question established forms of identity and community (2009: 152).

By characterising Finbar as a queer wanderer, his movements can be understood as disruptive catalysts for subversion and transformation that extend beyond his individual body. As Danny traces Finbar's earlier movements, he is brought into contact with identities and cultures that challenge the solidity of national culture and the myth of a unified European community. At the airport he walks by African and Indian migrants sitting at the immigration desk, with their physical detainment contrasting with Danny's ease of mobility. A Swedish bartender directs Danny to a city district 'where all the lost people go' and there Danny encounters a Moroccan immigrant blasting music on his stereo and a Chinese couple who sing him an old Chinese folk song in 'a forlorn and homesick air' (Cubitt 1996: 23). As Danny travels into Lapland, he meets a Swedish couple and a Finnish truck driver who all make claims for their country having invented the tango. Danny's journey, via Finbar's presumed journey, undermines stable notions of home, community and belonging within an increasingly globalised Europe.

Sue Clayton describes a central theme in the film as being 'the new European diaspora, the idea of a Europe at once both more local, and more expansive and boundless' (2007: 140). The three main settings in the film, Aachen Close, Stockholm and Lapland, are devoid of any distinct cultural markers or national signifiers. Clayton chose to film in Aachen Close for its feeling of being 'anywhere in Europe' (Wayne 2002: 16), Stockholm is presented as a global and multicultural city that encompasses diverse and displaced identities, and Lapland is represented by an expansive and largely empty snow-swept landscape. Through these spaces, which refute the notion of a 'centre', the film re-imagines Europe as a postmodern space that denies any strong relationship between identity and place. Finbar and Danny's relationship reflects this spatial representation, with Mike Wayne describing the characters as signifying two contrasting sides of modernity: 'community and separation, continuity and rupture' (2002: 85).

These conflicting characteristics embodied by Finbar and Danny are combined within the character of Kitten in *Breakfast on Pluto*. Like Finbar, Kitten emerges as first a 'queer child' and then a 'queer wanderer', with her movements through space undermining and subverting stable forms of identity, community and place. *Breakfast on Pluto* is set against the backdrop of the Troubles in 1970s Ireland and is about the journey of Patrick 'Kitten' Brady, a transgender woman raised by a foster mother and sister in the fictional border town of Tyllerin. Kitten's life in Tyllerin is defined by the institutions of the home and the Catholic Church, with her foster mother and the school priests set up as enforcers of strict moral and social codes by policing and reprimanding non-normative behaviours. Early in the film she is caught dressing up in her foster sister's dress and lipstick by her foster mother, who then forces her into a bath and demands she repeat: 'I am a boy, not a girl!' At her parochial school Kitten attempts to subvert religious doctrine by naming herself after Saint Cettin, a saint she claims was an ambiguously gendered accolade of Saint Patrick. When one of the priests presents the students with a question box where they can place notes asking questions about issues that are troubling them, Kitten asks about a good place to receive a sex change operation and is promptly expelled.

Through Kitten's antagonistic relationship with her home town the film sets up a central tenet of Kitten's narrative as being about feeling out of place and misunderstood. Her out-of-placeness is further emphasised by her childhood friends, who consist of other child 'misfits': Charlie, an Ethiopian-Irish girl; Lawrence, a boy with Down Syndrome; and Irwin, a boy who desperately wants to embody the hard-bodied masculine ideal of Irish republicanism but falls short. As a highly visible form of queerness, Kitten embodies a disruptive presence within Tyllerin. She not only fails to conform to familial and religious social norms but, as the illegitimate child of the town priest, Father Liam, and his English housekeeper, inherently represents national and religious transgression. Finding herself at odds with the conservative norms of her home town as well as the growing political conflict in Ireland, Kitten embarks on a wandering journey around Ireland and later to England in search of her birth mother. Along her journey she temporarily aligns with those she meets, resulting in brief stints as a glam rock band singer, a children's entertainer, a magician's assistant and a peep show performer.

Similarly to Finbar and Danny's wandering movements, Kitten's journey does not follow a clear linear path. The film's narrative is divided into episodes that mirror the stop-and-start quality of Kitten's journey. This discontinuous mobility is produced by Kitten's attachment to the idea of 'home', as representative of a space of love and protection, and her dependence on mobility as a mode of survival. Gorman-Murray argues for the importance of understanding queer migration in terms of emotional geographies, driven by 'yearnings to test new sexual identities, practices and ways of being; finding, consolidating or leaving intimate relationships; and seeking communities of belonging' (2009: 44). Even as Kitten utilises mobility to escape the repressive effects of nationalist and religious ideologies, her mobility remains motivated by her constant search for home, acceptance and belonging. Her journey subsequently becomes shaped by those she meets and with whom she temporarily aligns.

For example, after leaving Tyllerin she flags down the passing tour bus of Irish glam rock band Billy Hatchett and the Mohawks as she walks along a country road. She asks the driver if she can hitch a ride and he tells her to hop in. The camera tracks Kitten's movement as she moves to the back of the bus, opens the door and climbs inside. The camera stays in place as Kitten closes the door and the bus drives away, with the bus moving away from the static camera. Up until this point in the scene the camera's mobility mirrors Kitten's, with her movements dictating those of the camera; however, by having the camera become stationary once Kitten gets into the bus, the film implies that she is surrendering her personal mobility to that of the bus.

The start-and-stop quality of her journey represented in this scene can be understood as reflecting her various attempts to find spaces of 'home' to which she can belong, with such constructions of home becoming an ongoing boundary-marking exercise through which she attempts to make sense of her place in the world. Like Finbar she operates as a 'queer wanderer'. The disruptive nature of Kitten's mobility emerges in how her encounters with others effectively queer them by making visible paradoxical identities and contradictory ways of being. An example can be found in a sequence of scenes after Kitten climbs into Billy Hatchett's bus. The film cuts from the shot of the bus driving away to a shot of Kitten inside the bus, sitting in the far right corner beside the rear door. She is addressed by Billy (Gavin Friday) from off-screen, who asks her what she thinks of the trouble in Northern Ireland. As they begin to converse, the camera crosscuts between individual and increasingly close-up shots of Billy and Kitten. Billy tells Kitten about British guards torturing IRA prisoners and this, along with the Irish flag hanging behind him, his framing in close-up, and his control over the conversation and command over the bus space, position him within a republican and hard-bodied hypermasculine ideal.

When Billy discovers that Kitten has no idea who he is, he reacts with surprise, bringing the other band members into their conversation: 'Hear that lads? Never heard of Billy Hatchett and the Mohawks?!' As Billy speaks, the film cuts to a longer shot that opens up the confined space and shows the other band members on the bus as they begin to sing the background harmonies to 'Wig Wam Bam'. The film cuts back to a close-up of Billy as he joins in with the melody. The camera then moves from this shot across the bus space to rest on a close-up shot of Kitten's face, who begins

Figure 7.3 Billy Hatchett (Gavin Friday) shifts from hard-bodied republican masculinity, left, to glam rock performer, right, in *Breakfast on Pluto*. (*Source*: screen grab.)

to nod her head and hum along. The film cuts back to the close-up of Billy and then, using a sound bridge, cuts to a medium close-up shot of Billy singing the same song on-stage in a dance hall, in full glam rock costume and make-up, and lit by a stage spotlight (see Figure 7.3).

Here, the film's shift between the space of the bus and the space of the dance hall undermines the perceived solidity of Billy's hard-bodied masculinity by linking it with performance and a camp sensibility. Billy stands in full view on the middle of the stage and the cheering, dancing crowd suggests that this form of queer masculinity is allowed within the 'safe' space of performance. Following this scene, Billy's heterosexual masculine identity is further destabilised outside of performance when he expresses an attraction to Kitten and they begin to date. Kitten begins to perform on-stage alongside Billy, dressed as a Native American woman. Yet while Billy's public embodiment of queer masculinity and camp sensibility remain firmly located within a form of performance, Kitten's embodied queerness more explicitly challenges stable relations between biological sex, gender and sexuality. As a biological man that identifies with a female gender and that performs a different female persona, Kitten embodies a disconnect between biological sex, gender identity and gender performance. Recalling Judith Butler, Kitten's constant displacement among these three identities challenges stable forms of identity and hegemonic norms by '[constituting] a fluidity of identities that suggests an openness to resignification and recontextualisation' (2004: 176).

Both Judith Halberstam (2005) and Susan Stryker (1998) have commented on the use of the transgender body as a postmodern marker of fluidity and flexibility, with Halberstam arguing that 'the potentiality of the body to morph, shift, change, and become fluid is a powerful fantasy in transmodern cinema' (2005: 76). As emblematic of the postmodern condition, Kitten exposes those identities and spaces around her as similarly fluid, fragmented and multiple. This is made evident in her various interactions, including with Billy Hatchett (hypermasculine/queer), Mr Silky String (a well-dressed gentleman who elicits Kitten for sex then attempts to murder her) and Bertie (a friendly magician who befriends Kitten yet also takes advantage of her by making her perform in his magic shows). Yet even as the transgender body may represent a fluidity and 'embodiment in motion', it may simultaneously be used to reinforce normative gender identities and social processes (Stryker quoted in Alexander 2005: 56. For Jonathan Alexander, the transgender body has the potential to 'evoke tropes both of boundary crossing and the power of boundaries to (re)inscribe norms' (2005: 71).

The transgressive nature of Kitten's performance and presence on-stage becomes evident when the band moves into Northern Ireland (made evident by the presence of road patrols and the increasing amount of IRA propaganda). The band's audiences in Northern Ireland react more violently to Kitten's presence on-stage, and this points to the need for more rigidly defined gender and sexual identities within the context of heightened political tensions, since anything resisting easy classification represents a particular threat to national stability.

Kitten's peripatetic path of ongoing relocation allows her to experiment with new and unfamiliar identifications and belongings. Therefore, even as Kitten utilises mobility as a life mode and form of survival, that mobility is motivated by her strong desire to settle down and belong. The conflicting desires to settle down and to remain in motion that emerge through Finbar and Danny's relationship are combined within the figure of Kitten. Recalling Wayne's (2002: 85) characterisation of the men as representing two sides of modernity, 'community and separation, continuity and rupture', these same contrasting characteristics emerge simultaneously and in often traumatic ways through Kitten.

An example of how these tensions converge into a form of hysteria is found in a sequence of scenes later in the film, shortly after Kitten leaves Billy Hatchett and arrives in London. Kitten goes to a nightclub that is filled with British soldiers who have just returned from a tour of duty in Ulster. She is approached by one of them, who offers to buy her a drink and then asks her to dance. They are dancing when a bomb suddenly explodes inside the club. Kitten survives; however, when she is taken to the hospital and discovered to be biologically male, her gender performance is framed by the media and the police as a form of disguise and she is arrested on suspicion of planting the bomb in service of the IRA.

Kitten is taken to a police interrogation room where she is violently questioned and beaten by two police officers. The officers, convinced of Kitten's guilt, demand that she confesses. Kitten finally agrees, and is given a pen and paper on which to write her confession. Yet rather than admitting to planting the bomb she begins to narrate a fantastical account about Patricia Kitten Braden (aka 'Deep Throat'), a James Bond-esque alter-ego who enters into an IRA hideout and overpowers those inside with her deadly perfume spray. Kitten's narration is accompanied by a camp sequence in which Kitten, dressed in a black leather catsuit, plays the part of 'Deep Throat' as Buffalo Springfield's 'For What It's Worth' plays in the background. After defeating the IRA soldiers in this fantasy, Kitten looks directly at the camera and sings along to the song. She then sprays her perfume at the camera, and fragments of glass float up and assemble together to form the previous night's scene of Kitten dancing in the club. However, her dancing partner has been replaced by her childhood friend Lawrence, who was killed by a bomb when they were children. The film then cuts back to the interrogation room, where Kitten is collapsed on the table sobbing. The two police officers look at each other uncomfortably and then leave the room to review their facts: 'Did he or did he not, dressed as a woman, get caught by his own bomb?'

As Charlotte McIvor (2009) has also noted, by assuming Kitten's guilt based solely on her nationality and by understanding Kitten's cross-dressing as a disguise rather than an expression of gender identity, the officers fail to consider how Kitten's queerness operates at odds with the heteronormative and hypermasculine ideals of the IRA. Further, Kitten's state of hysteria at the end of the fantasy results from feeling forced into competing identifications. Like the relationship between Danny and Finbar, Kitten is situated within the contested terrain between filiation and affiliation: between 'what we are born into' and 'what we aspire to' (Holohan 2007: 145). Just as Danny's subjectivity is at once shaped by his closeness to Finbar and his distance from him, Kitten's subjectivity both engages with but is not wholly defined by the structuring forces of British colonialism and Irish Catholic nationalism.

According to Conn Holohan, Kitten avoids becoming too closely filiated and 'asphyxiated by the pressure of proximity' and yet does not achieve so great a distance as to become detached 'to the point of indifference' (2007: 145). Instead she remains implicated within her own culture even as she resists becoming defined by dominant discourses, and this positions her within a state of alterity. Holohan argues that this negotiation affords Kitten a unique subjectivity as she 'refuses the available subject positions within [her] immediate cultural milieu' (2007: 147). Such refusal can be located within the film's camp aesthetics and fantastical elements, as well as the various characters' shifting personas, such as Billy Hatchett's shift from a hypermasculine to glam rock identity.

Conclusion

This discussion of queer mobility indicates the ways in which globalisation has redefined the national as a structuring or appropriative rather than totalising force. In its appropriation of the road movie, *I Went Down* reconfigures cultural conventions associated with this American genre within a distinctly Irish setting. *The Disappearance of Finbar* was funded by the European MEDIA programme and the IFB, co-produced by British, Irish and Swedish production companies, and filmed in Ireland and Sweden. Its production context as well as its representation of transnational movement situate its Irishness in direct relation to a European sensibility.

Finally, in *Breakfast on Pluto* queerness emerges as a universal signifier of unbelonging that opens up the film's historical setting of the Troubles in Ireland to global audiences. For filmmaker Neil Jordan (2005), the story is relevant to contemporary audiences dealing with the threat of terrorism in a post 9/11 world:

> I looked back on my memories of the '60s and '70s in Dublin and London and found an eerie resemblance to that time – think of the London bombings that just happened – and it made me a little reluctant to do this film . . . but then I finally decided that the experience that the film represents is really quite instructive for anybody living in these times. With all these nasty ideologies trying to tell you what you should be, in a world where you can go into a bar and the bar may explode, how do you make your way in the world? Patrick does a pretty good job.

Not only does *Breakfast on Pluto* use queer mobility to destabilise and reconfigure dominant gender and sexual norms produced by national paradigms, but it highlights the ability of queerness to bridge the local and the global and to offer a more universal mode of address. Therefore, in all three films queer mobility operates as a disruptive position of alterity that not only destabilises those norms underpinning dominant Irish culture, but challenges the idea of the 'nation' itself in the context of globalisation.

In the ordering of these three case studies, this chapter further reveals an evolution in tensions surrounding queer mobility, from suggestions of its potential to reconstitute hegemonic masculinity, to its ability to undermine the stable relationship between identity and place, to its subversion of dominant norms and established meanings that reveal identity and space as inherently contested. In these films, queer mobility implies the freedom of movement and the dissolution of political, economic and social constraints. For Sara Ahmed, the lack of orientation offers new potential: 'The hope of changing direction is that we don't always know where some paths may take us: risking departure from the straight and narrow makes new futures possible, which might involve going astray, getting lost, or even becoming queer' (2006a: 21). From Bunny and Git's car moving into the distance as they travel towards the airport, to Finbar, Danny and Kitten's wandering movements, the shift away from a clearly demarcated path opens up new life modes and identifications. At the same time, all three films allude to the alienation, fragmentation and isolation that are symptomatic of such mobility.

CHAPTER 8

Contested Belongings within Diasporic Space

This chapter interrogates the dynamics of diaspora in relation to Irish queer masculinity in *2by4* (Smallhorne 1998) and *Borstal Boy* (Sheridan 2000), exploring how the queer male subject's physical displacement from Ireland and process of settling down elsewhere is negotiated in relation to his sexuality. Nationalist discourses have historically positioned homosexuality as a foreign contaminant or form of national treason, defining post-colonial Ireland as inherently heteronormative by imagining homosexuality as occurring outside the nation-state. As Ed Madden (2010) and Tina O'Toole (2013) have argued, this positioning of queer sexuality as outside the nation has resulted in cultural representations of sexual desire which posit migration out of Ireland as central to the Irish coming out narrative; subsequently, as Madden asserts, Irish queer sexuality itself constitutes a diasporic project.

Yet even as national belonging may appear to preclude sexual becoming, social identities and sexual behaviours continue to be policed within the diasporic context. Drawing from the memoirs of Italian-American author Mary Cappello (*Night Bloom*, 1998), where she describes her struggles with reconciling her lesbianism with the sex and gender norms set out by her Italian immigrant family, Anne-Marie Fortier argues that for Cappello 'ethnicity is an obstacle in her queer becoming' (2003: 7). In his study of Irish diasporic literature Madden notes similar struggles for Irish queer emigrants. He cites Máirtín Mac an Ghaill's study on young Irish gay men living in London in the 1990s ('Irish Masculinities and Sexualities in England', 1996) and Anne Maguire's autobiographical account of being a lesbian and an Irish emigrant out of place in both Ireland and New York ('The Accidental Immigrant', 1995) as evidence of how Irish diasporic communities continue to maintain ethnic boundaries by policing sexual behaviours. Thus, 'even when located elsewhere, Irish queer sexuality could be rendered other, *not*-Irish' (Madden 2010: 177; original emphasis). Ongoing conflicts surrounding LGBTQ activists' right to march under their own banners in the Boston and New York St Patrick's Day parades further reveal how heterosexuality continues to be a powerful symbol of Irish national identity used to police the boundaries of cultural territory and how dominant social norms continue to shape constructions of Irishness even within the diasporic context.

Such examples not only reveal how diaspora is mediated in relation to powerful sexual ideologies, but characterise diaspora itself as an inherently unstable space in which relations of 'here' and 'there', 'home' and 'away' are in constant negotiation: '[weaving] new webs of belonging that trouble spatial fields of "nation", "home", territory, "community"' (Fortier 2000: 16). Within this context diasporic identity emerges 'as a positionality that "is not a process of absolute othering, but rather of entangled tensions"' (Fortier 2000: 16). This conceptualisation of diasporic identity as unstable, in flux and contested is key to understanding how queerness and diaspora intersect in *2by4* and *Borstal Boy*. Both films operate as queer diasporic narratives that suggest the transgressive potential of diasporic space to enable queer subjectivities and life modes. In *2by4*, Irish immigrant Johnnie Maher (Jimmy Smallhorne) lives in the Bronx in New York City and works as the foreman for his Uncle Trump's (Chris O'Neill) construction company, Trump Consolidated. Johnnie works and socialises with other members of the city's Irish male immigrant working-class community, has an American girlfriend named Maria (Kimberly Topper) and also experiments with his sexuality, frequenting gay clubs and picking up men. At night Johnnie suffers from nightmares linked to a traumatic childhood experience that he is unable to recall until the end of the film when he remembers being abused as a child by Trump.

Borstal Boy is based on Irish author and former IRA volunteer Brendan Behan's autobiography of the same name, and recounts his experience of being arrested in Liverpool with bomb-making equipment during World War II and sentenced to a prison term in a borstal in East Anglia. Although this film is not a diasporic narrative in the conventional sense, it is included in this chapter because of its productive comparisons with *2by4*. Like New York, the borstal functions as a contested space where the displaced Irish subject negotiates his sexuality in relation to familiar and strange identifications. As Brendan (Shawn Hatosy) forms strong bonds with the other prisoners, he begins to question the rigid identity politics embedded within Irish republican nationalism. In particular, his discovery of the works of Oscar Wilde in the borstal library and his budding romance with English soldier Charlie (Danny Dyer) force him to re-evaluate his heterosexist understandings of Irishness through an exploration of his own sexuality.

Reconstituting 'Home' within Diaspora

In both films, the men's process of leaving Ireland and settling down elsewhere can be understood in terms of a process of estrangement: 'of becoming estranged from that which was inhabited as home' (Ahmed 2000: 92). Sara Ahmed argues for migration as involving both 'spatial dislocation', a separation and distance from the homeland, and 'temporal dislocation', an experience of discontinuity between past and present. This dual spatial-temporal experience of dislocation produces the migrant body as out of place and uncomfortable through 'the failure to fully inhabit the present or present space' (2000: 92). Here, the process of estrangement becomes the condition for new communities to form, as the migrant subject combats feelings of alienation and displacement through the creation of new social bonds. Ahmed's notion of estrangement is the starting point for this chapter's examination of queer diasporic space. As displaced bodies, Johnnie and Brendan attempt to settle down and feel 'in place' within their surroundings by establishing strong social bonds and fixed forms of community. Yet even as they attempt to carve out new spaces of belonging, the fixity and solidity of these communities are undermined by 'processes of decentring' (Brah 1996: 206) taking place within diaspora.

Specifically, the concept of home for both men becomes reconstituted as they negotiate new geographies of identity across multiple terrains of belonging. Chapter 8 explored how movement within and between national borders can be theorised as an act of liberation for the queer individual that functions as part of a broader coming-out narrative. At the same time, the analyses of *The Disappearance of Finbar* and *Breakfast on Pluto* revealed how such mobility takes place in relation to what Avtar Brah (1996) terms 'homing desires': desires to feel 'at home' within the context of migration. Questions of home carry a particularly complex resonance within the queer diasporic narrative, whereby 'home', as familial and national space, operates an inherently heteronormative construct that operates as an exclusionary and alienating space for the queer subject. The dominant queer migration narrative maps out the queer subject's process of coming out alongside their movement away from home, reinforcing 'home' and 'away' as opposing terms.

Yet it is important to understand the queer subject's relationship to home as more complex than a 'traumatic displacement from a lost heterosexual "origin"' (Eng 1997: 32). Instead, 'home' occupies an inherently ambivalent role within the queer diasporic imagination whereby it 'must be negotiated as a site of estrangement and nostalgia, complex (dis)affiliations and (dis)identifications' (Madden 2012: 177). Drawing from

Brah's 'homing desires', Fortier suggests that queer migrations involve the 'reprocessing' of home so that 'the identities of "home" as well as those who inhabit it are never fixed, but are continuously re-imagined and re-defined' (2003: 116).

In *2by4* and *Borstal Boy* 'home' emerges as a conflicted site of meaning that becomes reshaped by the men's changing relationships to Ireland (as homeland) and their lived localities (New York and the borstal). Both films suggest that Johnnie and Brendan's departures from Ireland enable their expression and experimentation with non-normative sexual behaviours and desires, linking their physical displacement with a subsequent psychic release from rigidly defined Irish identities and sexual norms. Yet even as these films imply the queer potential of diasporic space, they emphasise an ongoing tension between Irishness and queerness that is being constantly negotiated within a diasporic context. Rather than understanding the men's displacement from Ireland in terms of a linear development from closeted to 'outed' as they move from a conservative and intolerant Ireland to a more progressive and tolerant elsewhere, these films offer more complex intersections of Irishness and queerness that disrupt social binaries and dichotomised relations to space, and that are informed by broader relationships of antagonism surrounding gender, sexuality, race and ethnicity.

2by4

2by4 opens with shots of Johnnie and the other Irish immigrant men working on a building site. Dressed in blue jeans and shown painting walls, hammering nails and carrying wall sheeting, the men are immediately implicated within a blue collar, working-class and male homosocial identity. The film then cuts to Johnnie at home with Maria, who has bought him a pair of leather trousers. He initially refuses to try them on, telling her that if he walks into the pub wearing them he will 'have the lads break me balls'. However, at her insistence he puts them on and the film shows him standing in front of the mirror admiring his reflection. Commenting that they are not very Catholic, he proceeds to praise the trousers exclaiming 'I've never felt like that before Maria – woo!' He further expresses an embodied enjoyment in the physical sensation of wearing the unfamiliar clothing, bending and stretching his legs, running his hands down the sides of his hips and taking a few tentative steps around the room.

By juxtaposing these two scenes, the opening of *2by4* introduces Johnnie through competing forms of masculinity within the diasporic setting of New York. The construction site is represented as a male homosocial space where the men's similar dress and familiarity with one another produce connotations of affiliation and community. Johnnie's later comment to Maria that the lads will 'break me balls' and that the trousers are not very Catholic suggest the persistence of underlying Irish cultural mechanisms. As Ed Madden (2010) has also argued, this scene places emphasis on the performance of male sexuality and the influence of popular culture, namely glam rock. This opening sequence thus sets up Johnnie's diasporic life in relation to the familiar (the Irish immigrant community) and the strange (New York and American popular culture).

The Irish immigrant community plays a central role in Johnnie's life in New York and operates as his primary source of identification and belonging. This community links Johnnie's place of origin (Ireland) to his lived locality (New York) through a shared cultural heritage that is preserved through the men's collective performance of Irish culture. As displaced bodies, the men form 'migrant belongings' that involve 'creating momentary coherence – of place, of culture, of history – which is deemed central to the definition and duration of identities' (Fortier 2000: 174). Referencing Judith Butler's theory of gender performativity, Fortier considers how migrant belongings rely on the collective performance of particular cultural norms whereby 'ethnic identities may stem from the "stylised repetition of acts" [that] produces an effect of substantialisation and naturalisation of cultural belonging (2000: 6). In *2by4*, the men work and socialise with one another, play on a hurling team and frequent an Irish pub called The Lansdowne owned by Trump. These practices of group identity work to regulate social behaviours and maintain cultural boundaries, 'manufacturing cultural and historical belongings that mark out terrains of commonality, through which the social dynamics and politics of "fitting in" are delineated' (Fortier 2000: 2). In particular, the men police the boundaries of their community through casually enforced homophobia and racism.

In one scene, as the men travel to work on the back of a truck, Johnnie tells two newly hired Irish men, recently arrived in America, that 'the first week in New York, you get a hooker, right? The second week in New York, you get the crabs. After six months in New York, you get the first blow job off a bloke. Seamus, show him the blow job.' The men all laugh as Seamus quickly replies, 'I don't know how to do that.' In this exchange, New York is constructed in the Irish migrant imaginary as a space of sexual promiscuity and abandon. Madden notes that 'the uneasy humour of the scene lies in the way that sexuality, including homosexuality, presumably located in the foreignness of New York, is suddenly relocated among their own, in a joke, but one that foregrounds the uneasy status of homosexuality in Irish culture' (2010: 77). Even as the men may experiment with their sexuality in New York, such experimentation becomes associated with their surroundings rather than attributed to their own desires.

This type of disassociation recurs throughout the film. For example, as Johnnie and another Irish man, Billy (Terry McGoff), watch a hurling match, Billy comments that he finds hurling creepy since it involves 'folks running around, grabbing each other, you know? Communal showers and all that shite.' Later in the film, when Trump is arrested for indecent exposure in Central Park, he tells Johnnie that he was wrongfully arrested and 'how the hell was I supposed to know all the queers go there'. He then derides the 'big fucking black nigger of a fucking cop' for arresting him. Here, Trump's use of homophobic and racist slurs is an attempt to compensate for his weak explanation of what he was doing in a well-known gay cruising spot.

Even as both Johnnie and Trump participate in this process of boundary maintenance, they transgress these boundaries. The film shows Johnnie picking up and having sex with an Australian rent boy named Christian (Bradley Fitts), and later reveals Trump paying for sadomasochistic sex with a black male prostitute. Although both scenes open up tensions surrounding queerness and otherness, they are framed very differently. The scene with Johnnie and Christian begins with Christian approaching Johnnie on the street and asking him for a cigarette. Both men appear intoxicated, with their slurred speech and slow movements, and when Christian asks Johnnie to go somewhere 'to have some fun', Johnnie allows himself to be led down the street. Christian leads Johnnie to a derelict house run by prostitutes and drag queens who rent rooms for the night. Standing in a room, the men slowly undress and kiss each other, and later lie in bed, tenderly kissing and staring into each other's eyes. Soft instrumental music floods in as the camera cuts to a longer shot of the two men embracing in bed (see Figure 8.1).

The scene is initially imbued with a seediness by associating the men's sexual encounter with a deviant world of drugs and prostitution. However, as Martin McLoone suggests, this is undermined by the film's use of romantic signifiers: it 'is shot in a warm and hazy glow of soft lights and candles, and is remarkable for the way in which it shows the lovers engaged in a sensitive exploration of each other rather than in hard-core sexual activity' (2000: 197). The use of long takes in this scene and the relaxed interactions between the two characters frame Johnnie and Christian's sexual encounter in sharp contrast to the fragmented and frantic style of filming used when Johnnie and Maria have sex earlier in the film.

Later in the film Johnnie overhears Trump and the prostitute having sex. The prostitute, a black, muscular and tattooed black man, spanks

Figure 8.1 Johnnie (Jimmy Smallhorne) and Christian (Bradley Fitts) lie in bed together in *2by4*. (*Source*: screen grab.)

and anally penetrates Trump while deriding him as a 'dirty white mother fucker'. Here, it is via the racialised body that Trump both expresses and distances himself from his queerness. While earlier in the film Trump uses a derogatory slur when referring to a black police officer, in this scene he positions himself in a submissive and degraded position in relation to the black prostitute. This scene thus begins to further complicate tensions surrounding queerness and otherness that the film previously sets up through Johnnie and Christian's encounter by introducing racial difference and sexual acts of sadomasochism and debasement. In *Beautiful Bottom, Beautiful Shame*, Kathryn Bond Stockton (2006) uses 'shame' as a conceptual framework for exploring potential links between the signs 'black' and 'queer'. Both black and queer groups have been publicly marked as abject and socially debased; however, the focus of Stockton's book is on why certain forms of shame have been embraced by these groups. In particular, she explores 'the value of debasement as a central social action' that, rather than forging harmonious and homogenous communities, creates 'a kind of social solitude of people who are set, in some deep measure, apart from each other – but in an apartness they create together' (2006: 27). Furthermore, rather than attempting to concretely define relations between 'black' and 'queer', Stockton posits these as unstable and composite forms to 'explore more specific collisions, collusions, and borrowings' between them (2006: 33).

Returning to the scene between Trump and the prostitute in *2by4*, rather than attempting to fully define or understand this scene, it is its unfathomability that offers a compelling point of analysis. It encompasses tensions surrounding familiarity and strangeness, togetherness and apartness, and identification and difference that are not set up in strict opposition but rather intersect in complex ways. Both of these sex scenes solidify a characterisation of New York as a diasporic space where 'multiple subject positions are juxtaposed, contested, proclaimed or disavowed' (Brah 1996: 208). They also suggest the limitations of the Irish community, since both men not only secretly seek out particular sexual pleasures through the anonymity afforded by New York's sexual subcultures but are shown in more vulnerable and intimate terms with these two strangers than with their Irish community.

Due to his feelings of loyalty, Johnnie decides not to tell the other men about Trump. Trump plays a significant role in the Irish immigrant community by employing Irish immigrants in Trump Consolidated, coaching their hurling team and running an Irish pub that the men frequent. Trump is not only the patriarch of the Irish community in *2by4*, but acts as a surrogate father for Johnnie and a depository of memory that binds Johnnie to Ireland. Throughout the film, Johnnie makes several comments regarding his biological father that suggest he was largely absent from Johnnie's life. In Trump and Johnnie's conversations together, Trump frequently recalls an event when Johnnie was a child that Johnnie does not remember. In retelling these events, Trump not only positions himself as an ever present paternal figure in Johnnie's past but ties Johnny's present life in New York to his past in Ireland. In one scene Johnnie and Trump sit on a riverbank as Johnnie complains about Maria wanting to move in with him and him not wanting to pick out curtains with her just yet. At this mention of curtains, Trump asks: 'Curtains? Hey, do you remember sitting your ma's curtains on fire? . . . You don't remember? God Almighty man, you nearly burnt the house down.' Fortier suggests that ritualised acts of remembering within migrant communities are 'embodied and lived as expressions of an inherent, core and enduring identity that is organically linked to a larger, imagined community' (2000: 173). As they perform these communal forms of remembering, Johnnie reconstructs his past by reliving these memories with Trump and, in doing so, strengthens his ties to Ireland as homeland and as a stable place of origin. Thus, as Ahmed notes, the 'failure of individual memory is compensated for by collective memory' in which Johnnie is positioned into a past he has forgotten (2000: 77).

However, when Johnnie has a sudden and visceral flashback to his childhood and remembers being abused by Trump, he is forced to re-orient his present self in relation to a revised past. Throughout the film, Johnnie suffers from nightmares that are somehow linked to his childhood in ways that he does not understand. These nightmares consist of over-exposed and indistinct images and the sound of a garbled voice in the background. The source of these nightmares is revealed in one of the film's final sequences when Johnnie goes to a gay nightclub after getting into a fight with a Hispanic convenience store clerk. This fight results in Johnnie being badly beaten up with a bat by one of the clerk's friends. As Johnnie moves through the nightclub, the viewer is positioned alongside Johnnie, evidenced by the handheld motion of the camera that mimics his movements and the other patrons' direct eye contact with the camera. They have surprised and concerned expressions on their faces, implying the extent of Johnnie's physical injuries from the attack. The space is darkly lit, full of writhing bodies, and a heavy techno bass beat plays in the background.

A young black man whose face is covered in piercings begins to dance in front of Johnnie, with his face framed in a close-up shot from Johnnie's point of view. The film cuts between this close-up shot of the black clubgoer and the flashback close-up shot of Trump's face as he has sex with the black prostitute, with the sounds of Trump crying out heard over the club music. The film then cuts to Johnnie's childhood flashback shots, where the images remain blurry and overexposed, then cuts quickly between shots of Johnnie in the club and shots of him from earlier in the film. This sequence and the film's use of fast cuts suggest that Johnnie is beginning to mentally link together these different moments and memories from his past and present, and this leads him to uncover Trump as the source of his nightmare flashbacks.

The sound of heavy breathing can be heard over the sound of the club music as the film cuts to a longer shot of Johnnie, who pulls off his shirt and then stands with his arms outstretched, staring into space. In slow motion, he falls to the ground and the film then cuts back to the close-up shot of Trump's face crying out as the prostitute penetrates him. The film cuts to a close-up shot of Johnnie lying on his stomach on the ground, with other bodies visible standing in a circle around him. The club music disappears and speaking voices are heard in the background, including Maria's, although it is unclear what they are saying apart from Johnnie's name. Johnnie begins to groan in pain, lying on the ground but stretching his upper back and head upwards. The film cuts between this close-up shot of him and the unclear, blue-tinted and over-exposed flashback shots. His groaning turns into cries of what appears to be real physical pain and his movements begin to mimic being anally raped, with his legs spread, his arms clutching the ground and the veins in his neck bulging as he churns his head upwards. With a last loud cry, he begins to silently shake and sob, and the film cuts back to the indistinct shape of a head as the muffled sound of a child's voice is heard. The camera cuts back to a close-up of Johnnie's face, gasping for air as he sobs.

In this scene, Johnnie mentally and physical recollects being abused as a child by Trump when separate individual memories come together to converge with Johnnie's lived present. He remembers the abuse through physical motions that re-enact his experience of being raped, presenting this recollection as an extremely painful and bodily experience, and recalling Homi K. Bhabha's description of remembering as 'never a quiet act of introspection or retrospection. It is a painful re-membering, a putting together of the dismembered past to make sense of the trauma of the present' (Bhabha 1986: xxxv). Similarly to the earlier discussion of the scene with Trump and the black prostitute, in this scene race once again operates as a facilitator of queerness. Johnnie's violent confrontation with the Hispanic store clerk and his encounter with the young black man in the club are framed as leading to and triggering Johnnie's sudden process of remembering.

Johnnie's relationship to Ireland as homeland was largely forged via Trump and the other Irish men. Yet with this sudden recollection, his past, his relationship with Trump and Ireland all become sites of trauma. McLoone criticises the film for reducing homosexuality to a metaphor for the disjunction of family and nation: 'Thus, another male oedipal crisis reverberates with the symbolism of the abusive and incomplete family/nation and a crisis of cultural identity is rendered as a crisis of sexual identity' (2000: 197). Other critics have argued that the film problematically associates homosexuality with sexual abuse, with Jenny Murphy arguing that the film's 'hopes of a prolonged subversion of homosocial sexual boundaries are dashed' when the film ultimately pathologises Johnnie's sexuality by linking it to paedophilia and childhood abuse (2003: 73). Yet although the film's association of non-normative sexual desire with sexual abuse is potentially problematic by framing Johnnie's sexuality as a result of his childhood abuse and reinforcing negative associations between homosexuality and paedophilia, there is also something unfathomable about the complex constellations of tensions surrounding gender, sexuality, race and ethnicity in this film that positions it as an inherently queer text. Within these constellations, queerness emerges in *2by4* as an 'open mesh of possibilities, gaps, overlaps, dissonances and resonances, lapses and excesses of meaning when the constituent elements of anyone's gender, of anyone's sexuality aren't made (or can't be made) to signify monolithically' (Sedgwick 1993: 7).

After his painful recollection of Trump's abuse, Johnnie confronts his uncle at The Lansdowne. The final shot of the film then shows Johnnie in his living room, ironing, as the song 'Danny Boy' plays in the background. As an Irish ballad with strong nationalist connotations that is particularly embraced by Irish diasporic communities, 'Danny Boy' insinuates a reclaiming of Ireland as 'home'; yet, this final shot emphasises Johnnie's true displacement, with those previously stable notions of family and home having instead become sites of trauma and abuse.

Borstal Boy

In *Borstal Boy*, the borstal where Brendan is imprisoned can be productively compared to *2by4*'s New York as a diasporic space where 'boundaries of inclusion and exclusion, of belonging and otherness, of "us" and "them"' are contested' (Brah 1996: 208–9), renegotiated and reconstituted in relation to the displaced Irish queer body. Early on in the film the borstal is set up as an insular space removed from dominant society. Brendan's arrival in the port of Liverpool at the beginning of the film and his return to Dublin port at the end of the film provide visual bookends to Brendan's borstal narrative. Both scenes take place at night and are lit unevenly through smoke (in Liverpool) and fog (in Dublin). The respective ports are each marked as industrial spaces and characterised by systems of regulation, with male military personnel visible in the opening scene and a customs officer in the closing scene.

In contrast, the sequence of shots introducing the borstal frame it as an idyllic rural space. The sequence begins with a panning long shot of the prison bus containing Brendan and other prisoners driving along a country dirt road during the day, with trees and mountains visible in the background as instrumental music plays. As the bus drives up the borstal's long drive, trees are visible on either side with lush green fields beyond them and there is a visible lack of guards and barriers. The borstal's warden Joyce (Michael York) greets the prisoners and advises them against any attempts to escape since the surrounding area contains minefields planted by the nearby army base. He then announces, 'I trust we will have no further use of chains, you are borstal boys now.' One of the guards leads the boys away and the next shot shows them standing in a line outside the reception building, dressed in identical uniforms that consist of a beige collared shirt, navy blue sweater, green khaki long shorts, long dark green socks and black boots. The boys' identical clothing and their characterisation within the communal identity of 'borstal boys' work to strip away their past affiliations. Here, a sense of commonality amongst the boys is created through their shared experience of displacement within unfamiliar surroundings.

The Irish community in *2by4* is formed through the continuous performance of a shared cultural heritage, which maintains a common identity that bonds the men together. Alternatively, in *Borstal Boy* the prisoners' community is formed through a process of what Ahmed (2000) terms 'uncommon estrangement': the forming of community through the lack of a common identity. Ahmed uses the example of *Flaming Spirit* (1994), an edited collection of works by migrant Asian women authors produced by the Asian Women's Writing Collective in the United Kingdom. She argues that the collection produces a community through the authors' shared experiences of not feeling fully at home, and yet the unstable politics of 'Asian' as an identity label along with differences amongst the contributors in terms of class, sexuality and religion make apparent 'the lack of common identity that would allow its form to take one form' (Ahmed 2000: 94). The identity of 'borstal boys' is similarly unstable, representing a culturally diverse group of bodies that are linked by their shared experiences of physical displacement. For Ahmed, the lack of clarity found in such identities 'makes a definition and redefinition of the community possible; it allows the group to emerge in the need to "redefine our identity as a group"' (2000: 94). Through this act of displaced bodies 'remak[ing] what it is they might have in common' (2000: 94), new social relations and forms of belonging can emerge that challenge normative models of 'home' and 'nation'.

At the borstal, Brendan finds himself in the company of boys from England, Scotland, Wales, Poland and Canada. Rather than sharing a common homeland and collective history, the borstal community '"makes a place" in the act of reaching out to the "out-of-place-ness" of other migrant bodies' (Ahmed 2000: 94). Ahmed's emphasis on movement in this type of community formation, 'reaching out' to 'make a place', offers a compelling framework for understanding how the physical interactions between the boys produce them as a community. The boys are kept occupied at the borstal through physical labour, including gardening and digging, and sports such as rugby and wrestling.

One day, as the boys are digging in the fields, Brendan begins to whistle. Jerzy (Viko Nikai), a Jewish boy from Poland, begins to whistle the same tune. When Charlie asks Jerzy how he knows an Irish song, Brendan replies that it is a German song his Communist grandmother taught him. Another boy comments that he wishes he had a grandmother like that, and the boys begin to laugh and playfully throw dirt clods at each other. Here, the physical interactions between the boys suggest the breaking down

Figure 8.2 The borstal boys' tangled intertwined bodies as they celebrate their rugby win in *Borstal Boy*. (*Source*: screen grab.)

of national antagonisms. In a later scene, the boys challenge the soldiers from a nearby military base to a game of rugby. After the boys win, they run around the field cheering, and then jump on each other in jubilation, forming a tangled mass of writhing, intermingled bodies (see Figure 8.2). Later that night they enter their dorms in high spirits, singing with their arms around each other. Both scenes suggest that bodily encounters between the boys work to produce new social bonds that allow them to 'remake what it is they might have in common' (Ahmed 2000: 94).

At the same time that Brendan is participating in the production of a borstal community, he develops a growing friendship with English soldier Charlie. Brendan first meets Charlie in prison in Liverpool as he awaits sentencing. The film initially sets up the men's relationship as antagonistic after Brendan wakes up from a nightmare to find Charlie stroking his face in an attempt to console him. Brendan accuses Charlie of trying to come on to him and his hostile feelings towards Charlie continue after they arrive at the borstal. Yet as the film progresses the two boys begin to develop a close friendship that later turns into a romantic relationship. The climactic moment of the film occurs when Brendan and Charlie kiss on-stage in front of the entire borstal community during a performance of Oscar Wilde's *The Importance of Being Earnest*.

In the play Brendan plays the leading role of Jack while Charlie dresses in drag to play Jack's love interest Gwendolen. As the play begins, the film cuts between medium long shots of the stage framed straight on from the position of the audience, and medium long shots of the audience from the position of the actors on-stage. These framing techniques emphasise the stage as a performance space and highlight the active presence of the watching boys, guards and warden, who laugh loudly and cheer throughout the play, particularly during the performances of those who are impersonating female characters. The humour these performances elicit derives largely from the excessiveness of the boys' costume; for instance, the borstal librarian and Charlie appear on-stage in big wigs, ill-fitting dresses and heavily applied make-up. While Butler argues that drag offers the potential for subversion, claiming that 'in imitating gender, drag implicitly reveals the imitative structure of gender itself – as well as its contingency' (2004: 137), the excessive parody of the men's gender masquerade in fact reinforces the actors' maleness to undermine that potential. As Stella Bruzzi (1997) argues, while androgyny softens the contours of fixed identities and elicits eroticism through ambiguity, overt cross-dressing can work to desexualise the subject by deflecting the subversiveness of their performance through humour and comedic effect.

The tones of hilarity and excessiveness within the performance suddenly shift in a scene in which the characters of Cecily and Gwendolen kiss their male suitors, Algernon and Jack. While the pair of boys playing the roles of Algernon and Cecily dramatically air kiss each other on the cheeks as the watching boys clap and cheer, Brendan and Charlie, as Gwendolen and Jack, softly kiss on the mouth for an extended amount of time. Their kiss is framed in a close-up shot followed by a series of close-up shots of various audience members, who all watch with shocked expressions. During the kiss the audience's cheers taper off and the atmosphere becomes almost silent. As Brendan and Charlie break away from their embrace, the librarian steps forward to deliver his next line: 'Gwendolen, what does this mean?' The librarian's question moves beyond the performance to connect the boys' on-stage actions to their lived reality. Charlie then replies with Gwendolen's line ('merely that I am engaged to be married'), shifting the play back towards performance. The film cuts to the play's ending and Brendan's final lines as the audience claps and cheers.

Brendan and Charlie's kiss momentarily destabilises the performance space of the stage. Working within a theatrical context, John M. Clum (1994) argues that drag and two men kissing on-stage function differently. While drag may connote homosexuality, it is not transgressive for a heterosexist audience since it 'merely underscores the connection between homosexuality and effeminacy' (1994: 29). On the other hand, a kiss shared between two men on-stage is often seen as a highly subversive act because it transgresses the established and 'naturalised' gender order: 'The kiss is an act that brings alien homosexual desire into the realm of the known and thus asserts a threatening parity between homosexual and heterosexual desire' (Clum 1994: 12). Consequently, a kiss between two men on-stage threatens the heterosexist audience with embodied homosexuality by not only making homosexual desire visible but by openly acting upon that desire. Therefore, while the drag costumes in the boys' performance are set up as 'safe' forms of gender transgression for public consumption by allowing the audience to maintain an imaginative distance from the performer and their gender, the kiss between Brendan and Charlie blurs reality and fantasy and 'brings alien homosexual desire into the realm of the known' (Clum 1994: 12) to momentarily destabilise the surrounding space.

As in *A Man of No Importance* (Krishnamma 1994), discussed in Chapter 4, in *Borstal Boy* Wilde becomes a vehicle for the expression of queerness. Brendan discovers Wilde's work shortly after arriving at the borstal, when the borstal librarian suggests Brendan might find parallels between himself and the playwright: 'Fellow Irishman, fellow jailbird, rebel. You know what he was down for, don't you? He was put in jail for buggering the son of Marquess of Queensberry!' While Brendan initially rejects Wilde, telling the librarian that Wilde 'was no Irish man if he was up to that caper', he later begins to read Wilde's work. When a borstal guard refers to Wilde as a 'bloody poofter', Brendan responds: 'Wasn't he a jailbird like meself?' By aligning himself with Wilde, Brendan begins to consider new configurations of Irishness outside of rigid nationalist identity politics. In reassessing his nationalist politics Brendan simultaneously develops a more liberal sexual attitude that enables him to explore his relationship with Charlie.

Brendan and Charlie's relationship is further complicated by Brendan's desire for Elizabeth (Eva Birthistle), warden Joyce's daughter who lives in the borstal. In contrast to his relationship with Charlie, which develops over the course of the film, Brendan's attraction to Elizabeth is made explicit after she first arrives at the borstal and remains an undercurrent throughout the film. Yet *Borstal Boy* frames Elizabeth, the heterosexual object of desire, as a disruptive figure. There are two scenes in the film that make visible the triangulated structure of desire between Brendan, Charlie and Elizabeth. In a scene early on in the film, Brendan and Charlie compete in a wrestling match in the borstal gym when Elizabeth peers around the door of the gym to watch them fight. Catching sight of her, Brendan is momentarily distracted and Charlie is able to overpower him. Here, her sudden appearance within the male homosocial space of the gym disarms Brendan and results in an unequal distribution of power between the two men.

She operates in a similarly disruptive manner in a scene near the end of the film, after the boys have returned to their dorms following the performance of *The Importance of Being Earnest*. Charlie arrives at the dorms to discover that another boy, Dale (Lee Ingleby), has opened Charlie's suitcase and found belongings that Charlie had stolen from the other boys. Charlie and Dale begin to fight, and Dale instructs the other boys to hold Charlie down and bend him over in an apparent rape attempt. Elizabeth suddenly arrives, acting on Brendan's earlier invitation to visit the dorms, and Dale begins to force her down on one of the beds in a second rape attempt. When Brendan walks in, he immediately defends Elizabeth by knocking Dale unconscious and then leaves the dorms with Elizabeth, despite Charlie's cries for Brendan not to leave him. Even as the borstal enables Brendan's sexual self-discovery, it is simultaneously revealed as a space structured by heterosexist norms. This scene undermines the utopian qualities of the borstal and reveals the limits of the borstal community.

Shortly following Brendan's public disavowal of Charlie, Charlie is released from the borstal and returns to active duty in the British Royal Navy. After Charlie leaves, the film begins to develop a romantic subplot between Brendan and Elizabeth. Brendan begins spending time with her in her art studio and they later kiss. Yet filmmaker Peter Sheridan stresses Brendan and Charlie's relationship as the film's primary romance, since,

> we [the audience] would much prefer him to be with the guy than the girl. I guarantee you that a heterosexual audience would want Brendan to be with Charlie. That's the real relationship of the story. That's the relationship where necks are on the block. (Sheridan quoted in Barter 2001: 20)

This emphasis on Brendan and Charlie's relationship as the film's central narrative tenet becomes evident when Brendan discovers that the ship Charlie was stationed on was bombed and Charlie is dead. After hearing the news, Brendan runs through the borstal grounds as dramatic non-diegetic instrumental music plays. The film cuts quickly between close-up shots of Brendan's face as he runs and various shots of Charlie that are set up as flashback memories: Charlie washing his face at the mirror, Charlie sleeping clutching the rugby ball, Charlie laughing outside. Many of these flashbacks are framed from a voyeuristic point of view that implies Brendan was watching Charlie in these moments without Charlie's knowledge. Thus, despite Brendan's more public pursuit of Elizabeth and his decision to choose her over Charlie in the dorms following Dale's attack, these flashbacks and Brendan's emotional reaction to the news of Charlie's death suggest that Charlie, rather than Elizabeth, is his true object of desire. At the same time, by having Charlie die and Brendan consequently 'discover' the straight path through Elizabeth, *Borstal Boy* can be aligned with *The Last Bus Home*, *Cowboys & Angels* and *The Disappearance of Finbar*, since all four films celebrate heterosexuality at the demise or exclusion of the non-heterosexual character.

However, Brendan retains a sense of queerness that distinguishes *Borstal Boy* from the other three films. Prior to leaving the borstal, Brendan tells Elizabeth that 'I've had it both ways – just like Oscar Wilde'. This admission demonstrates the evolution of his sexual ideologies and yet also firmly situates this experience in the past through the use of past tense. In the film's final scene Brendan is shown approaching the customs officer in Dublin port. The Irish customs officer (Ronnie Drew) glances at Brendan's expulsion order and comments that it 'must be wonderful to be free', to which Brendan replies 'it must'. An expression of confusion passes over the officer's face as Brendan retrieves his order and walks out of the station. In this final shot, Brendan walks away from the camera, disappearing into the fog, and the unknown, as dramatic instrumental music swells in the background. Brendan's final comment underlines the reality of his circumstances, whereby his experience of political and sexual liberation at the borstal will not extend into his life in Ireland, where he has no such freedom of choice.

Conclusion

2by4 and *Borstal Boy* suggest the potential of diasporic space to reconfigure national and sexual identities, and to produce new forms of belonging and community. As Johnnie and Brendan settle down within their respective diasporic contexts, their encounters within these spaces work to redefine their relationships to Ireland as (home)land. Both films challenge the opposition of home and away by revealing the potential of diasporic space to 'make strange' the idea of home. This process of 'making strange' causes the men to question what they had previously perceived as a stable and fixed site of belonging and enables new articulations of queerness that challenge heteronormative assumptions of home as both a familial and national space. In doing so, these films further reveal how diaspora itself operates through social and spatial structures of belonging and alienation, and familiarity and strangeness that work to produce and regulate forms of difference.

Both films also imply an incompatibility between Irishness and queerness. Johnnie's queer sexuality is linked to his sexual abuse at the hands of Trump and by rejecting Trump at the end of the film, Johnnie subsequently disavows his past and cuts his ties to Ireland. The community in *Borstal Boy* is set up as a temporary formation that is dependent on the borstal's physical and cultural insularity from dominant society. The film suggests that the bonds tying the boys together will dissolve once they leave the borstal and return to their respective nation-states. Specifically, Brendan's final comment to the customs officer at the end of the film highlights how his return to Ireland will entail his re-assimilation back into repressive nationalist identity politics.

Thus the two films emphasise diasporic space as a space of crisis, characterised by competing and conflicting modes of identification that simultaneously enable and restrict the articulation and formation of queer sexual subjectivities. Within these Irish queer diasporic narratives, the concept of home becomes reconstituted as the men move through unfamiliar surroundings. Recalling Ahmed's characterisation of migration in terms of a spatial and a temporal dislocation, the ending of both films imply the characters' conflicting relationships to home, with Ireland in *2by4* and the borstal in *Borstal Boy* representing '"the past" [that] becomes associated with a home that it is impossible to inhabit, and be inhabited by, the present' (Ahmed 2000: 343).

CHAPTER 9

The Irish Queer Short Film

This chapter concludes this study of Irish queer cinema by focusing on the queer potential of the Irish short film. The short film has played a crucial role in the development of an indigenous film culture in Ireland. While the IFB's closure in 1987 led to a marked decline in the production of feature films, there was a sharp increase in the number of short film productions from 1987 to 1993. In contrast to the two Irish shorts produced in 1986, there were 13 productions in 1987 and 30 productions in 1993 (Monahan 2009: 87). Shorts were viewed as a film practice that allowed filmmakers to retain a public profile and develop their filmmaking skills despite a lack of State funding. They further became a means for the Irish film community as a whole to maintain its cultural visibility and train new filmmakers. During this period two colleges, Dun Laoghaire School of Art and Design and the College of Commerce, Rathmines (now part of the Dublin Institute of Technology) offered filmmaking courses. As a result, many filmmakers associated with this early wave of short filmmaking emerged from art college or film school backgrounds and approached film as an artistic endeavour rather than a commercial practice.

Short film production in Ireland has also been critical to the development of an Irish queer cinema. Both Lance Pettitt (1997) and Martin McLoone (2000) have argued for the short film as an arena where LGBTQ struggles have been documented. Less costly to produce with a quicker production cycle than the feature-length film, the short film is a medium available to filmmakers with precarious resources. The temporal limitations of the medium also provide new narrative and aesthetic possibilities. For instance, Ruth Barton considers how short films are 'more fluid in the construction and less dependent on the three-act structure still widely favoured by Hollywood and non-Hollywood practitioners alike' (2007: 154). Building on Barton's argument, Barry Monahan (2009) claims that shorts are not only less dependent on the traditional narrative structure but inherent in the form is an awareness of its spatial and temporal limitations.

Subsequently, the short film must place a particular emphasis on the visual or what Monahan terms 'visual density': 'a stylistic and visceral condensation that occurs within the more restricted form' (2009: 95).

To a certain extent, short films are able to combat some of the criticisms associated with films explored in the preceding chapters. While queer representations in Irish cinema are frequently described as stereotypes or allegorical, Conn Holohan (2010b) underscores the potential of the short film to challenge reductive gender stereotypes. He argues that the temporal limitations of the short film does not allow for the same level of character development and complexity as found in the feature-length film. While this limitation may suggest more of a reliance on stereotypes, he instead argues that the transgressive potential of the short can be found in its construction 'around a singular moment of character revelation' (2010b: 289). Through such moments of brief narrative disruption the short film is able to offer more complex, and subversive, cinematic subjectivities. Indeed, for Holohan 'it is the very brevity of the moment that the true power of the short is contained' (2010b: 289).

Further, while Irish cinema as a whole has been shaped by commercial demands, McLoone (2000) considers how the development of short film production in Ireland as a training strategy and the availability of public funding for short film projects offer the potential for filmmakers to experiment more with the medium's formal and aesthetic possibilities. Although he notes that many Irish shorts remain delimited by similar mainstream conventions affecting Irish cinema in general, McLoone believes low-budget films that are furthest removed from the high-end commercial budgets are more able to resist these pressures and retain strong radical potential. Pettitt similarly associates radical potential with low-budget filmmaking, and argues that low-budget and student short films have been a key arena where the struggles of LGBTQ people have been documented. Writing in 1997, Pettitt claims that films such as *Chaero* (Hayes 1988), *Bent out of Shape* (Walsh 1995) and *Summertime* (Morrison 1995) reveal that despite changes in legislation in Ireland, young LGBTQ people 'still have to face various kinds of social and institutionalised forms of homophobia in schools, within the churches, and in everyday domestic family situations' (Pettitt 1997: 274).

Building on Pettitt's work, this chapter argues that the Irish short film has emerged as a rich and dynamic site where representations of queerness can remain an 'open mesh of possibilities, gaps, overlaps, dissonances and resonances' (Sedgwick 1993: 7). Subsequently, queer short film production in Ireland can be understood as constituting a counterpublic space. José Esteban Muñoz defines counterpublics as 'communities and relational chains of resistance that contest the dominant public sphere' by producing and validating minoritarian public spheres (1999: 146). Drawing on this definition, this chapter considers how the space of Irish short film production operates as a space of resistance against hegemonic representations of sexuality and provides a platform for more diverse articulations of queer identity. The following sections focus on specific case studies linked together in terms of distinct spatial themes: the contested nature of public space, the destabilisation of domestic spaces and the spatiality of lesbian desire.

The Contestation of Public Space

In showcasing the everyday struggles of young people against institutionalised forms of homophobia, Irish queer shorts have emphasised the contested nature of public space. Referring to Sally Munt's (1995: 124) 'politics of dislocation', Nancy Duncan (1996: 138) suggests that 'public space can be used as a site for the destabilisation of unarticulated norms'. In territorialising queerness within public space, Irish queer shorts publicise issues of sexuality and homophobia to legitimate them as public discourse. This section focuses specifically on how such 'politics of dislocation' are incorporated within two early shorts, *Chaero* (Hayes 1988) and *Bent out of Shape* (Walsh 1995), and two more recent ones, *Chicken* (Dignam 2001) and *Elephant Shoe* (Early 2009).

Both *Chaero* and *Bent out of Shape* have been acknowledged by McLoone (2000) and Pettitt (1997) as especially ground-breaking early queer films that realise the radical and confrontational potential of the short film medium. Pettitt describes *Chaero* as 'a simple, realistic and largely conventional film, but its narrative contains deeply subversive elements within an Irish context' and characterises *Bent out of Shape* as an example of 'a more mainstream screen social realism' (1997: 263, 279). For Pettitt, even as these films use more conventional narrative structures in ways that could be perceived as making them less radically queer, they retain radical political potential through their content. Specifically, both films showcase queer identities on-screen during a time period when such cultural representations of queerness were largely absent.

Chaero is the first Irish film made by an openly gay filmmaker, Matt Hayes. It follows two boys, Richie (Kevin Murphy) and Chaero (Vincent Burke), as they go to an abandoned building site and begin to wrestle. They kiss and another boy, Doyle (Declan Walsh), witnesses them and threatens to tell 'the lads'. Doyle's ability to use his act of seeing the boys kiss as a form of blackmail reveals the marginalised status of sexual minorities within Ireland. Further, like in *The Last Bus Home* (Gogan

1997) public space in *Chaero* enables the articulation of queer desire (encouraging Richie and Chaero's kiss) and simultaneously produces this act as a form of social deviance through a witness (Doyle) who operates as a heteronormative regulatory apparatus. Later, Richie and Chaero get Doyle drunk and once he is passed out they take a photo of Chaero kissing him. After Doyle recovers, Chaero shows him the photo and tells him that 'We're not the only fags here', ending the film with an act of extortion that ensures Doyle's silence.

Richie and Chaero are able to subvert Doyle's act of blackmail by threatening to 'out' him. Yet in doing so they continue to frame homosexuality as an act of social deviance that must remain closeted for survival and maintain a private/public distinction surrounding the regulation of non-normative sexuality. The film thus refuses an easy happy ending by framing the boys' small victory in relation to a wider unresolved issue regarding homophobic discrimination in Ireland.

Similar tensions around the heteronormativity of public space are found in *Bent out of Shape*. The film is about a friendship between Danny (Des O'Byrne), a man in his twenties who works in a video store in suburban Dublin, and Stephen (Stuart Dannell), a young boy who is being bullied. The video store also rents under-the-counter adult videos, and through Danny's willingness to help Stephen the film sets him up as a more ethical figure in comparison to the sleazy group of men that frequent the store for pornography. Through Danny's guidance, Stephen becomes more comfortable with being different and this comfort becomes reflected in his changing style, as he begins to incorporate leather pants, a silver jacket and gelled hair. When a patron complains to Danny's boss that Danny is 'messing about with a youngster', his boss confronts him, to which Danny replies that he is gay but that doesn't make him a child molester. One evening a group of men decide that these accusations are enough proof to attack Danny, and their attack leaves Danny hospitalised. When Stephen overhears his bullies saying that Danny got what he deserved, he subsequently attacks them and the film ends with Stephen and the girl from the shop next door going to visit Danny at the hospital.

Danny's public attack reveals his vulnerability within public space. Recalling the boys' taunting Jimmy and the man after they leave the gay bar in *Pigs* (Black 1984), this attack scene in *Bent out of Shape* reveals how heteronormative structures are maintained through the social policing and regulation of sexuality within public space. The film also reveals the persistence of heteronormative ideologies that define what constitutes 'normal' sexualities and socialities. Among the men who attack Danny are customers of the video store who rent pornography. Whereas Danny's friendship with Stephen is called into question because of his sexuality, with his perceived sexual deviance framed as a moral threat, the men's ability to cite moral regulation as justification for the attack reveals uneven social standards surrounding other forms of sexual expression, specifically pornography. Further, like in *Chaero*, *Bent out of Shape* ends with a reversal in power relations, as the queer subject adopts the strategies of their oppressor (blackmail in *Chaero* and physical violence in *Bent out of Shape*). Thus, both films imply that strategies of survival for the queer subject rely on utilising existing systems of repression embedded within public space rather than attempting to contest or change them.

Two more recent short films, *Chicken* and *Elephant Shoe*, can be aligned with these earlier films in terms of documenting everyday systems of sexual repression whilst representing new forms of male intimacy. Yet both films represent highly charged moments in time rather than the more traditional, linear narratives of their earlier counterparts. Beginning with *Chicken*, the film opens with two boys hanging out by the railroad tracks, drinking ciders and throwing rocks at empty cans. Mick (Darren Healy) shows Kev (Niall O'Shea) how to pierce a hole in the cider can to shotgun drink it, and when Kev tries he is unprepared for the sudden burst and spills cider over himself. Mick gives Kev his jacket, telling him to put it on before he freezes, and goes and sits by the tracks. He tells Kev, 'Do you want to show you're not a wuss?' and then says that he needs to take a little test to prove it, 'unless of course you're chicken?' Taking Kev's hand, Mick places Kev's palm on the ground and spreads out his fingers. He then puts his hand over top of Kev's, telling him that way if he slips he gets it first. He then begins stabbing the knife into the ground in between each of their fingers. As Mick speeds up his movements, the camera cuts between slow zoom-in shots of each of the two boys. The sound of the knife hitting the ground and an approaching train further add to the increasing tension of the moment. As the train speeds past the boys, they look down to see the knife has slightly cut one of their fingers. Their fingers then intertwine and they begin to embrace. The film then cuts to a longer shot of the train moving off into the distance.

Madden describes the film as one that 'seems to place male intimacy at the limits of intelligibility' (Madden 2011: 78), subverting traditional characteristics of hegemonic masculinity and transforming violence and aggression into intimacy. Through 'a singular moment of character revelation' (Holohan 2010b: 289), the tone shifts and the boys' act transforms from one of violent possibility to one of queer possibility. *Chicken* therefore disrupts narrative coherence to suggest the complexity of male representation. It is significant that this moment of disruption occurs within public space, beside railroad tracks as a train (likely containing watching passengers) passes by. The boys' spatial isolation in the countryside by the railroad tracks symbolises their social marginalisation. As the train moves past the boys, it is probable that passengers are able to witness their public embrace. As discussed in Chapter 6 in relation to *The Last Bus Home*, the countryside operates as a space for the public expression of queerness even as this expression of queerness itself reveals the inherently contested nature of public space.

Elephant Shoe is similarly constructed around a singular moment that reveals public space as a conflicted site. The film opens with a man (Barry Keegan) sitting in a café, writing in a notebook and drinking a coffee. Another man (Frank McGovern) joins him, dressed more formally in a suit and tie. The men smile at one another but do not speak, and only the background sounds of the busy café are heard. Food arrives at the table and the second man begins to eat quickly. The first man tries to feed him using his own fork, but the second man silently refuses, shaking his head. He looks down at his phone as he eats and this, along with his attire, implies that he is on a quick break from work. He then stands up and puts on his jacket, preparing to leave. The first man pulls out a folded piece of paper to give him but the second man has already walked away from the table. The first man stares in dismay at the off-screen movements of the man out of the café. There is a cut to a close-up of the first man's face as he looks down at the table with an expression of disappointment. At the off-screen sound of someone knocking on the café window he looks up, and the film cuts to a shot of the second man standing at the window (see Figure 9.1). The men smile at one another as the second man mouths something. He then walks off as Mississippi John Hurt's 'It Ain't Nobody's Business' begins to play and the film cuts to credits.

Figure 9.1 Man shows moment of intimacy to his partner through the safety of the café window in *Elephant Shoe*. (*Source*: screen grab.)

Elephant Shoe reveals the closeted lives that queer men continue to live in contemporary Ireland. The café window as a physical demarcation between the two men reveals the mediation of sexual identity through public/private divides. In doing so, it challenges the representation of the liberated and openly outed queer man found in feature-length queer films such as *Goldfish Memory* (Gill 2002) and *Cowboys & Angels* (Gleeson 2003). Both *Chicken* and *Elephant Shoe* subvert traditional meanings to introduce queer possibility. Just as the knife, a representation of violence and phallic power, becomes the catalyst for male intimacy in *Chicken*, the window, signifying physical separation, becomes the catalyst for the men's connection in *Elephant Shoe*.

Disrupting Domestic Spaces

As with Irish queer cinema more generally, the family is a recurring trope with a number of Irish queer shorts, including *Dream Kitchen* (Dignam 1999) and *Fantabulous* (Goldyn 2009). Both films set up normative images of domestic spaces that are then destabilised through brief fantastical sequences. For Holohan (2011), this type of strategy aligns the short film with the literary short story. He cites Charles May's (2002: 52) argument regarding how the short story develops characters not through detailed description or scenes of social interaction but instead through a 'focus on the revelatory break-up of the rhythm of everyday reality' (Holohan 2011: 289). This disruption is achieved by first establishing an everyday world characterised by recognisable spaces and then providing a moment of insight that cannot be contained within that recognisable world.

Dream Kitchen opens with the protagonist (Andrew Lovern) walking home from school. He passes his father, Da (Frank Coughlan), who is covered in grease as he works on the car in the driveway, and then enters into his darkly lit home to see his heavily pregnant sister (Sarah Pilkington) sitting in front of the television smoking a cigarette. He walks into the kitchen to find his mother, Ma (Caroline Rothwell), on the phone complaining about her husband and drinking vodka. The film cuts to a close-up shot of the son's face looking directly at the camera and there is a fade to another close-up shot of his face as the camera pulls back to reveal him standing in the same kitchen; however, this space is cleaner and much more brightly lit and classical music plays in the background. As the camera pulls back it reveals Ma still standing in the room, although she is now holding a martini glass in place of a glass of vodka and coke and wearing a high collared blue suit in place of a vinyl pink jacket. The son reveals to Ma that he is gay, at which point she tells him that 'this is truly wonderful news' and embraces him. Along with the visual changes in the space, the characters' speech has also changed and they use more formal, theatrical English. For McLoone (2000), the highly stylised Shakespearean dialogue contributes to the film's absurdist effect whilst highlighting the fantasy's contrast to the son's real world experiences of alienation and isolation.

Ma calls Da into the room to share the news, and the boy's father walks into the room. The son announces 'Father – I'm gay!' to which his father replies that he is 'not deserving of such good fortune'. His sister then comes into the room, again transformed from her previously dishevelled state, and is told of the news by the rest of her smiling family. As the son embraces his sister, the doorbell rings and he moves off-screen to answer it. The film then cuts to the son reappearing in the kitchen to present his boyfriend, Andrew (Loclann Aiken). The shot of Andrew is backlit and the music hits a crescendo, serving to emphasise the character's model looks. The family welcomes Andrew as the film fades to show the son still sitting at the kitchen table, returned to his dreary surroundings. The son stands and appears about to come out to Ma as he reminds her of the programme they were watching the evening before after the news, to which she replies, 'the one about those odd fellows?' Da comes into the kitchen and, upon hearing them, comments: 'Bloody perverts'. The doorbell rings and the son goes to the door to find Andrew, the same boyfriend from the fantasy, standing on the doorstep. Looking directly at the camera and smiling, the son closes the door as the film cuts to show him and Andrew getting into a red car and driving away.

In juxtaposing reality and fantasy, the film presents the domestic sphere as both a restrictive apparatus and a catalyst for change. Interestingly, the film implies the significance of class to social liberalism, with the family's more formal and upper-class speech in the fantasy linked to the ease with which they embrace the son's homosexuality. The son's fantasy is therefore not only about a new context where his family is accepting of his sexuality but also one where they are living as a more affluent upper class.

Fantabulous was made in Joasia Goldyn's third year at the National Film School IADT Ireland. Shot on 16-mm film and edited with Final Cut Pro, it epitomises the type of low-budget, independent filmmaking that McLoone has stressed as necessary for Irish short films to be truly radical. The film opens with a teenaged boy (Arron Rogers) lying in bed as his mother (Mel Ryan) brings him food on a tray. She leaves and the film cuts to a close-up shot of make-up being placed in a careful row, and then shows the boy sitting in front of the camera and removing his sweater. He puts on a headband to hold his hair back and looks directly into the camera, which acts as a mirror. There is a series of close-up shots of him applying make-up: shaking off his foundation brush, applying lip gloss, painting nails, putting on purple eye shadow. He puts on sparkly tights and then retrieves a feathered collar from a hat box. As the camera circles him, it cuts to a shot of him on a stage. He dances, lit by a spotlight as 'Gimme Some More' by Irish electronic-rock band Jape plays in the background and as an invisible crowd cheers and claps. He finishes dancing and acknowledges the crowd, mouthing 'Thank you' as he waves. There is a cut to a close-up of his shoes as he walks along a plush pink carpet. He stands in front of a dressing-room mirror, adorned with boas, and poses, before sitting and smiling at his reflection.

In a close-up profile shot, he begins to converse with an invisible presence as he continues looking into the mirror. He turns his head to look off-screen and there is a cut to him back in his bedroom, looking off-screen. The colours are more muted and his face registers fear before he looks back into the mirror. His aura of confidence is replaced by an expression of fear and shame. His mother moves into the shot while he continues staring at his reflection. The film cuts to a close-up shot of his face, still covered with make-up, as he sits huddled in the shower with his arms around his legs. In a longer shot, we see his mother forcibly taking off his false eyelashes and scrubbing his face. She hands him the pink cloth and leaves. He looks off-screen and, presumably seeing her leave the bathroom, stands in the shower and begins to dance, with the same music from his fantasy flooding back in (see Figure 9.2). The film then cuts to credits.

As with *Dream Kitchen*, family and home become sites of conflict in *Fantabulous*. The private space of the boy's bedroom enables him to

Figure 9.2 Forced back into the 'closet', boy (Arron Rogers) performs a defiant dance in *Fantabulous*. (*Source*: screen grab.)

freely experiment with gender performance. Yet the mother's sudden reappearance within that space makes it evident that even this seemingly private site continues to be policed by heteronormative structures. Both *Dream Kitchen* and *Fantabulous* also use fantasy to emphasise the crossing of public and private divides. Recalling Chapter 5's argument surrounding compartmentalisation, both films represent their respective domestic spaces as compartmentalised spaces. Their containment within these spaces reflects their subsequent feelings of being closeted. Indeed, the end of *Fantabulous*, where the boy is forced into the shower by his mother, implies the shower itself is a closet, whereby his mother is forcing him back inside. Yet both films end with their protagonist in a state of movement: in *Dream Kitchen* the son escapes his domestic confines as the red car drives away into the distance and in *Fantabulous* the film ends with the boy dancing in the shower. Through the contrast between compartmentalised space and character mobility, both films at once acknowledge the family as a continued structure of repression even as they evoke defiance against such repression. It remains unclear in *Dream Kitchen* where the son has gone and if he will return. Similarly, in *Fantabulous* even as the teenager's dance at the end of the film suggests a powerful resistance it remains ambiguous how and whether such resistance will figure in his life after the fade to black.

The Spatiality of Lesbian Desire

The Irish queer short film has also been a space where more diverse representations of Irish lesbianism have been showcased. As with Irish queer cinema more generally, representations of queer men outnumber those of queer women; at the same time, there are a number of important shorts showcasing non-normative female sexuality. In particular, the Irish language short film *Olive* (Neasa Hardiman 2003), Colette Cullen's films *The Last Time* (1993) and *The Magician* (1995), and the more recent *Me First* (Byrne 2014) are significant contributions to representations of queer women within Irish cinema.

As previously discussed in Chapter 5, queer women in Irish films are frequently denied agency and subjectivity. The shorts explored here challenge the representational containment queer women have been subject to as symbols of national morality, narrative devices or objects for male viewing pleasure. The formal properties of the short film allow for the creation of an aesthetic of intimacy that in turn enables new forms of female agency and subjectivity to emerge.

Beginning with *Olive*, the short is a coming of age story about teenaged

Deirdre (Isabel Claffey) who does not have any friends at school, listens to 1970s punk rock and is battling a secret crush for Olive (Lisa Lambe), the rebellious girl in her class. The film opens with what Deirdre's voice-over narration describes as her first kiss with Brian O'Rahilly. As they pull away from their lip lock, Deirdre appears largely underwhelmed, telling him thanks as they both wipe their mouths. She then walks out of the space and turns directly to the camera to describe the kiss as 'like having a wet slug in your mouth'. Deirdre's good grades, alternative music tastes and disinterest in pursuing boys set her apart from her peers; like in *The Disappearance of Finbar* (Clayton 1996) and *Breakfast on Pluto* (Jordan 2005), Deirdre is framed as a queer child who feels out of sync with her peers and 'may prefer growing sideways' in relation to them (Stockton 2009: 52).

Olive also stands out from her peers. In an early scene, she arrives to class late and while the other students are dressed in their white and navy school uniforms Olive wears a red leather jacket over hers. The film cuts to show various teachers describing Olive as 'a brat', 'a special child' and 'just nuts'. When Deirdre and Olive bond over punk rock music and begin to develop a friendship, it appears these two out-of-place bodies will align together. They begin to hang out regularly, with Deirdre's voice-over stating that she is no longer on her own. When they go to a club one night Deirdre has the courage to kiss Olive in public. In a series of close-up shots, the girls move closer together. Olive touches Deirdre's lip and they begin the kiss. The camera then cuts into a longer shot that circles around the girls as they openly kiss. Olive leads Deirdre to the back of the club and they continue to kiss, with a series of close-up shots emphasising their lips, their hands. There is then a cut to someone dropping coins into an overturned hat and Deirdre and Olive turn to see others in the club laughing and clapping. Olive begins to laugh too, while Deirdre looks disappointed that the moment has ended.

In its shift between close-up to longer shots, the film at once isolates Deirdre and Olive's embrace within the space of the club and then emphasises it as a public act subject to the looks of the other patrons. The next scene shows Deirdre running into Olive, who is holding hands with a boy. Looking deflated, Deirdre greets Olive, who replies 'Oh hi there' in English and then turns away from her friend. Olive's English reply to Deirdre's Irish greeting further emphasises her attempt to distance herself from Deirdre, since the girls' relationship has been developed via the Irish language. For Gerry McCarthy (2004b), this final scene reveals that 'sexual and linguistic betrayal go together', and through this dual betrayal it becomes evident that these two queer bodies are no longer aligned with one another. Yet the film ends on an upbeat note, with Deirdre turning to the camera and declaring that Olive's betrayal does not matter and that she is better off.

Cullen's shorts provide glimpses into the intimate experiences and spaces of queer women in Ireland. A graduate of the London College of Printing Film School who now works in both film and theatre, Cullen has a large body of work that, according to Pettitt (1997), aims to address the almost complete lack of images of Irish lesbians on-screen. Beginning with *The Last Time*, the short is described by Cullen as 'a light hearted look at lesbian culture and explores lesbian sexual and erotic images' (Cullen quoted in Pettitt 1997: 277). The story follows Mary's (Rachel Grimstead) various sexual crushes and fantasies. Beginning with her crush on a carpenter named Ann, who works at a country western bar, Mary recalls her various sexual fantasies about other women. These fantasies are loosely linked by the use of chapter titles and her voice-over narration. Beginning with 'The Meeting' and ending with 'The Last Time', the use of chapter titles would imply creating a coherent structure. Yet the film remains a somewhat incoherent text, firmly located within Mary's subjectivity and combining reality and fantasy. The short ends with Mary's contrite promise to herself that she will not fall for another woman and that Ann is 'the last time'.

In *The Last Time* the lesbian body is presented as an active body, with the narrator's sexual desires propelling her body through space and shifting the direction of the narrative. In emphasising the need to think about the production of a sexed lesbian space in terms of bodies desiring other bodies, Elspeth Probyn suggests repositioning the lesbian body 'in a more positive structure of possibilities and try[ing] to unleash her desire for another woman's body as productive, as that which may produce alternative conceptions of space' (1995: 78–9). Through Mary's sexual fantasies, possibilities for new alternative narratives are created. The desiring lesbian body thus produces new ways of being. The film also depicts rarely represented lesbian spaces, specifically a lesbian nightclub and a lesbian country western bar.

While a key criticism of films produced during the Celtic Tiger is that they are largely apolitical texts, the opening of *The Last Time* immediately situates the short within Ireland's broader socio-political climate. The first scene in the film shows Mary getting up from her couch to answer the doorbell and the camera then pans through the space. On the wall are various news clippings and an Act Up Fight AIDS poster. Here, the home is depicted as a political space and the queer woman herself rendered a political body, bringing her out of the private realm into the public sphere.

Cullen's later film, *The Magician* (1995), is about Helen (Valerie Abbey) who is a magician. One evening, after her show, two of her friends come to her dressing room and bring Jackie (Rachel Grimstead). After Helen tricks Jackie into agreeing to a dinner date, the two begin a relationship. Within the film there is also an undercurrent of an AIDS narrative, as Helen and her friends grieve over their friend Nick's recent death. When Helen discovers Jackie is in remission from leukaemia she begins to distance herself, unwilling to deal with a similar situation of having someone close to her ill. One evening Jackie appears to be getting ill but brushes off Helen's questions by responding that she is simply tired. That night Helen spoons her in the bed. The film then cuts to the next morning, showing Helen leaving the house and boarding a train. It is unclear where she is going and whether she is leaving Jackie due to fears she is having a relapse. The final shot of the film shows the train moving off-screen through the Irish countryside.

Whereas Irish lesbians have historically been rendered invisible within public discourses, here a queer woman controls what is made visible. The film opens with Helen performing a magic show and a later scene in the film shows her performing various tricks, ostensibly to the camera. Through this play with reality and illusion, Helen is placed in a privileged position of knowledge in relation to the on-screen and off-screen audience. The crossing of boundaries, between reality and illusion, visibility and invisibility, further add to the complexity of the text. Using the documentary short *Undressing My Mother* (Wardrop 2004), Holohan (2011: 89) examines how the formal properties of the short enable 'an aesthetic of intimate engagement' that is constructed through the crossing of boundaries between intimate and public space, closeness and distance, and visibility and ambiguity. As Helen performs her magic tricks, the viewer is invited to share the performance space she creates, and yet she remains distanced, from both Jackie and the viewer, through the magnitude of the grief she continues to feel for her friend Nick. The juxtaposition of the final two scenes, between proximity (as Helen spoons Jackie in bed) and distance (as the train moves off-screen and out of sight) create conflicting tensions that produce more complex characterisation.

Finally, *Me First* (Byrne 2014) was directed by a Masters film student, Leanne Byrne. It explores the struggles of Sarah (Naimh Walsh), a middle-aged woman, as she comes out and starts a relationship with her daughter, Sinead's, friend Alex (Siobhán Bolton). The film opens with Sarah ironing and cooking dinner as her hostile husband Tom (Ray Reilly) watches television. Sinead (Seána Woods) invites a Canadian friend, Alex, from university over to work on a school project. Alex represents a younger generation than Sarah, one who believes marriage is an archaic institution imprisoning women. After a fight with Tom that turns physical, Sarah calls Alex and meets her downtown. Sarah reveals to Alex that she no longer loves her husband and Alex tells Sarah that she moved to Ireland in order to get over a bad break-up. That night they kiss and when they go to a play together a following night, they return back to Sarah's home. The next morning Sinead walks into her mother's bedroom to find Sarah and Alex in bed together.

By having Sinead discover the two women in bed together rather than framing this discovery through the male gaze of the husband the film retains a female-centric narrative. Although this discovery is somewhat implausible, with Sarah both bringing Alex home with her and then leaving the bedroom door open, it establishes that the story is more about Sarah's experience of sexual rediscovery and her relationship with her daughter than her relationship with Tom. The film ends with Sarah and Sinead's reconciliation. The family has without a doubt become unravelled, and yet the film avoids characterising Sarah's relationship with Alex as a form of sexual deviance that has disrupted the normative family. While this short has a more conventional narrative and arguably more reductive characterisation than the other shorts discussed here, it challenges the positioning of queer female sexuality as disruptive to familial structures. Heteronormative familial relations and queer desires intertwine, and the film ends with neither of these being fully disavowed.

Conclusion

The space of the short film enables new forms of intimate storytelling and queer subjectivities that further counter dominant representational trends with regards to non-normative identities in Irish cinema. Irish queer cinema, including feature-length and short filmmaking, is only one dimension of the emergence of a unique queer culture in Ireland. Other developments in Ireland and elsewhere have begun to offer more varied and complex understandings of Irish sexual identities and their place within contemporary Irish shorts. Film competitions such as the Dublin Pride Film Shorts Competition, the growing public presence of festivals such as GAZE (Dublin's Lesbian and Gay Film Festival) and the Craic Gay and Lesbian Irish Film Festival in New York, the development of archival and digital spaces through, for instance, the Cork LGBT Archive Project, and the housing of the Irish Queer Archive in the National University of Library, are further contributing to the development of a queer cultural space in Ireland.

CHAPTER 10

Concluding Remarks

The 2015 same-sex marriage referendum was a ground-breaking moment for queer politics and identities in Ireland. In 2017 famed Irish drag queen Panti Bliss spoke about the impact of the referendum, which 'has had a liberating effect and it had a transformative effect on the country' (Knox 2017). For Panti, the popular vote in favour of same-sex marriage resulted in a new national imagining predicated on the political and social inclusion of sexual minorities: 'we – Irish queers – are in a unique position where we know quantifiably how the rest of the country feels about us because we had a huge debate and voted on it' (Knox 2017). In looking at how Ireland has evolved from a past of sexual repression and homophobic persecution, 'it's wild how queer Ireland has become' (Knox 2017).

Panti's comments underscore the queer–national relationship that is a key focus of this book. Queer theory undermines the idea of a national community as a natural and unified formation by exposing the gaps and forms of unbelonging that are necessary for sustaining the nation's claims of hegemony and by revealing those who are excluded and marginalised within the national narrative. At the same time that queerness has the disruptive potential to dismantle the national, it opens up new possibilities for national re-imaginings. This book has not only explored how queerness reveals the inconsistencies of the nation and the national subject, but how it in turn enables new socialities and spatialities to form. It therefore suggests that the relationship between 'queer' and 'national' is not one that is wholly incompatible but rather one where the terms inform one another in multiple and complex ways.

In the wake of Ireland's marriage referendum, this book is a timely intervention into debates surrounding the role of sexuality within the constitution of Irish national culture. *Irish Queer Cinema* focuses on feature-length and short films released between 1984 and 2016 to provide the first extensive critical study of Irish queer cinema. It moves beyond a more traditional historical approach to Irish cinema by developing spatial models of queer society that explore the ways in which particular socio-cultural spaces (the family, the pub, the city, the countryside, the nation-state, diaspora, the short film) encode queer relations and how these spaces are simultaneously re-inscribed into a national narrative that represents 'Ireland'. Through its different case studies, it draws out queer thematics and spatial relationships that produce new insights and enable new productive comparisons between films.

This book is indebted to previous work on gender and sexual representation in Irish cinema. There remain films that for reasons of timing, cohesion and accessibility were not included here. There is also future work to be done on those culturally significant non-fiction works that make up Ireland's queer cinema. *Irish Queer Cinema* is therefore part of an ongoing interrogation into Irish queer culture that needs to take place. Like Ireland itself, Irish queer cinema can be viewed as an ever-changing space, in a state of constant revision via new local, transnational and global connections, reformed by evolving filmmaking practices and policies and the increasing accessibility of the digital, and reshaped by those economic and socio-political developments affecting Irish society and culture.

Select Filmography

Adam & Paul (Lenny Abrahamson, 2004, IR)
About Adam (Gerard Stembridge, 2001, IR/UK)
Bent Out of Shape (Orla Walsh, 1995, IR)
Borstal Boy (Peter Sheridan, 2000, IR/UK)
Breakfast on Pluto (Neil Jordan, 2005, IR/UK)
Chaero (Matt Hayes, 1988, IR)
Chicken (Barry Dignam, 2001, IR)
Clash of the Ash (Fergus Tighe, 1987, IR)
Cowboys & Angels (David Gleeson, 2003, IR)
Crush Proof (Paul Tickell, 1998, UK/IR)
The Crying Game (Neil Jordan, 1992, UK)
A Date for Mad Mary (Darren Thornton, 2016, IR)
The Disappearance of Finbar (Sue Clayton, 1996, IR/SWE/FIN)
Dream Kitchen (Barry Dignam, 1999, IR)
Elephant Shoe (Alan Early, 2009, IR)
Fantabulous (Joasia Goldyn, 2009, IR)
Garage (Lenny Abrahamson, 2007, IR)
Goldfish Memory (Liz Gill, 2002, IR)
Handsome Devil (John Butler, 2016, IR)
I Went Down (Paddy Breathnach, 1997, IR/UK)
The Last Bus Home (Johnny Gogan, 1997, IR)
The Last Time (Colette Cullen, 1993, IR)
The Magician (Colette Cullen, 1995, IR)
A Man of No Importance (Suri Krishnamma, 1994, IR/UK)
Me First (Leanne Byrne, 2014, IR)
Olive (Neasa Hardiman, 2003, IR)
Pigs (Cathal Black, 1984, IR)
Reefer and the Model (Joe Comerford, 1988, IR)
Snakes and Ladders (Trish McAdam, 1996, IR)
The Stag (John Butler, 2013, IR)
2by4 (Jimmy Smallhorne, 1998, IR/USA)

Bibliography

Ahmed, Sara (2000), *Strange Encounters: Embodied Others in Post-Coloniality*, London: Routledge.
Ahmed, Sara (2006a), *Queer Phenomenology: Orientations, Objects, Others*, Durham, NC: Duke University Press.
Ahmed, Sara (2006b), 'Orientations: toward a queer phenomenology', *GLQ: A Journal of Lesbian and Gay Studies*, 12 (4), pp. 543–74.
Aitken, Stuart C. and Christopher Lee Lukinbeal (1997), 'Disassociated masculinities and geographies of the road', in Steven Cohan and Ina Rae Hark (eds), *The Road Movie Book*, London: Routledge, pp. 349–70.
Alexander, Jonathan (2005), 'Transgender rhetorics: (re)composing narratives of the gendered body', *College Composition and Communication*, 57 (1), pp. 45–82.
Alexander, M. Jacqui (1994), 'Not just any (body) can be a citizen: the politics of law, sexuality and postcoloniality in Trinidad and Tobago and the Bahamas', *Feminist Review*, 48, pp. 5–23.
Anderson, Benedict (1983), *Imagined Communities: Reflections on the Origin and Spread of Nationalism*, London: Verso.
Barry, Aoife (2016), 'This Irish film about prison, a wedding, and female friendship is being called a triumph', *The Journal.ie*, 6 September, available at http://www.thejournal.ie/date-for-mad-mary-interview-2967010-Sep2016/ (last accessed 14 September 2017).
Barry, Todd (2009), 'Queer wanderers, queer spaces: dramatic devices for re-imagining Ireland', in David Cregan (ed.), *Deviant Acts: Essays on Queer Performance*, Dublin: Carysfort Press, pp. 151–69.
Barter, Pavel (2001), 'Peter Sheridan interview', *Film West: Ireland's Film Quarterly*, 43 (1), pp. 20–1.
Barton, Ruth (1999), 'Feisty colleens and faithful sons: gender in Irish cinema', *Cineaste*, xxiv (2/3), pp. 40–5.
Barton, Ruth (2001), 'Kitsch as authenticity: Irish cinema and the challenge to romanticism', *Irish Studies Review*, 9 (2), pp. 193–202.
Barton, Ruth (2004), *Irish National Cinema*, London: Routledge.
Barton, Ruth (2007), '"The Ireland they dream of": *Éireville*, *Coolockland*, and the appropriation of science fiction and fantasy narratives in Irish short filmmaking', in Brian McIlroy (ed.), *Genre and Cinema: Ireland and Transnationalism*, London: Routledge, pp. 151–62.

Battel, Róisín Ní Mháille (2003) 'Ireland's "Celtic Tiger" economy', *Science, Technology & Human Values*, 28 (1), pp. 93–111.

Baudrillard, Jean (1996), 'Coming out of hibernation? The myth of modernization in Irish culture', in Luke Gibbons (ed.), *Transformations in Irish Culture*, Cork: Cork University Press in association with Field Day, pp. 82–93.

Bauman, Zygmunt (1996), 'From pilgrim to tourist – or a short history of identity', in Stuart Hall and Paul du Gay (eds), *Questions of Cultural Identity*, London: SAGE Publications, pp. 18–36.

Beaumont, Caitriona (1997), 'Women, citizenship and Catholicism in the Irish Free State, 1922–1948', *Women's History Review*, 6 (4), pp. 563–85.

Bech, Henning (1997), *When Men Meet: Homosexuality and Modernity*, Cambridge: Polity Press.

Bell, David and Jon Binnie (2000), *The Sexual Citizen: Queer Politics and Beyond*, Cambridge and Oxford: Polity Press and Blackwell Publishing.

Berlant, Lauren and Michael Warner (2002), 'Sex in public', in Michael Warner (ed.), *Publics and Counterpublics*, New York: Zone Books, pp. 187–208.

Bhabha, Homi K. (1986), 'Foreword to the 1986 edition', in Franz Fanon, *Black Skin, White Masks*, London: Pluto Press, pp. 21–37.

Binnie, Jon (2004), *The Globalization of Sexuality*, London: SAGE Publications.

Boller, Alessandra (2017), 'Celtic Tiger Ireland and the car as a liminal space: movement and paralysis in Gerard Donovan's *Country of the Grand*', *Estudios Irlandeses*, 12, pp. 12–25.

Brah, Avtar (1996), *Cartographies of Diaspora: Contesting Identities*, London: Routledge.

Browne, Kath, Jason Lim and Gavin Brown (eds) (2007), *Geographies of Sexualities: Theory, Practices and Politics*, Aldershot: Ashgate Publishing.

Bruzzi, Stella (1997), *Undressing Cinema: Clothing and Identity in the Movies*, London: Routledge.

Buchanan, Jason (2009), 'Living at the end of the Irish century: globalization and identity in Declan Hughes's *Shiver*', *Modern Drama*, 52 (3), pp. 300–25.

Bunreacht na hÉireann (Constitution of Ireland) (1999), Dublin: Government Publications Sale Office.

Butler, Judith (2004), *Gender Trouble: Feminism and the Subversion of Identity*, 3rd edn, New York and London: Routledge.

Clarke, Donald (2004), 'Rude awakening', *The Irish Times*, 31 January, available at http://infoweb.newsbank.com/ (last accessed 21 June 2012).

Clayton, Sue (2007), 'Visual and performative elements in screen adaptation: a film-maker's perspective', *Journal of Media Practice*, 8 (2), pp. 129–45.

Clum, John M. (1994), *Acting Gay: Male Homosexuality in Modern Drama*, New York: Columbia University Press.

Connell, R. W. (2005), *Masculinities*, Cambridge: Polity Press.

Connolly, Linda and Tina O'Toole (2005), *Documenting Irish Feminisms: The Second Wave*, Dublin: The Woodfield Press.

Conrad, Kathryn A. (2004), *Locked in the Family Cell: Gender, Sexuality, and Political Agency in Irish National Discourse*, Madison: University of Wisconsin Press.

Corrigan, Timothy (1992), *A Cinema Without Walls: Movies and Culture after Vietnam*, New Brunswick, NJ: Rutgers University Press.

Coulter, Colin (2003), 'The end of Irish history? An introduction to the book', in Colin Coulter and Steve Coleman (eds), *The End of Irish History? Critical Approaches to the 'Celtic Tiger'*, Manchester: Manchester University Press, pp. 1–33.

Creed, Gerald W. and Barbara Ching (1997), *Knowing Your Place: Rural Identity and Cultural Identity*, New York: Routledge.

Cregan, David (ed.) (2009), *Deviant Acts: Essays on Queer Performance*, Dublin: Carysford Press.

Cresswell, Tim (1996), *In Place/out of Place: Geography, Ideology, and Transgression*, Minnesota: University of Minnesota Press.

Crone, Joni (1988), 'Lesbian Feminism in Ireland', *Women's Studies International Forum*, 11 (4), pp. 343–7.

Cronin, Michael (2004), '"He's My Country": liberalism, nationalism, and sexuality in contemporary Irish gay fiction', *Eire-Ireland*, 39 (3–4), pp. 250–67.

Crosson, Séan (2009), 'Gaelic games and "the movies"', in Mike Cronin, William Murphy and Paul Rouse (eds), *The Gaelic Athletic Association 1884–2009*, Dublin: Irish Academic Press, pp. 111–36.

Cubitt, Sean (1996), 'The Disappearance of Finbar II', *Vertigo*, 1 (6), available at https://www.closeupfilmcentre.com/vertigo_magazine/volume-1-issue-6-autumn-1996/the-disappearance-of-finbar-ii/ (last accessed 9 January 2016).

Désert, Jean-Ulrick (1997), 'Queer space', in Gordon Brent Ingram, Anne-Marie Bouthillette and Yolanda Retter (eds), *Queers in Space: Communities, Public Places, Sites of Resistance*, Seattle: Bay Press, pp. 17–26.

Detamore, Mathias (2012), 'Queering the hollow: space, place, and rural queerness', in Andrew Gorman-Murray, Barbara Pini and Lia Bryant (eds), *Sexuality, Rurality, and Geography*, Plymouth: Lexington Books, pp. 81–94.

Duncan, Nancy (1996), 'Introduction: (re)placings', in Nancy Duncan (ed.), *BodySpace: Destabilising Geographies of Gender and Sexuality*, London: Routledge, pp. 1–12.

Dyer, Richard (2002), *The Culture of Queers*, London: Routledge.

Edge, Sarah (1995), '"Women are trouble, did you know that Fergus?": Neil Jordan's "The Crying Game"', *Feminist Review*, 50 (Summer), pp. 173–86.

Eng, David L. (1997), 'Out here and over there: queerness and diaspora in Asian-American studies', *Social Text*, 52/53, pp. 31–52.

Fahey, Tony (1995), 'Family and household in Ireland', in Patrick Clancy (ed.), *Irish Society: Sociological Perspectives*, Dublin: Institute of Public Administration, pp. 205–34.

Flanagan, Martin (2001), 'Paul Tickell', in Yoram Allon, Del Cullen and Hannah

Patterson (eds), *Contemporary British and Irish Film Directors: A Wallflower Critical Guide*, London: Wallflower Press, p. 333.

Fortier, Anne-Marie (2000), *Migrant Belongings: Memory, Space, Identity*, Oxford: Berg.

Fortier, Anne-Marie (2003), 'Making home: queer migrations and motions of attachment', Lancaster: Department of Sociology, Lancaster University, available at http://www.lancaster.ac.uk/sociology/research/publications/papers/fortier-making-home.pdf (last accessed 1 July 2013).

Foucault, Michel (1978), *The History of Sexuality: Volume 1: An Introduction*, trans. Robert Hurley, New York: Pantheon Books.

Foucault, Michel (1986), 'Of other spaces', trans. Jay Miskowiec, *Diacritics*, 16 (1), pp. 22–7.

Foucault, Michel (1996), 'Friendship as a way of life', in S. Lortinger (ed.), *Foucault Live: Collected Interviews, 1961–1984*, New York: Semiotext(e).

Freeman, Elizabeth (2007), 'Queer belongings: kinship theory and queer theory', in George E. Haggerty and Molly McGarry (eds), *A Companion to Lesbian, Gay, Bisexual, Transgender, and Queer Studies*, Oxford: Blackwell Publishing, pp. 295–314.

'Garage' (2008), *Soda Pictures*, available at http://www.sodapictures.com/media/499cb22fb36986cea7caf7668612cd94.pdf (last accessed 21 May 2012).

Gibbons, Luke (2005), 'Projecting the nation: cinema and culture', in Joe Cleary and Claire Connolly (eds), *The Cambridge Companion to Modern Irish Culture*, Cambridge: Cambridge University Press, pp. 206–24.

Gibson, Chris (2013), 'The global cowboy: rural masculinities and sexualities', in Andrew Gorman-Murray, Barbara Pini and Lia Bryant (eds), *Sexuality, Rurality and Geography*, Plymouth: Lexington Books, pp. 199–218.

Giffney, Noreen and Margrit Shildrick (eds) (2013), *Theory on the Edge: Irish Studies and the Politics of Sexual Difference*, Basingstoke: Palgrave.

Gillespie, Michael Patrick (2008), *The Myth of an Irish Cinema: Approaching Irish-Themed Films*, Syracuse: Syracuse University Press.

Ging, Debbie (2002), 'Screening the Green: cinema under the Celtic Tiger', in Peadar Kirby, Luke Gibbons and Michael Cronin (eds), *Reinventing Ireland: Culture, Society and the Global Economy*, London: Pluto Press, pp. 177–95.

Ging, Debbie (2008), 'Goldfish memories? On seeing and hearing marginalised identities in contemporary Irish cinema', in Borbála Faragó and Moynagh Sullivan (eds), *Facing the Other: Interdisciplinary Studies on Race, Gender and Social Justice in Ireland*, Newcastle: Cambridge Scholars Publishing, pp. 182–203.

Ging, Debbie (2013), *Men and Masculinities in Irish Cinema*, New York: Palgrave Macmillan.

Gosling, Tim (2004), '"Not for sale": the underground network of anarcho-punk', in Andy Bennett and Richard A. Peterson (eds), *Music Scenes: Local, Translocal, and Virtual*, Nashville: Vanderbilt University Press, pp. 168–86.

Gorman-Murray, Andrew (2007), 'Rethinking queer migration through the body', *Social and Cultural Geography*, 8 (1), pp. 105–21.
Gorman-Murray, Andrew (2009), 'Intimate mobilities: emotional embodiment and queer migration', *Social and Cultural Geography*, 10 (4), pp. 441–60.
Graham, Brian (1997), 'Ireland and Irishness: place, culture and identity', in Brian Graham (ed.), *In Search of Ireland: A Cultural Geography*, London: Routledge, pp. 1–16.
Gray, Mary L. (2007), 'From websites to Wal-Mart: youth, identity work, and the queering of boundary publics in small town, USA', *American Studies*, 48 (2), pp. 49–59.
Gray, Mary L. (2009), *Out in the Country: Youth, Media and Queer Visibility in Rural America*, New York: New York University Press.
Halberstam, Judith (2005), *In a Queer Time and Place: Transgender Bodies, Subcultural Lives*, New York: New York University Press.
Halperin, David M. (1995), *Saint Foucault: Towards a Gay Hagiography*, Oxford: Oxford University Press.
Hannam, Kevin, Mimi Sheller and John Urry (2006), 'Editorial: mobilities, immobilities and moorings', *Mobilities*, 1 (1), pp. 1–22.
Hayward, Susan (2000), 'Framing national cinemas', in Mette Hjort and Scott Mackenzie (eds), *Cinema and Nation*, London: Routledge, pp. 88–102.
Hill, John (1987), 'Images of violence', in Kevin Rockett, Luke Gibbons and John Hill (eds), *Cinema and Ireland*, London: Croom Helm, pp. 147–93.
Holohan, Conn (2007), 'Trauma, narrative and subjectivity in *Breakfast on Pluto*', in Martin McLoone and Kevin Rockett (eds), *Irish Films, Global Cinema*, Studies in Irish Film 4, Dublin: Four Courts Press, pp. 140–49.
Holohan, Conn (2009), 'Queering the green: the limitations of sexuality as metaphor in recent Irish film', in Isabelle le Corff and Estelle Epinous (eds), *Cinemas of Ireland*, Newcastle upon Tyne: Cambridge Scholars Publishing, pp. 137–45.
Holohan, Conn (2010a), *Cinema on the Periphery: Contemporary Irish and Spanish Film*, Dublin: Irish Academic Press.
Holohan, Conn (2010b), 'Aesthetics of intimacy', *Short Film Studies*, 1 (1), pp. 87–90.
Holohan, Conn (2011), 'Disturbing types: gender stereotypes and the short film', *Short Film Studies*, 1 (2), pp. 287–90.
Hopkins, Jeff (1994), 'Mapping of cinematic places: icons, ideology, and the power of (mis)representation', in Stuart C. Aitken and Leo E. Zonn (eds), *Place, Power, Situation, and Spectacle: A Geography of Film*, Lanham: Rowman & Littlefield, pp. 47–65.
Inglis, Tom (1998), *Moral Monopoly: The Rise and Fall of the Catholic Church in Modern Ireland*, 2nd edn, Dublin: UCD Press.
Inglis, Tom (2008), *Global Ireland, Same Difference*, New York: Routledge.
Inglis, Tom (2009), GAA has tapped into growth of sport as substitute for religion', *The Irish Times*, 24 August, available at https://www.irishtimes.com/opinion/

gaa-has-tapped-into-growth-of-sport-as-substitute-for-religion-1.724754 (last accessed 29 October 2017).

The Irish Independent (1995), 21 April, pp. 26.

Jagose, Annamarie (1996), *Queer Theory*, Melbourne: Melbourne University Press.

Johnston, Trevor (2017), 'A Date for Mad Mary: a romcom about real people', *British Film Instititute*, 20 February, available at http://www.bfi.org.uk/news-opinion/sight-sound-magazine/interviews/date-mad-mary-darren-thornton (last accessed 9 September 2017).

Jordan, Neil (2005), 'Breakfast on Pluto', *Sony Pictures Classics*, available at http://www.sonyclassics.com/breakfastonpluto/main.htm (last accessed 1 November 2012).

Keogh, Dermot (1995), *Ireland and the Vatican: The Politics and Diplomacy of Church-State Relations 1922–1960*, Cork: Cork University Press.

Kirby, Peadar, Luke Gibbons and Michael Cronin (2002), 'Introduction: The reinvention of Ireland: a critical perspective', in Peadar Kirby, Luke Gibbons and Michael Cronin (eds), *Reinventing Ireland: Culture, Society and the Global Economy*, London: Pluto Press, pp. 1–20.

Knell, Jenny (2010), 'North and south of the river: demythologizing Dublin in contemporary Irish film', *Éire-Ireland*, 45 (1&2), pp. 213–41.

Knopp, Larry (2004), 'Ontologies of place, placelessness, and movement: queer quests for identity and their impacts on contemporary geographic thought', *Gender, Place and Culture: A Journal of Feminist Geography*, 11 (1), pp. 121–34.

Knopp, Larry (2007), 'From lesbian and gay to queer geographies: pasts, prospects and possibilities', in Kath Browne, Jason Lim and Gavin Brown (eds), *Geographies of Sexualities: Theory, Practices and Politics*, Farnham: Ashgate Publishing, pp. 21–8.

Knox, Kirsty Blake (2017), 'Panti Bliss: "It's wild how queer Ireland has become"', *Independent*, available at http://www.independent.ie/entertainment/panti-bliss-its-wild-how-queer-ireland-has-become-35621403.html (last accessed 10 September 2017).

Laderman, David (2002), *Driving Visions: Exploring the Road Movie*, Austin: University of Texas Press.

Lapointe, Michael Patrick (2006), *Between Irishmen: Queering Irish Literary and Cultural Nationalisms*, PhD thesis, Vancouver: University of British Columbia, available at https://circle.ubc.ca/bitstream/handle/2429/31090/ubc_2007-267486.pdf?sequence=1 (last accessed 4 August 2011).

Lefebvre, Henri (1991), *The Production of Space*, trans. Donald Nicholson-Smith, Oxford: Blackwell Publishing.

Lloyd, David (2011), *Irish Culture and Colonial Modernity 1800–2000: The Transformation of Oral Space*, Cambridge: Cambridge University Press.

Loter, Jim (1999), 'Cathal Black's *Pigs*: ambivalence, confinement, and the search for an Irish sense of place', in James MacKillop (ed.), *Contemporary Irish*

Cinema: From The Quiet Man to Dancing at Lughnasa, New York: Syracuse University Press, pp. 128–38.

Madden, Ed (2010), '"Gently, not gay": proximity, sexuality, and Irish masculinity at the end of the twentieth century', *Canadian Journal of Irish Studies*, 36 (1), pp. 69–87.

Madden, Ed (2011), 'Exploring masculinity: proximity, intimacy and *Chicken*', in Caroline Magennis and Raymond Mullen (eds), *Irish Masculinities: Reflections on Literature and Culture*, Dublin: Irish Academic Press, pp. 77–88.

Madden, Ed (2012), 'Queering the Irish diaspora: David Rees and Padraig Rooney', *Eire-Ireland*, 47 (1&2), pp. 172–200.

Madden, Ed (2013), 'Get your kit on: gender, sexuality, and gay rugby in Ireland', *Eire-Ireland*, 48 (1&2), pp. 246–81.

Maher, Kevin (1999), 'Crush Proof', *Sight and Sound*, 9 (5), available at http://old.bfi.org.uk/sightandsound/review/ (last accessed 14 November 2016).

Mahon, Evelyn (1987), 'Women's rights and Catholicism in Ireland', *New Left Review*, I (166), pp. 53–77.

McCarthy, Conor (2000), *Modernisation: Crisis and Culture in Ireland 1969–1992*, Dublin: Four Courts Press.

McCarthy, Esther (2017) 'Handsome Devil is in the detail for John Butler', *Irish Examiner*, available at http://www.irishexaminer.com/lifestyle/artsfilmtv/handsome-devil-is-in-the-detail-for-john-butler-448117.html (last accessed 10 September 2017).

McCarthy, Gerry (2004a), 'A sexy young Limerick rises from the ashes', *The Sunday Times*, 18 April, p. 10.

McCarthy, Gerry (2004b), 'Gay culture has gone from the margins to the mainstream in Ireland, with surprising results', *The Sunday Times*, Eire Culture, 25 July, p. 18.

McDevitt, Patrick F. (2004), *'May the Best Man Win': Sport, Masculinity and Nationalism in Great Britain and the Empire, 1880–1935*, New York: Palgrave.

McElroy, Naomi (2003), 'Hit film turns Stab City into Fab City', *The Sunday Mirror*, 19 October.

McIvor, Charlotte (2009), '"Crying" on "Pluto": Queering the "Irish question" for global film audiences', in David Cregan (ed.), *Deviant Acts: Essays on Queer Performance*, Dublin: Carysford Press, pp. 151–69.

McLoone, Martin (1994), 'National cinema and cultural identity: Ireland in Europe', in John Hill, Martin McLoone and Paul Hainsworth (eds), *Border Crossing: Film in Ireland, Britain and Europe*, Belfast: Institute of Irish Studies/BFI, pp. 146–73

McLoone, Martin (1999), in James MacKillop (ed.), '*December Bride*: a landscape peopled differently', *Contemporary Irish Cinema: From the Quiet Man to Dancing at Lughnasa*, Syracuse: Syracuse University Press, pp. 40–53.

McLoone, Martin (2000), *Irish Film: the Emergence of a Contemporary Cinema*, London: British Film Institute.

McLoone, Martin (2007), 'Cinema, city and imaginative space: "hip hedonism" and recent Irish cinema,' in Brian McIlroy (ed.), *Genre and Cinema: Ireland and Transnationalism*, London: Routledge, pp. 205–16.

McLoone, Martin (2008), *Film, Media and Popular Culture in Ireland: Cityscapes, Landscapes, Soundscapes*, Dublin: Irish Academic Press.

McLoone, Martin (2009), 'National cinema and global culture: the case of Irish cinema', in Isabelle le Corff and Estelle Epinous (eds), *Cinemas of Ireland*, Newcastle upon Tyne: Cambridge Scholars Publishing, pp. 14–27.

McLoone, Martin (2010), ' Landscape and Irish cinema', in Graeme Harper and Jonathan Rayner (eds), *Cinema and Landscape*, Bristol: Intellect, pp. 131–46.

Monahan, Barry (2009), 'The pedagogical culture of Irish film production: a short history', in Isabelle le Corff and Estelle Epinoux (eds), *Cinemas of Ireland*, Newcastle upon Tyne: Cambridge Scholars Publishing, pp. 87–99.

Moore, Coinín (2009), 'Ireland and Hollywood standards', in Isabelle le Corff and Estelle Epinous (eds), *Cinemas of Ireland*, Newcastle upon Tyne: Cambridge Scholars Publishing, pp. 102–13.

Mulvey, Laura (1975), 'Visual pleasure and narrative cinema', *Screen*, 16 (3), pp. 6–18.

Muñoz, José Esteban (1999), *Disidentifications: Queers of Color and the Performance of Politics*, Minnesota: University of Minnesota Press.

Munt, Sally (1995), 'The lesbian flâneur', in David Bell and Gill Valentine (eds), *Mapping Desire: Geographies of Sexualities*, London: Routledge, pp. 104–14.

Murphy, Jenny (2003), '"The quare ones": finding a male homosexual space within Irish cinema', *Film and Film Culture*, 2, pp. 69–77.

Nash, Catherine (1993), 'Remapping and renaming: new cartographies of identity, gender and landscape in Ireland', *Feminist Review*, 44, pp. 39–57.

Neale, Steve (1983), 'Masculinity as spectacle: reflections on men and mainstream cinema', *Screen*, 24 (6), pp. 2–17.

Ní Laoire, Caitríona (2002), 'Young farmers, masculinities and change in rural Ireland', *Irish Geography*, 35 (1), pp. 16–27.

Ní Laoire, Caitríona (2005), '"You're not a man at all!": masculinity, responsibility, and staying on the land in contemporary Ireland', *Irish Journal of Sociology*, 14 (2), pp. 94–114.

O'Connell, Díóg (2010), *New Irish Storytellers: Narrative Strategies in Film*, Bristol: Intellect.

O'Connell, Díóg (2016), 'Revisiting old themes in recent Irish cinema', in Estelle Epinoux and Frank Healy (eds), *Post Celtic Tiger Ireland: Exploring New Cultural Spaces*, Newcastle upon Tyne: Cambridge Scholars Publishing, pp. 160–74.

O'Regan, Tom (1996), *Australian National Cinema*, London: Routledge.

O'Toole, Fintan (2015) 'Ireland has left "tolerance" far behind: LGBT community has given all of Irish democracy one of its greatest days', *The Irish Times*, 25 May, available at https://www.irishtimes.com/news/politics/fintan-o-toole-ireland-has-left-tolerance-far-behind-1.2223838? (last accessed 9 September 2017).

O'Toole, Tina (2013), 'Cé leis tú? Queering Irish migrant literature', *Irish University Review*, 43 (1), pp. 131–45.
Pettitt, Lance (1997), 'Pigs and provos, prostitutes and prejudice: gay representation in Irish film, 1984–1995', in Éibhear Walshe (ed.), *Sex, Nation and Dissent in Irish Writing*, Cork: Cork University Press, pp. 252–84.
Pettitt, Lance (1999), 'A construction site queered: "gay" images in new Irish cinema', *Cineaste*, 24 (2–3), pp. 61–3.
Pettitt, Lance (2000), *Screening Ireland: Film and Television Representation*, Manchester: Manchester University Press.
Pramaggiore, Maria (2006), '"Papa don't preach": pregnancy and performance in contemporary Irish cinema', in Diane Negra (ed.), *The Irish in Us: Irishness, Performativity, and Popular Culture*, Durham, NC: Duke University Press, pp. 110–29.
Probyn, Elspeth (1995), 'Lesbians in space: gender, sex and the structure of missing', *Gender, Place and Culture: A Journal of Feminist Geography*, 2 (1), pp. 77–84.
Rascaroli, Laura (2003), 'New voyages to Italy: postmodern travellers and the Italian road film', *Screen*, 44 (1), pp. 71–91.
Rich, Adrienne (1980), 'Compulsory heterosexuality and lesbian existence', *Signs: Journal of Women in Culture & Society*, 5 (4), pp. 631–60.
Roberts, Shari (1997), 'Western meets Eastwood: genre and gender on the road', in Steven Cohan and Ina Rae Hark (eds), *The Road Movie Book*, London: Routledge, pp. 45–69.
Rockett, Kevin (1987), 'History, politics and Irish cinema', in Kevin Rockett, Luke Gibbons and John Hill (eds), *Cinema and Ireland*, London: Croom Helm, pp. 3–144.
Rockett, Kevin (1994), 'Culture, industry and Irish cinema', in John Hill, Martin McLoone and Paul Hainsworth (eds), *Border Crossing: Film in Ireland, Britain and Europe*, Belfast: Institute of Irish Studies, pp. 126–39.
Rockett, Kevin, Luke Gibbons and John Hill (eds), (1987), *Cinema and Ireland*, London: Croom Helm.
Rose, Kieran (1994), *Diverse communities: the evolution of lesbian and gay politics in Ireland*, Cork: Cork University Press.
Rushbrook, Dereka (2002), 'Cities, queer space and the cosmopolitan tourist', *GLQ: A Journal of Lesbian and Gay Studies*, 8 (1&2), pp. 183–206.
Scheib, Ronnie (2003), 'Goldfish Memory', *Variety*, 14 April, 390 (9), p. 24.
Schneider, Elizabeth M (1991), 'The violence of privacy', *Connecticut Law Review*, 23 (973), pp. 973–99.
Sedgwick, Eve Kosofsky (1992), *Between Men: English Literature and Male Homosocial Desire*, New York: Columbia University Press.
Sedgwick, Eve Kosofsky (1993), *Tendencies*, Durham, NC: Duke University Press.
Simpson, Mark (1994), *Male Impersonators: Men Performing Masculinity*, New York: Routledge.
Sinfield, Alan (1994), *The Wilde Century*, New York: Columbia University Press.

Soja, Edward W. (1996), *Thirdspace: Journeys to Los Angeles and Other Real-and-Imagined Places*, Oxford: Blackwell Publishing.
Stivers, Richard (2000), *Hair of the Dog: Irish Drinking and its American Stereotype*, New York: Continuum.
Stockton, Kathryn Bond (2006), *Beautiful Bottom, Beautiful Shame*, Durham, NC: Duke University Press.
Stockton, Kathryn Bond (2009), *The Queer Child, or Growing Sideways in the Twentieth Century*, Durham, NC: Duke University Press.
Stoneman, Rod (2005), 'The sins of commission II', *Screen*, 46 (2), pp. 247–64.
Stryker, Susan (1998), 'The transgender issue: an introduction', *GLQ: A Journal of Lesbian and Gay Studies*, 4 (2), pp. 145–58.
Stychin, Carl F. (1998), *A Nation by Rights: National Cultures, Sexual Identity Politics, and the Discourse of Rights*, Philadelphia: Temple University Press.
Valentine, Gill (1996), '(Re)negotiating the "heterosexual street": lesbian productions of space', in Nancy Duncan (ed.), *Bodyspace: Destabilizing Geographies of Gender and Sexual*, London: Psychology Press, pp. 146–55.
'Video Releases' (2000), available at http://www.irishtimes.com/news/video-releases-1.298131 (last accessed 13 April 2017).
Viegener, Matias (1993), '"The only haircut that makes sense anymore": queer subculture and gay resistance', in Martha Gever, John Greyson and Pratibha Parmar (eds), *Queer Looks: Perspectives on Lesbian and Gay Film and Video*, New York: Routledge, pp. 116–33.
Walsh, Fintan (2008), 'Cock tales: homosexuality, trauma and the cosmopolitan queer', *Film Ireland*, 120, pp. 16–18.
Walsh, Fintan (2010), *Queer Notions: New Plays and Performances from Ireland*, Cork: Cork University Press.
Walsh, Fintan (2012), 'Mourning sex: the aesthetics of queer rationality in contemporary film', in Claire Bracken and Emma Radley (eds), *Theorising the Visual: New Directions in Irish Cultural Studies*, Cork: Cork University Press.
Walsh, Fintan (2013), 'Mourning sex: the aesthetics of queer relationality in contemporary film', in Claire Bracken and Emma Radley (eds), *Viewpoints: Theoretical Perspectives on Irish Visual Texts*, Cork: Cork University Press, pp. 215–28.
Walsh, Fintan (2016), *Queer Performance and Contemporary Ireland: Dissent and Disorientation*, Basingstoke: Palgrave.
Walshe, Éibhear (1997), *Sex, Nation and Dissent in Irish Writing*, Cork: Cork University Press.
Walshe, Éibhear (2009), 'Queering Oscar: versions of Wilde on the Irish stage and screen', in David Cregan (ed.), *Deviant Acts: Essays on Queer Performance*, Dublin: Carysfort Press, pp. 7–24.
Wayne, Mike (2002), The *Politics of Contemporary European Cinema: Histories, Borders, Diasporas*, Bristol: Intellect Books.
Weeks, Jeffrey (2010), *Sexuality*, 3rd edn, London: Routledge.

Weston, Kath (1991a), *Families We Choose: Lesbians, Gays, Kinship*, New York: Columbia University Press.

Weston, Kath (1991b) 'Get thee to a big city: sexual imaginary and the great gay migration', *GLQ: A Journal of Lesbian and Gay Studies*, 2 (3), pp. 253–77.

Whatmore, Sarah, Terry Marsden and Philip Lowe (eds) (1994), *Gender and Rurality*, London: Fulton.

White, Jerry (2001), 'Trish McAdam', in Yoram Allon, Del Cullen and Hannah Patterson (eds), *Contemporary British and Irish Film Directors: A Wallflower Critical Guide*, London: Wallflower Press, p. 222.

Wills, Clair (2001), 'Women, domesticity and the family: recent feminist work in Irish cultural studies', *Cultural Studies*, 15 (1), pp. 33–57.

Wilson, Angelica (2000), 'Getting your kicks on Route 66! Stories of gay and lesbian life in rural America', in Richard Phillips (ed.), *De-Centering Sexualities: Politics and Representations Beyond the Metropolis*, New York: Routledge, pp. 199–216.

Index

About Adam, 8, 23, 24, 67
Abrahamson, Lenny, 8, 23, 25, 49, 60, 61, 65
Adam & Paul, 8
Ahmed, Sara, 17, 70, 126, 130, 135, 139, 145
Aitken, Stuart C., 109, 111

Barry, Todd, 120
Barton, Ruth, 3, 12, 13, 20, 21, 22, 24, 28, 30, 34, 67, 86, 88, 97, 107, 115–16, 146
Behan, Brendon, 55, 82, 129
Bent Out of Shape, 147, 148, 149, 150
Black, Cathal, 2, 21, 29, 49
Bliss, Panti, 13, 160
Borstal Boy, 20, 23, 128, 129, 131, 138–44, 145
Brah, Avtar, 130, 131, 135, 138
Breakfast on Pluto, 23, 24, 49, 109, 110, 111, 114, 117–26, 156
Breathnach, Paddy, 8, 49, 109
Butler, John, 26, 87, 102, 104, 105
Butler, Judith, 123, 132, 141
Byrne, Leanne, 155, 158

Casement, Roger, 10
Catholicism, 1, 9, 12, 13, 19, 26, 27, 28, 31, 40, 51, 52, 71, 91, 92, 97, 121, 125, 131, 132
Cathleen ni Houlihan, 81, 90
Celtic Tiger, the, 3, 12, 13, 18, 22–5, 26, 27, 50, 62, 66, 87, 89, 90, 106, 108, 157
  cinema of, 3, 22–5, 26, 50, 62, 66, 89, 157
  post-, 23–7, 66, 87, 90, 106, 108
Chaero, 147, 148, 149, 150
Chicken, 148, 150, 152

Clash of the Ash, 21, 22, 26, 91, 92, 94, 98–104, 105, 106, 107
Clayton, Sue, 20, 109, 120
Comerford, Joe, 2, 21, 29, 49, 107
coming out, 11, 26, 46, 92, 128, 128, 153
Conrad, Kathryn A., 10, 31, 37, 45, 81
Cork Gay Collective, 11
Cowboys & Angels, 3, 5, 23, 24, 46, 68, 69–76, 78, 80, 81, 82, 83, 86, 87, 88, 89, 144, 152
criminal, 5, 7, 10, 24, 26, 49, 64, 73, 90, 94, 96
cross-dressing, 125, 144
Crush Proof, 5, 23, 24, 80, 82, 84, 85, 86, 87, 88, 89, 90, 117, 156, 157
Crying Game, The, 18, 19, 20, 49
Cullen, Colette, 155, 157

Date for Mad Mary, A, 5, 26, 87, 88, 90
Désert, Jean-Ulrick, 15, 53, 54, 59, 96, 112
diaspora, 17, 24, 120, 128, 129, 130, 131, 132, 135, 138, 144, 145, 161
Dignam, Barry, 148, 152
Disappearance of Finbar, The, 20, 24, 109, 110, 111, 114, 117–26, 126, 130, 144, 156
Dream Kitchen, 152, 154, 155
Dublin, 10, 11, 13, 16, 29, 30, 33, 39, 40, 46, 50, 54, 58, 65, 66, 68, 76, 77, 78, 82, 84, 89, 111, 114, 116, 117, 126, 138, 144, 146, 149, 159
Dublin Institute of Technology, 146
Dun Laoghaire School of Art and Design, 146

Early, Alan, 148
Elephant Shoe, 148, 150, 151, 152

INDEX

emigration, 12, 13, 21, 22, 28, 104, 107
ethnicity, 48, 50, 52, 65, 72, 74, 128, 131, 132, 137

family, 9, 10, 11, 12, 15, 17, 22, 28, 29, 30–4, 37, 39, 40, 41, 44–5, 47, 53, 67, 80, 85, 94, 96, 97, 100, 101, 107, 110, 119, 121, 128, 130, 137, 138, 144, 147, 152, 153, 154, 155, 159, 161
  nuclear, 31, 100
  queer re-organisation of, 32–3, 92
Fantabulous, 152, 153, 154, 155
feminism, 12, 82, 84, 86
  second-wave, 81
First Wave, the, 18, 20, 21, 22, 23, 25, 26, 27, 29, 92
Fortier, Anne-Marie, 128, 129, 130, 131, 132, 135
Foucault, Michel, 9, 14, 16, 31, 50, 53, 54, 68
Freeman, Elizabeth, 32, 32, 38

gangster, 112
Garage, 8, 23, 25, 49, 50, 52, 54, 60–6, 93
Gill, Liz, 3, 23, 89, 152
Ging, Debbie, 3, 5, 21, 24, 37, 49, 75, 77, 89, 96
Gleeson, David, 3, 23, 69, 89, 152
Gogan, Johnny, 2, 29, 49
Goldfish Memory, 3, 5, 23, 24, 26, 68, 69, 76–80, 81, 82, 85, 86, 87, 88, 89, 152
Goldyn, Joasia, 152, 153
Gorman-Murray, Andrew, 110, 116, 121
Gray, Mary L., 92, 100

Halberstam, Judith, 16, 17, 33, 92, 93, 123
Handsome Devil, 26, 103
Hardiman, Neasa, 155
Hayes, Matt, 147, 148
Hollywood, 24, 107, 146
Holohan, Conn, 3, 4, 78, 125, 147, 151, 152, 158

homophobia, 3, 10, 15, 16, 26, 27, 29, 42, 44, 61, 68, 73, 96, 103, 105, 106, 132, 133, 147, 148, 149, 160
homosociality, 7, 8, 36, 49, 50, 51, 53, 54, 59, 60, 61, 63, 64, 65, 83, 101, 108, 112, 113, 131, 137, 143

I Went Down, 8, 20, 24, 49, 109, 110, 111–16, 117, 126
Importance of Being Earnest, The, 140, 143
Irish Film Board (IFB), 2, 4, 19, 22, 23, 126, 146
Irish Gay Rights Movement (IGRM), 11, 66, 81
Irish Republican Army (IRA), 18, 19, 42, 89, 94, 96, 97, 122, 124, 125, 129

Jordan, Neil, 18, 19, 20, 22, 23, 49, 109, 126

Knell, Jenny, 89
Knopp, Larry, 110
Krishnamma, Suri, 10, 23, 49, 55

Last Bus Home, The, 24, 29, 30, 32, 33, 39–47, 49, 68, 93, 97, 144, 149, 151
Last Time, The, 155, 157
lesbian feminism, 12, 16, 81
Limerick, 69, 70, 75, 76
Lloyd, David, 51, 52
Lukinbeal, Christopher Lee, 109, 111

Madden, Ed, 3, 5, 49, 103, 128, 130–1, 132, 150
Magician, The, 155, 157
male gaze, the, 159
Man of No Importance, A, 10, 23, 24, 49, 50, 52, 54–60, 66, 96, 142
McAdam, Trish, 5, 23, 80, 86, 89
McIvor, Charlotte, 19, 125
McLoone, Martin, 3, 4, 12, 13, 20, 24, 25, 30, 39, 46, 67, 68, 91, 92, 95, 107, 133, 137, 146, 147, 148, 153
Me First, 158
MEDIA programme, 24, 126
metrosexuality, 104, 105

Mother Ireland, 81, 84, 90
Mulvey, Laura, 82
Murphy, Jenny, 3, 7, 8, 39, 40, 108, 137

neoliberalism, 3, 90
New Ireland, 50, 68, 76
New Queer Cinema, 7
New York, 11, 20, 24, 46, 128, 129, 131, 132, 133, 135, 138, 159

Olive, 155, 156, 157

Panti Bliss, 13, 160
Pettitt, Lance, 2, 3, 7, 8, 19, 20, 40, 146, 147, 148, 157
Pigs, 2, 7, 21, 22, 29, 30, 32, 33–9, 45, 47, 68, 97, 149
postmodernism, 6, 68
Probyn, Elspeth, 54, 59, 157
punk rock, 29, 30, 39, 40, 45, 46, 47, 156

Quiet Man, The, 48, 65, 92

Reefer and the Model, 2, 7, 21, 22, 26, 49, 83, 92, 94–7, 100, 102, 105, 106, 107
religion, 9, 19, 21, 24, 26, 28, 31, 41, 102, 103, 121, 122, 139
republicanism, 12, 13, 19, 121, 122, 123, 129
road movie, the, 24, 52, 111, 113, 114, 115, 117, 126
Rose, Kieran, 9–10, 11, 12, 16
rugby, 26, 27, 103, 104, 139 140, 143
rural, 1, 17, 22, 23, 26, 48, 49, 60, 65, 68, 69, 71, 89, 91–108, 138
  rural queerness, 93, 96
Rushbrook, Dereka, 74

Second Wave, the, 22, 23, 24
  Sedgwick, Eve Kosofsky, 61, 83, 117, 137, 147
Sheridan, Peter, 23, 28, 128, 143
Smallhorne, Jimmy, 23, 24, 128, 129, 134

Salome, 55
Snakes and Ladders, 23, 82, 84, 86, 87, 89
space
  centre/periphery, 57, 65, 74, 76, 88
  cinematic, 4, 14, 17, 52
  compartmentalisation of, 69, 87, 88, 155
  diasporic, 128, 130, 131, 135, 138, 144, 145
  heterotopic, 50, 53, 54, 68, 104
  proximity, 38, 74, 87, 98, 125, 158
  queer, 42, 53, 59, 74, 75, 76, 91, 93, 96, 100, 107, 112
Sedgwick, Eve Kosofsky, 61, 83, 117, 137
Stag, The, 26, 104–6, 108
Stembridge, Gerard, 8, 23, 67
Stockton, Kathryn Bond, 117, 134, 156
Stonewall Riots, the, 11
Stivers, Richard, 50, 51, 52
suicide, 12, 49

Thornton, Darren, 26, 80, 87
Tickell, Paul, 5, 23, 80
Tighe, Fergus, 21
transgender, 6, 16, 18, 121, 123, 124
transnational, 49, 105
Troubles, the, 19, 120, 126
2by4, 20, 23, 24, 128, 129, 131–8, 139, 144, 145

urban, 1, 13, 21, 23, 50, 67, 68, 69, 80, 81, 82, 86, 88, 89, 90, 91, 92, 97, 101, 104, 110
  'urbanisation', 12, 14

Valera, Éamon de, 107

Walsh, Fintan, 3, 7, 8, 13, 23, 24, 58, 61, 66, 90
Walsh, Orla, 147, 148
Weston, Kath, 32, 92, 93
Wilde, Oscar, 10, 54, 55, 56, 58, 59, 65, 66, 129, 140, 142, 144
Wilson, Angelica, 100